Developing TEACHER LEADERS

Second Edition

Frank Crowther

with Margaret Ferguson and Leonne Hann

Developing TEACHER LEADERS

Second Edition

How Teacher Leadership Enhances School Success

Foreword by
Andy Hargreaves

A Joint Publication

For information:

Corwin Press
A SAGE Company
2455 Teller Road
Thousand Oaks, California 91320
www.corwinpress.com

SAGE Ltd.
1 Oliver's Yard
55 City Road
London EC1Y 1SP
United Kingdom

SAGE India Pvt. Ltd.
B 1/I 1 Mohan Cooperative
  Industrial Area
Mathura Road, New Delhi 110 044
India

SAGE Asia-Pacific Pte. Ltd.
33 Pekin Street #02-01
Far East Square
Singapore 048763

Printed in the United States of America.

Library of Congress Cataloging-in-Publication Data

Crowther, Frank, 1942-
Developing teacher leaders : how teacher leadership enhances school success/Frank Crowther, Margaret Ferguson, Leonne Hann. 2nd ed.
    p. cm.
Previous ed. entered under title: Developing teacher leaders.
Includes bibliographical references and index.
ISBN 978-1-4129-6374-9 (cloth: acid-free paper)
ISBN 978-1-4129-6375-6 (pbk.: acid-free paper)
    1. Teacher effectiveness. 2. Educational leadership. I. Ferguson, Margaret, 1953- II. Hann, Leonne. III. Title.

LB1025.3.D487 2009
371.1'06—dc22   2008019169

This book is printed on acid-free paper.

08 09 10 11 12 10 9 8 7 6 5 4 3 2 1

Acquisitions Editor:	Debra Stollenwerk
Associate Editor:	Desirée Enayati
Production Editor:	Eric Garner
Copy Editor:	Gretchen Treadwell
Typesetter:	C&M Digitals (P) Ltd.
Proofreader:	Theresa Kay
Indexer:	Sheila Bodell
Cover Designer:	Monique Hahn

Contents

Foreword to the Second Edition

Bringing Teacher Leadership Back In

More than two decades ago, after increasing exasperation with the assault that British Thatcherism was making upon all the professions, but most of all on those that involved education, I applied for a job in Canada at the Ontario Institute for Studies in Education. The job was in a regional field center, assisting improvement and innovation efforts in local schools. Some months later, I received a telephone call inviting me to an interview for a completely different job in the same institution—to be an associate professor in educational administration. It was a flattering approach, but I had to admit the truth. "I haven't actually applied for a job in educational administration," I said. "We know you haven't," came the reply. "But I don't actually know anything about educational administration," I confessed. "No, we know you don't," they reassured me.

Months and even years later, I slowly unpacked the truth behind this mystery. One member of the search committee for the educational administration position was also on the search committee for the field center job. I had been poached! More than this, after an external review, the department had been told it must appoint an international scholar with qualifications in a discipline outside educational administration (mine was sociology) but who had interests and expertise that were compatible with the field. The last piece to fit in place explaining the almost unanimous support for my appointment was that I had a field of interest completely different from and therefore not competing with any other member of the department—teachers. My colleagues were safe. In the field of educational administration someone who studied teachers would pose no challenge to them whatsoever!

Even as late as the 1980s, the field of educational administration that would in many places later evolve into educational leadership had little or no place for research on teachers and teaching—except where teachers got in the way of administrators' plans. Courses in collective bargaining and in principal supervision and evaluation of teachers were enough to deal with those eventualities. Apart from some academically internal and largely esoteric debates within the field about abstract theoretical directions, leadership was mainly something practiced either heroically or managerially by big men in big suits. Teachers were not the leaders, but the led.

With a doctorate and a book on cultures of middle school teaching in England behind me (Hargreaves, 1986), I came upon an intriguing opportunity for a new study. Elementary teachers in Ontario had gained legislated increases in preparation time. Would they use it to perpetuate a long-standing culture of alleged individualism of teaching in and preparing for their own classes or would they use the time to work together and overcome the barrier of time that many had said impeded their efforts to collaborate in the past? From England especially, there was a growing literature pointing to exemplary instances of collaboration in English primary schools, with primary teachers also taking on roles of subject leaders and advisors for their colleagues within the school. And in Ontario, I was able to construct a natural experiment by studying the use of newly provided preparation time in two large school districts—one with an explicit focus on collaboration, one without. After decades of classic critiques that teaching was diminished and made conservative by being performed in a culture of isolation and individualism, I found myself part of an emerging field of work that did not merely complain about how most teachers failed to work together, but that began to document the examples of collaborative professional practice that already existed.

The most interesting critical findings of the preparation time study came not from the district that had no focus on collaboration, but from the one that did. Under confident, outstanding yet strangely low-key principals, some schools were able to energize the collective leadership of their teachers as they collaborated together to make improvements that benefited their students. They were able to develop what I called strong cultures of collaboration. But other principals tried to drive collaboration through their staffs, telling them where and when to meet, with whom and for what purpose. In this context of what I called forced collaboration or contrived collegiality, many teachers actually started to collaborate less (Hargreaves, 1994). Although I did not use the language of teacher leadership at the time, principals in the first schools were able to acknowledge and advance the power of teacher leadership, while those who were less comfortable in their own skin were either unaware or afraid of it.

Building on this work, my new Canadian colleague, Michael Fullan, and I linked the findings on teacher collaboration to his foundational work on educational change. We developed a series of short texts addressed to the teaching profession and accompanied this with a demanding worldwide program of intensive systemwide training to build teachers' capacities and skills in collaboration for school improvement, and to develop principals' skills and capacities so they could foster stronger collaborative cultures while avoiding contrived collegiality (Fullan & Hargreaves, 1996; Hargreaves & Fullan, 1998). In many ways, this effort to reculture schools and systems on more collaborative lines formed the precursor to contemporary emphases on creating professional learning communities. Again, although we did not pose it in these words, we were trying to grow more teacher leadership across schools and systems.

Then came the standards movement. In the early stages, the idea of high standards, broadly defined, was a spur to stronger and more focused teacher collaboration. With my co-founder of the International Centre for Educational Change, Lorna Earl, I set about examining how reputationally successful junior high school teachers made sense of a curriculum reform effort to develop a more rigorous and relevant interdisciplinary curriculum for young adolescents through a small number of common learning outcomes, linked to alternative forms of assessment (Hargreaves, Earl, Moore, & Manning, 2001). Left to their own devices, even the best teachers struggled to interpret outcomes that seemed either too specific or too vague, they found it difficult to map the curriculum backwards from the outcomes to their teaching, and they became frustrated with formatively assessed interdisciplinary outcomes that seemed to be in conflict with summatively described subject-based report cards. However, when teachers worked together under the quiet yet firmly facilitative leadership of principals who understood teaching and learning, and when they had access to the outside expertise of process consultants who supported their planning efforts, they collaborated magnificently to team teach classes together, looping with them from one year to the next; or to mount inventors' festivals to showcase students' interdisciplinary achievements to corporate judges; or to create three-way parent interviews where parents, teachers, and students met to discuss students' work portfolios together. Supported by high quality principalship, teachers demonstrated once more how, given the chance, they were able to succeed and also to lead.

Then standards turned into standardization. Reformers tried to bypass the principal and the teacher and take their highly prescribed changes straight into the classroom. They loaded up curriculum content in narrowly defined basics linked to high stakes tests, and took away time and resources for teachers to think through the implementation. Apart from a very few teachers who took on roles as centralized curriculum writers, implementation experts or coaches who enforced fidelity and compliance, professional collaboration went underground and teacher leadership went into reverse. Research funded by the Spencer Foundation and conducted with my colleagues Ivor Goodson, Dean Fink, and others revealed how the age of standardization reduced the amount and quality of professional collaboration and formalized what was left into hurried meetings dedicated to implementing unwanted government priorities—contrived collegiality on a massive scale (Hargreaves, 2003). Overwhelmed and insecure, teachers either abandoned their leadership and retreated into their classrooms, or invested their leadership in union activism to oppose the reforms that inflicted harm on their students and themselves.

The purpose of the Spencer-funded study was not just to examine the impact on teachers of contemporary reforms, but to see how teachers in eight secondary schools had experienced and responded to change over more than thirty years. Four of the selected schools were traditional and four were innovative. Interestingly, the archaeology of change in the innovative schools unearthed decades of evidence of extraordinary teacher leadership that far preceded modern discussions of the subject (Hargreaves & Fink, 2006). Frustrated teachers in one inner city created a school without walls in the 1970s to respond to the diverse needs of students unable to succeed in conventional high school settings. Assertive women in another high school, at a time when even pant suits were regarded as a sign of dangerous rebellion, formed a women's group in the school that secured gender neutral language and curriculum across the district, and a mentoring program for young women teachers. Decades later, these young women leaders would become some of the most prominent leaders of not only their district but of the entire province. Outstanding teacher leadership today creates outstanding school and system leadership for the future. And such leadership has been in existence for at least four decades.

Two of these innovative schools became fully fledged professional learning organizations or learning communities. While elsewhere, so-called professional learning communities and the teachers who lead within them have degenerated into stilted teams of teachers thrown together after school to examine numerical data and generate short-term solutions that boost student achievement in tested subjects, these schools were living and lively communities where teachers were committed to deep learning not just tested achievement, where they collaborated informally as well as formally, and where they cared about their students' and each others' lives as people as well as the formalities of their work and performance (Giles & Hargreaves, 2006). Teacher leadership, we learned, is powerful when it is grounded in cultures of trust and responsibility around genuinely shared goals for improved student learning, but it is often corrupted and contorted when it becomes colonized by external agents who want to use it merely to deliver government or system targets in narrowly conceived objectives (Hargreaves, 2008).

An especially instructive case that highlights this contrast is that of Finland—the highest performer in the world on OECD PISA tests, as well as being the country with the narrowest achievement gaps. In 2007, I took a team to Finland for OECD to examine the relationship between leadership and school improvement (Hargreaves, Halász, & Pont, 2007). In Finland, within broad steering guidelines of the state, teachers create curriculum together in each municipality. Within their schools, they feel responsible for all the children in the school, not just in their own class, grade, or subject. Trust, cooperation, and responsibility are at the heart of Finnish teachers' culture. And if the principal should become ill, indisposed, or ineffective, then teachers say that they simply take over the school because the school does not belong to the principal—it belongs to all of them. In Finland, teacher leadership is not a plan, a career structure, or a set of tasks, but a defining feature of how the entire national system operates. In Finland, teachers are able and expected to lead because there are things of substance worth leading.

Most recently, my Boston College colleague, Dennis Shirley, and I have investigated the power of teacher leadership and collaboration across schools, identifying how the majority of schools in a network of underperforming schools can significantly lift student achievement by sharing ideas and practices with each other and also connecting with higher performing mentors. These practices of teachers helping teachers and schools supporting schools demonstrate the power of networked teacher leadership to yield significant and more sustainable results than implementation of imposed, standardized practices (Hargreaves & Shirley, in press).

From this body of work on teachers and teaching over 30 years, it is evident that there is a long and distinguished though often understated and even unsung tradition of teacher leadership in our schools. All teachers in schools know who their leaders are—the ones who teach well, work hard, are prepared to stand up for what they believe, are able to work with and command respect among diverse colleagues, and are in it for the children rather than for themselves. Teacher leadership often paradoxically requires confident but low-key principalship in order to prosper, but in some systems like Finland it is a defining feature of how the system operates. Teacher leadership thrives in innovative environments and is driven underground by standardized ones, where it may resurface to turn against the system itself, in defense of teachers' dignity and of the students they serve. Teachers can and do lead across schools as well as within them, raising the performance of their own institutions as they do so. In recent years, however, teacher leadership has sometimes become so formalized and data-driven that long-term reflection and deep conversation have been replaced by the pressure to meet short-term targets in hurried meetings. In its deeper and most authentic sense, it is time to bring teacher leadership back in as a collective collegial effort through conversation, inquiry, and action to transform curriculum and pedagogy together so that all students' needs can be served effectively.

Developing Teacher Leaders by Frank Crowther, Margaret Ferguson, and Leonne Hann brings teacher leadership back in with a vengeance. After years of soulless standardization and sometimes in direct defiance of it, a very small club of outstanding scholars committed to teacher professionalism has asserted the importance of teacher leadership for educational change, and also exemplified it in practice. These writers, in this important second edition, are, with Alma Harris in Britain and Ann Lieberman and Lynne Miller as well as Joe Murphy in the United States, in the very forefront of advocacy for and analysis of teacher leadership.

Conceptually and strategically, in this much developed second edition, Crowther and colleagues demonstrate the importance of teacher leadership in developing a mission and a vision without being exclusionary of the purposes of others; they emphasize how teacher leadership is a vital part of community and culture building in schools; they stress how credible teacher leadership is not merely vague talk about missions and plans but also grounded in and insistent upon pedagogical excellence; they indicate how effective teacher leadership turns ideas into action and overcomes barriers by turning obstacles into opportunities; and they show that the best teacher leadership is asset-based rather than deficit-driven—building on existing records and early indications of achievement and success.

Teacher leadership, this book acknowledges, is not always good leadership and it can take many different forms. The links to pedagogy, community-building, an action-orientation and a problem-solving mentality are more likely, they argue, under strong and supportive principals. In Anglo-Saxon contexts at least, teacher leadership, like distributed leadership, does not mean weaker leadership for principals but principals who have strong leadership capacities of their own—a clear sense of direction and an ability to lead with and through rather than over others in pursuit of these purposes. Strong principals in cultures of teacher leadership know when to challenge and to push and also when to step back. These are some of the essential lessons of this leading text in the field of teacher leadership.

Developing Teacher Leaders, though, is not just a book based in theory or a few opportunistic examples from practice. Rather, it arises out of collaborative improvement work between universities and schools in places where teacher leadership has been central. Most important of all, perhaps, is the broad-based IDEAS improvement network established by the authors after their first edition where schools network with each other and, with outside assistance, come together to develop a pedagogical focus and build communities of inquiry and improvement around it. From personal experience, I can vouch that this is the liveliest and most challenging of networks where teachers push and support each other across schools in the non-sanctimonious, fun-filled way that only teachers can, to make real changes that benefit all their students, especially those who are most at risk. Endless examples of exemplary practice from this improvement work, most often written by teacher leaders themselves, demonstrate what teacher leadership looks like in the busy world of practice as well as the elegant formulae of theory.

Last of all, unlike the other leading texts on this topic, Crowther, Ferguson, and Hann set out a collection of activities or CLASSES for readers who want to develop and deepen their own teacher leadership. This book is theoretical and practical, inspiring and informative, constructive yet also critical. Australia and New Zealand have been at the very leading edge of some of the world's most effective initiatives in education—literacy practices and Reading Recovery being among the best known. *Developing Teacher Leaders* adds to this impressive lineage, giving to the world a vision, a set of values, and vivid examples in practice of how and why more and better teacher leadership can and should lead to more and better improvement for all the students that we serve. It brings teacher leadership out of the marginal shadows of educational administration and into the forefront of successful educational change.

—Andy Hargreaves

REFERENCES

Crowther, F., Kaagan, S. S., Ferguson, M., & Hann, L. (2002). *Developing teacher leaders: How teacher leadership enhances school success.* Thousand Oaks, CA: Corwin Press.

Fullan, M., & Hargreaves, A. (1996). *What's worth fighting for in your school?* New York, NY: Teachers College Press.

Giles, C., & Hargreaves, A. (2006). The sustainability of innovative schools as learning organizations and professional learning communities during standardized reform. *Educational Administration Quarterly, 42*(1), 124–156.

Hargreaves, A. (1986). *Two cultures of schooling: The case of middle schools.* New York, NY: Falmer Press.

Hargreaves, A. (1994). *Changing teachers, changing times: Teachers' work and culture in the postmodern age.* London: Cassell.

Hargreaves, A. (2003). *Teaching in the knowledge society: Education in the age of insecurity.* New York, NY: Teachers College Press.

Hargreaves, A. (2008). Leading professional learning communities: Moral choices and murky realities. In A. M. Blankstein, P. D. Houston, & R. W. Cole (Eds.), *Sustaining professional learning communities.* Thousand Oaks, CA: Corwin Press.

Hargreaves, A., Earl, L., Moore, S., & Manning, S. (2001). *Learning to change: Teaching beyond subjects and standards.* San Francisco, CA: Jossey-Bass.

Hargreaves, A., & Fink, D. (2006). *Sustainable leadership.* San Francisco, CA: Jossey-Bass.

Hargreaves, A., & Fullan, M. (1998). *What's worth fighting for out there?* New York, NY: Teachers College Press.

Hargreaves, A., Halász, G., & Pont, B. (2007). *School leadership for systemic improvement in Finland.* Paris: OECD.

Hargreaves, A., & Shirley, D. (in press). The coming of post-standardization. *Phi Delta Kappan.*

Preface to the Second Edition

> *Knowledge workers will give the emerging knowledge society its character; its leadership, its social profile. They may not be the ruling class of the knowledge society, but they are already its leading class. And in their characteristics, social position, values, and expectations, they differ fundamentally from any group in history that has ever occupied the leading position.*
>
> —Peter Drucker
> (1994, p. 64)

WHY THIS BOOK AND WHY NOW?

When Steve Kaagan, Margaret Ferguson, Leonne Hann, and I were preparing the first edition of *Developing Teacher Leaders* in 2001, we spent considerable time contemplating possible quotations with which to introduce our Preface. We settled on the statement from internationally renowned change theorist Peter Drucker that appears here. It seemed to capture our thoughts regarding the dynamic image of a proud teaching profession that we dared to believe might emerge at some point in the future.

As I finalize the second edition, some seven years later, I can think of no more appropriate statement with which to begin the Preface and, indeed, the book itself. I say this primarily because Drucker's statement remains as inspiring in 2008 as it was in 2001. But, a great deal has changed since 2001. Of particular note is that compelling evidence now exists that the time of the teaching profession is clearly on the horizon. Our profession is much closer to assuming a "leading class" place in society than we could possibly have imagined just seven years ago. Thus, our use of Drucker's statement in this second edition is marked by a fresh note of confidence.

In preparation for the first edition, my co-authors and I had worked for five years to attempt to uncover the deep meaning that we believed was inherent in the concept of teacher leadership. As researchers, we engaged with teachers and school principals in contexts as diverse as a Midwestern American city and an outback Australian bush town. As scholars, we searched for meaning through presentations at international conferences and through collegial discussions in the staff rooms of elementary and secondary schools. As our journey progressed, and our Teachers as Leaders Framework took shape, we became increasingly convinced that the emerging knowledge society might well be shaped by qualities that were part and parcel of the work of the teaching profession.

In the past seven years, I have been closely associated with concentrated R&D efforts to extend the concepts that defined our first edition. In so doing, my colleagues and I have been guided by two distinctive goals—to enhance the quality of the school as the most central site of human learning and development and to advance the cause of the teaching profession. These efforts have been undertaken primarily through the Leadership Research Institute of the University of Southern Queensland, with applications in a number of Australian State and Catholic school systems, as well as Singapore and Sicily. Most notably, the University of Southern Queensland's school revitalization initiative, the IDEAS Project, which is grounded in principles of teacher leadership and parallel leadership, provides the main database for this second edition. Additionally, a number of outstanding critiques of the core concepts of teacher leadership and parallel leadership have informed our thinking as we have prepared this second edition. Most notable has been a systematic analysis in 2005 by renowned educational leadership researcher and theorist Joseph Murphy.

As with the first edition, this book is for people who believe it is critically important to enrich the leadership of our schools—people who suspect that the models of school leadership that dominate worldwide are weary, worn, and inadequate; people who believe that the teaching profession's growth for the past several decades has been severely stunted and is overdue, not just for revitalization but also for renaissance; people who believe that the teaching profession must, in fact, be the centerpiece of the emerging knowledge society, creating schools that are dynamic sources of inspiration in a world that, for many, is confusing and alienating.

Indeed, it is difficult for us to imagine the evolution of a knowledge society without the teaching profession leading the way. For, as the six case study snapshots that are contained in the chapters of this edition illustrate, teacher leaders have unique capabilities to illustrate the complex dynamics of successful knowledge creation:

> Communities of people working together so that their collective intelligence results in creation of new knowledge that enhances their personal efficacy and their quality of life and enables them to contribute to a more sustainable and better world for others. (Crowther, 2003, p. 12)

In the context of current school reform efforts, this book is also for dedicated community and business leaders who want schools to be intellectually vibrant, morally disciplined, and aesthetically stimulating—and who know that teachers are, ultimately, the primary force in effecting such ends.

The Teachers as Leaders Framework (Table 1.1), along with the closely affiliated concepts of metastrategic principalship and parallel leadership, represents the essential source of the sense of optimism and confidence that pervades the second edition of *Developing Teacher Leaders*. Along with my coresearchers and coauthors, I have seen the Framework exemplified in a wide range of contexts and have witnessed its capacity, when allied to metastrategic principalship, to enhance not just school outcomes but also the quality of life of school communities.

Yet, we must be realistic. The mindset that schools have little effect on children's life chances, a widely accepted interpretation of the Coleman report four decades ago (Coleman, 1966), continues to impinge negatively on the work of teachers worldwide, their professional self-concept, and their public image. It cannot be denied that schools and teachers throughout much of the Western world seem to be assailed by a range of media commentators, politicians, business leaders, and academics as malevolently today as was the case in decades past. Unsurprisingly, the "I'm just a teacher" syndrome that came to dominate many teachers' self-concepts in the decades following the Coleman report persists. It demands of those of us who recognize its crippling effects that we generate inspiring alternatives and make those alternatives available for widespread professional and school-based application.

We believe that the Teacher as Leaders Framework does just that. It captures a view of the teaching profession that stands in stark contrast to the sense of negativity and paralysis that has come to dominate so much professional and lay thinking during the past half century. It makes clear that many teachers who currently work in our schools have leadership qualities that have not previously been recognized and that, if actualized, can transform not only schools but also communities. And, it points to the vitality and integrity of the concept that we call *parallel leadership* as a way forward for other professions wishing to reshape themselves as the emerging knowledge society envelops them.

A DIFFERENT APPROACH TO TEACHER LEADERSHIP

This book is different because it proposes that educational leadership for the emerging postindustrial world must embrace the leadership capabilities of teachers. The term *teacher leadership* refers not solely to pedagogical expertise, professionalism, enthusiasm, passion, and commitment. Certainly, schools need all these qualities from their teachers. But what we are talking about is a form of leadership that is responsive to the imperative that schools transform themselves and, in so doing, demonstrate for communities how organizational transformation can be managed positively and effectively. Ultimately, teacher leadership, as we intend it, is about action that enhances teaching and learning in a school, that ties school and community together, and that advances quality of life for a community. All these elements are part of the portfolio of teacher leaders. Thus this book is different, not just because it asserts the need for new forms of leadership in our schools, but also because we define teacher leadership as a transformative process that is grounded in definitive values and functions.

This book is also different because it postulates and describes the critical importance of teacher leadership in successful school reform. While it is true that the concept of distributed leadership now has a clear place in the educational leadership literature, and while it is equally true that teacher leadership is now widely regarded as a reality, the vast majority of educational leadership theorists and authors appear to us to continue to view teacher leadership as a peripheral rather than central plank in successful school improvement. The reason may be that evidence in support of the fundamental importance of parallel leadership in sustained pedagogical improvement is not yet widely known or understood. The role of the principalship that has emerged from half a century of development and promotion remains largely intact, its recognized shortcomings notwithstanding. But this book is different. It asserts the centrality of the teacher leader–metastrategic principal relationship in enhancing school capacity and provides a research-based conceptual explanation (Figure 3.1) that is unique in some important respects.

Moreover, this book is in part about advancing the cause of democracy. The construction of leadership that is the focus of the second edition of *Developing Teacher Leaders* is grounded in a belief that schools have a fundamental responsibility to practice mature forms of democracy and to demonstrate their practices to the wider community. Parallel leadership, we assert, represents a more advanced form of democratic process than is to be found in the bureaucratically-derived conceptions of leadership that have dominated schools in the past. Esteemed American educator John Goodlad (as cited in Goldberg, 2000) stated recently that "the workplace will not survive unless we educate people for democracy . . . and there needs to be a profound rethinking of what 21st century democracy requires of the schools" (p. 84). He pointed to the unequivocal importance of leadership roles for schools that have not yet been recognized. Our book represents a partial response to Goodlad's challenge.

In proposing a definitive concept of teacher leadership, in projecting a central role for the teaching profession in the knowledge society of the future, in linking teacher leadership to deliberate and sustained school reform, and in presuming to advance democratic thinking, this book is distinctive.

A SUMMARY OF CHANGES
FROM THE FIRST EDITION

The second edition of *Developing Teacher Leaders* should be regarded as both a refinement and an extension of the first edition. The central concept of teacher leadership has been refined, but not fundamentally recast, to take into account recent research outcomes. The same applies to the metas-trategic role of the principal. Furthermore, the second edition may be regarded as a refinement of the first in the sense that the optimistic future that was envisioned for the teaching profession in 2001 is rearticulated in this edition, though with much greater confidence.

In four important respects, however, this book represents a significant extension of the thinking that was contained in the first edition.

Most notably, five of the six snapshots that are presented in this edition are new. The sixth was featured in the first edition but has been extended to include an epilogue that provides insights regarding the complexity of teacher leadership when viewed longitudinally. Second, the international school development program that has been the basis for our research into teacher leadership, the IDEAS Project, is outlined in Appendix A. Third, the process of capacity-building that comes into effect when teacher leaders and principals act "in parallel" has been expanded and its dynamics described. Fourth, the CLASS Plan that is presented in Chapter 6 constitutes what we regard as an authoritative approach to the systematic development of teacher leadership and parallel leadership in school settings. It has been trialed in a wide variety of settings, evaluated by presenters and participants, and modified in accordance with their recommendations.

THE TEACHERS AS LEADERS RESEARCH
PROJECT, 1996 TO 2008 AND ONGOING

The frameworks for teacher leadership and parallel leadership that are the foundation of this book stem from research conducted in five phases over a period of more than a decade, with support from three research-funding agencies. The first two phases were completed in Queensland, Australia, and the third was undertaken as part of an Australia-wide research project with links to Michigan. The fourth phase involved a national trial and evaluation of a school revitalization initiative (the IDEAS Project) that is founded on principles of teacher leadership and parallel leadership. The fifth phase, which is continuing, involves major systemic implementation of the IDEAS Project in Australia and in a range of international settings. An overview of the decade-long research and development projects that provide the basis for this edition of *Developing Teacher Leaders* is contained in Appendix B.

In essence, a comprehensive longitudinal database exists for the concepts and processes that are presented in this book. Additionally, as is indicated in Appendix B, a number of research-based articles, books, and doctoral dissertations have been published recently by researchers associated with the Teachers as Leaders Project.

ORGANIZATION OF THE BOOK

Developing Teacher Leaders is both conceptual and developmental. It is conceptual in that it describes teacher leadership, parallel leadership, and ways that these ideas engender improved outcomes, including student achievement, teacher esteem, and community confidence. It is developmental in the sense that it provides a range of relevant professional learning exercises, and offers readers a platform for engaging the concepts of teacher leadership and parallel leadership in their own schools.

In Chapter 1, we explain the concept of teacher leadership that emerged from our research. Central to this chapter is a definition of teacher leadership and an associated framework that outlines the main elements of teacher leadership. Chapter 2 presents five premises derived from our research that we believe provide new direction for the teaching profession in the emerging knowledge society. A simple but profound conclusion emerges from these premises: All the essential elements of significant leadership theories are present in the work of some classroom teachers. As remarkable as this assertion may be, these elements do not represent the sum total of teacher leadership, nor do existing theories capture the full power of teacher leadership. Rather, teacher leadership has an extra dimension that distinguishes it from other leadership forms, namely, a focus on schoolwide excellence in teaching, learning, and assessment—a concept that is fundamental to successful school reform.

Chapter 3 introduces the concept of parallel leadership. Parallel leadership is necessary if school vision and classroom practices are to be aligned and if school revitalization is to be sustained over time. Parallel leadership, as we define it, encourages relatedness between teacher leaders and principal leaders that enables the knowledge-generating capacity of schools to be activated and sustained. Our diagram linking parallel leadership and successful school capacity-building (Figure 3.1) is a centerpiece of Chapter 3.

Chapter 4 outlines the metastrategic role of the school principal in successful school reform and describes the five key functions of metastrategy that have emerged from our research. We also discuss seven challenges that we have identified as confronting principals seeking to develop teacher leadership and parallel leadership in their schools. *Developing Teacher Leaders* also provides a basis for the professional learning of educators seeking to enrich the leadership of their schools. Complementing the concepts in Chapters 1 to 4 is a comprehensive (two to three years) professional learning program entitled The CLASS Plan (Creating Leaders to Accelerate School Successes). The rationale for the CLASS Plan is outlined in Chapter 5 and the fifteen exercises are presented in Chapter 6. The vision of the CLASS Plan is: An ever expanding cohort of teacher leaders who view themselves as shaping an advanced twenty-first century profession and enhancing student successes in their schools.

The four components of CLASS Plan are:

- Component One: Orientation to the program (three exercises)
- Component Two: Stimulating and nurturing teacher leadership capabilities (six exercises)
- Component Three: Developing parallel leadership relationships and strategies (three exercises)
- Component Four: Sustaining teacher leadership into the future (three exercises)

The fifteen exercises that are introduced in Chapter 5 and presented in Chapter 6 have three common qualities. First, they are experiential. Second, they are constructivist—they involve participants' analyses of their own thought processes, experiences, and emotions as they engage in professional learning. Third, they relate directly to the core concepts of the book, namely, teacher leadership, metastrategic principalship, and parallel leadership.

The exercises are designed to be used primarily by teachers and principals in schools aspiring to build their leadership capacity. There are explicit and detailed directions for each one. The exercises can be completed without external facilitation although, with qualified outside help, the impact will likely be greater. Having completed the exercises, preferably as part of a collaborative schoolwide or cluster process, participants should be well-equipped to undertake further leader development work on their own.

Appendix A contains a description of the IDEAS Project. Appendix B outlines the research methodology that has underpinned our ten years of developmental work. The five stages of the research are outlined, along with sample research data that indicate our confidence in a relationship between the leadership concepts and processes featured in this book and the enhancement of educational outcomes. Appendix C recounts discussions held in Michigan with teacher leaders and other educators concerning the main ideas in the book.

Chapters 1 to 4 rely heavily on six snapshots that describe teacher leadership and parallel leadership in real-life situations. These chapters also make significant use of research findings relating to IDEAS Project schools. Pseudonyms are used in all references to the schools and individual professionals in question.

CONCLUDING COMMENT

Basic to the thinking behind this second edition of *Developing Teacher Leaders* is that the world is not standing still, nor will the future resemble the present, let alone the past. The Teachers as Leaders Framework that is central to this book, and the related notion of parallel leadership, will undoubtedly evolve into new forms and acquire new meanings. Also of integral importance is the challenge of Drucker's assertion which introduces this Preface: In the emerging postindustrial world, leadership will be dominated by knowledge workers. The authors and other contributors to this book assert that teachers are ideally placed to become the central knowledge-generating profession. The concepts and the developmental activities that make up *Developing Teacher Leaders* reflect our optimism that, for members of the teaching profession, the journey into the postindustrial world will be increasingly meaningful and gratifying.

—Frank Crowther
February, 2008

Acknowledgments

Many professional educators have made constructive contributions to this edition of *Developing Teacher Leaders*.

The analytical and creative thinking of my coauthors in the first edition—Steve Kaagan, Margaret Ferguson, and Leonne Hann—is, I am sure, still very much in evidence in the second edition. Margaret and Leonne contributed editorially to the second edition and therefore have had a helpful ongoing impact.

The research staff of the Leadership Research Institute at the University of Southern Queensland have contributed many of the refinements that appear in the second edition through their ongoing work with the IDEAS Project. Dorothy Andrews, Director of the Institute, Marlene Barron, Joan Conway, Mark Dawson, Tom Hart, Mary Keeffe, Marian Lewis, Allan Morgan, Shauna Peterson, Helen Starr, and Sharon Taylor have individually and collectively modeled the dynamics of a successful professional learning community, and continue to do so. Dr. Bryan Connors, a Canadian Visiting Scholar, has also contributed immensely during his annual visits to the University of Southern Queensland.

Across education systems, I acknowledge the invaluable support of Gary Barnes, Steve Bell, Emma Brennan, Steve Brown, Trish Brown, Jan Darcy, Ross Dean, Sybil Dickens, Michael Gaffney, Janice Haydon, Lyn Healy, Doug Jeanes, Beverley Johnson, Jayne Johnston, Terry Kearney, Jenny Lewis, Mary L'Estrange, Kim Lloyd, Sally McCutcheon, Bob McHugh, Chris McRae, Keith Newton, Elizabeth O'Carrigan, Brett Rangiira, Rosemary Roberts, Marnie Rodriguez, Brett Shackleton, Alan Swan, Greg Thornton, Karena Wilson, and Alison Woodman. Internationally, Joy Chew, Senthu Jeyaraj, Giuseppe Micciche, David Foo Seong Ng, Ken Stott, Angela Tan, and Terry Wrigley have added a dimension to this book that enriches it greatly.

Among the many schools-based professionals whose leadership in action has provided the basis for the core content of this second edition of *Developing Teacher Leaders* I acknowledge in particular: Linda Abawi, Lesley Bath, Jason Beggs, Trish Bevan, Judy Boyle, Judy Dunn, Michael Fay, Dan Feehley, Ken Fischer, Sue Flood, Ian Fraser, Geri Hardy, Jan

Hargreaves, Peter Holcz, Norm Hunter, Julie King, Simon McGlade, Catherine O'Sullivan, Lynelle Rafton, Kathy Ritchie, Robyn Rodwell, and Loretta Simioni.

Finally, the ten years of research on which this book is based were made possible with funding support from the Australian Research Council; the Queensland, Victorian, and Western Australian Departments of Education; the Catholic Archdioceses of Sydney, Canberra-Goulburn, and Toowoomba; the Australian Commonwealth Department of Education, Training and Youth Affairs; and the Singaporean Ministry of Education. These generous forms of assistance are gratefully acknowledged.

Corwin Press gratefully acknowledges the contributions of the following individuals:

Richard Ackerman
Professor University of Maine
Orono, ME

Deborah Bambino
National School Reform Faculty
Pennsylvania Center of Activity
Philadelphia, PA

Gordon Donaldson
Professor University of Maine
Orono, ME

Ann Lieberman
Senior Scholar Carnegie Foundation
  for the Advancement of Teaching
Stanford, CA

Gayle Moller
Retired Assistant Professor
Western Carolina University
Cullowhee, NC

Jennifer York-Barr
Professor University of Minnesota
Minneapolis, MN

About the Authors

Frank Crowther is an internationally respected scholar and researcher in educational management and leadership. He is Emeritus Professor at the University of Southern Queensland, Australia. In 2006, he was awarded an Order of Australia (AM) for his lifetime of service to the teaching profession internationally.

Margaret Ferguson is District Manager of Education Services at Education Queensland. Her work focuses on capacity-building, curriculum leadership, and pedagogical enhancement in schools.

Leonne Hann is an educational leadership researcher and advisor. She has participated in national research projects in school innovation. Her postgraduate study dealt with teacher leadership and successful school reform.

1

Teachers as Leaders

Emergence of a New Paradigm

Within every school there is a sleeping giant of teacher leadership, which can be a strong catalyst for making change. By using the energy of teacher leaders as agents of school change, the reform of public education will stand a better chance of building momentum.

—Marilyn Katzenmeyer &
Gayle Moller (2001, p. 2)

NEEDED: A NEW PARADIGM
OF THE TEACHING PROFESSION

Even a cursory reading of the educational literature leads to the conclusion that the way the teaching profession is currently viewed is ill-founded and out of date—in a word, wrong.

A review of policy developments throughout most of the Western world reveals that the pressures and demands on teachers are greater than in living memory. This is evidenced in heightened parental expectations for individualized programs for their children; the implications of new neurological, genetic, and psychological research for learning and child development; duty of care legislation; performance-based pay schemes; and national and international assessment programs; not to mention the challenges associated with the distinctive characteristics of Generation Y. Indeed, a major weekend newspaper has recently devoted its editorial to the challenges confronting teachers as they prepare for a new school term:

> Almost 700,000 (students) will answer the rolls . . . this week. . . . Also shining their school shoes will be more than 37,000 teachers, who will shoulder a burden of responsibility second to none. And rarely have they faced so many challenges. Changing community expectations and social patterns have swept away the professional certainties of yesteryear . . . teachers are increasingly expected to step into the mentoring void created by inadequate parenting. Classroom relationships and dynamics are changing at a startling pace, and this year will represent a steep learning curve for teachers, children and the community as a whole. (*The Sunday Mail*, January 27, 2008, p. 60)

But, regardless of the ever-increasing complexity of teachers' work and in spite of their increasing credentials and professional maturity, the responsibility and authority accorded the profession have not grown or changed significantly in decades.

Thus, a new paradigm of the teaching profession is needed, one that recognizes both the capacity of the profession to provide desperately needed school revitalization and the striking potential of teachers to provide new forms of leadership in schools and communities. The Teachers as Leaders Framework (Table 1.1) that represents the core of this chapter—and, indeed of this book—substantiates the assertion that teacher leadership is an idea whose time has come. This assertion was advanced by Katzenmeyer and Moller (1996) in the first edition of their landmark publication, *Awakening the Sleeping Giant: Leadership Development for Teachers.* They claimed that teachers have the potential to exercise new and dynamic leadership in schools, thereby enhancing the possibility of social reform. They introduced the metaphor of a sleeping giant to illustrate not just the dormant status of teacher leadership at that time but also the power it might exert if aroused.

In the twelve years since publication of *Awakening the Sleeping Giant,* teacher leadership has drawn considerable attention worldwide and has acquired a degree of legitimacy in the educational literature and also in educational practice. But what does teacher leadership mean? Following an exhaustive review of international literature, Joseph Murphy reached the conclusion that in 2005 teacher leadership remained basically "a theory

Table 1.1   The Teachers as Leaders Framework

Teacher leaders . . .

Convey convictions about a better world by

- articulating a positive future for all students
- contributing to an image of teaching as a profession that makes a difference

Facilitate communities of learning by

- encouraging a shared, schoolwide approach to core pedagogical processes
- approaching professional learning as consciousness-raising about complex issues
- synthesizing new ideas out of colleagues' professional discourse and reflective activities

Strive for pedagogical excellence by

- showing genuine interest in students' needs and well-being
- continuously developing and refining personal teaching gifts and talents
- seeking deep understanding of significant pedagogical practices

Confront barriers in the school's culture and structures by

- standing up for children, especially disadvantaged and marginalized individuals and groups
- working with administrators to find solutions to issues of equity, fairness, and justice
- encouraging student "voice" in ways that are sensitive to students' developmental stages and circumstances

Translate ideas into sustainable systems of action by

- working with the principal, administrators, and other teachers to manage projects that heighten alignment between the school's vision, values, pedagogical practices, and professional learning activities
- building alliances and nurturing external networks of support

Nurture a culture of success by

- acting on opportunities to emphasize accomplishments and high expectations
- encouraging collective responsibility in addressing schoolwide challenges
- encouraging self-respect and confidence in students' communities

---

in action" (Murphy, 2005, p. 46). But, he also noted that a number of significant understandings are now in place, including three that we regard as particularly significant:

- Barth's contention (2001) that community development via teacher leadership nurtures democracy (as cited in Murphy, p. 56).
- Katzenmeyer and Moller's assertion (2001) that, as teachers begin to believe in their leadership capabilities, they take on increased

schoolwide responsibilities and in so doing affect teaching and learning throughout the school (as cited in Murphy, p. 53).

- Smyllie et al.'s claim (2002) that teacher leadership may make both independent and, with leadership from other sources, additive or multiplicative contributions to school improvement and outcomes for students (as cited in Murphy, p. 50).

To these powerful insights we add three provocative assertions that have emerged from international research since the first edition of *Developing Teacher Leaders* in 2002:

- Muijs and Harris' conclusion (2002) from British research that the impact of principals' leadership on student outcomes is mediated through the exercise of teacher leadership (as cited in Harris, 2004, p. 1).
- Durrant's conclusion (2004) from British research that holistic school reform without recognition of teacher leadership through agency, authority, and action is conceptually incomplete and unlikely to result in enhanced "capacity" (p. 27).
- Katyal and Evers' conclusion (2004) from their Hong Kong research that teacher leaders have sophisticated capabilities of both a pedagogical and a social nature. In combination, these capabilities enable them to influence student engagement beyond the classroom (p. 51).

The refined Framework for Teacher Leadership that we present in Table 1.1 emanates from our own research and developmental work over the past half decade, but it is noticeably consistent in intent with the outcomes of the research of these six authorities. It is therefore idealistic in its purposes, practical in its origins, and authoritative in its conceptualization.

Compared to many other conceptions of teacher leadership that have emerged over the past decade or more, the Framework also has characteristics of a role-based model (Getzels & Guba, 1957, as cited in Owens & Valesky, 2007, p. 136). That is, the Framework is grounded in a worldview that schools are social systems that (a) have clearly defined roles and expectations and (b) are managed and worked by individuals with personalities and needs-dispositions. Thus, the teacher leaders whom we describe in our case study snapshots perform highly complex formal educational functions in conjunction with, and on behalf of, their colleagues and their principals. They are also individually characterized by marked dispositions, styles, and ideals. In essence, our Teachers as Leaders Framework is therefore intended as more than a generic example of "distributed" leadership. Rather, it is intended to enable schools to achieve specified goals at the same time as its bonafide representatives achieve heightened personal reward and actualization.

To begin, we profile two schools where teacher leaders have exercised distinctive forms of leadership to shape meaning for their students and communities. The practical differences between the two forms are very considerable, but they each reflect the six key elements of the Teachers as Leaders Framework.

The snapshot that follows was prepared for the 2002 edition of *Developing Teacher Leaders*. It remains unchanged in this edition, but the epilogue that follows is new.

SNAPSHOT ONE: GREENHILLS STATE HIGH SCHOOL

Greenhills has 600 students and is situated in a small, economically depressed rural town. Because it is attractive in many ways, the casual visitor to Greenhills could be forgiven for not discerning that the surrounding community has endured a long-term slump in its primary industrial base, that it has one of the highest levels of economic disadvantage in the nation, and that as many as three generations of some families have experienced persistent unemployment.

According to a veteran teacher at the school, students used to "come to school with their shoulders dropped." It was in this context of limited opportunity and low levels of motivation that teacher leaders undertook to provide the material out of which success stories are made.

Where it all began is still not entirely clear. Perhaps it was the Student Aspirations Program, through which a small group of teachers built a system for student mentoring and peer support. This involved identifying students' interests or talents as a starting point for building self-esteem and proficiency and, ultimately, for broadening their horizons for future endeavors. Over the years, the Student Aspirations Program became part of the fabric of the school, changing regularly as new teachers, with new interests and capacities, joined the community. Conceivably, it was only when the school motto—*Success Breeds Success*—began to infiltrate the thinking of the whole school community that students' expectations and self-belief started to change.

A second possibility is that credit for initiating the turnaround should be assigned to the current principal. Among his considerable talents is his ability to convince students that personal demeanor—dress, speech, manners—is very important to their achieving enhanced levels of academic and postschool success. He also insisted that every achievement, no matter how small, or in what field, was worthy of celebration. Thus, he had no difficulty convincing Nancy and Lisa, two young teachers, of the impact of their public speaking initiatives and organized sports competitions on student motivation, self-expectation, and school pride. Nor did he have difficulty accommodating the school resources committee's recommendation that finances be made available to facilitate access to online career information for students and the community to improve career opportunities for all.

The positive effects of synergistic leadership at Greenhills State High are numerous. First, the school has achieved marked recognition for its academic, cultural, and sporting successes, having been honored in a statewide showcasing competition. Second, it has undertaken significant educational innovations in which teachers have challenged themselves to improve their teaching practices. Third, community surveys indicated that it has become regarded as the center of local community life to an extent seldom achieved by a high school.

The teacher leaders we observed at Greenhills were able to articulate clearly their goals and strategies. They spoke convincingly of the "we can do anything" mindset of the student body, the inseparability of school and community, the sense of reward that goes with overcoming immense odds, and the teamwork of the teachers—heightened further as it is matched by the facilitative support of the principal. They regarded their school as unique, and they treasured that uniqueness, despite, or maybe because of, the human disadvantage, and even despair, out of which it had emerged.

The question we asked ourselves as we left Greenhills was, "Could this dynamic leadership come from elsewhere in the community or does it point to something distinctive about the teaching profession?" Certainly, our analysis of the leadership processes in place at Greenhills, supported by the views of teachers and school administrators, is that the magic of Greenhills resides substantially in the power of teachers through their pedagogical and community-building practices—to transform their schools and enrich their communities.

Epilogue, November 2007

Readers may well ask, "What has happened at Greenhills since 2001? Has teacher leadership continued to thrive? If so, what forms does it take?"

We had heard about the pioneering work of one longstanding teacher leader, Andrew Fisher, in exploring pedagogical processes with cohorts of students. We asked him to provide a description of the work that had resulted in his receiving an international travel award in 2006:

> As a long-serving teacher at Greenhills, I had observed dramatic changes take place in students' perceptions of themselves, their school and the outside world under the influence of dynamic teacher leaders and programs such as the Student Aspirations Program. What, I wondered, were the implications for everyday classroom pedagogy? I thought I had particular expertise in relation to this question and determined to find out.
>
> As one member of the school management team for the implementation of a long-term process of school renewal, I saw the valuable input that students had in developing the school vision and an agreed set of principles of good teaching practices for the school. I also observed the enthusiasm and freshness of ideas that the students brought to the task. This confirmed my long-held belief that there is much that teachers and school communities can learn from listening respectfully to students. I determined to build on the students' enthusiasm by establishing a team of volunteer students who met every couple of weeks to explore further issues associated with the school. This enabled students to have the time and space to articulate their views on teaching and learning and schooling in general in a forum where their ideas were valued, discussed, challenged, and acted on in some way.
>
> Over time the group has had some remarkable successes—designing and painting a mural to depict the school vision, initiating workshops on learning styles, conducting workshops and presentations on teaching and learning to staff of the school and other schools, writing papers for and participating in a worldwide student conference via the internet, and developing a dialogue with their teachers on pedagogy. Along with a small number of other teachers I have facilitated the meetings, but the agendas have always been set by the students.
>
> At the same time, I initiated a quite unusual experiment with a year nine class (9D) that was becoming almost unmanageable. Having tried all in my teaching repertoire, but failing to change the class's behavior, I decided to listen to what the

students had to say. Together they developed a "9D Statement of Good Teaching and Learning" based on the students' ideas of what made a good lesson. This statement became the core of classroom learning experiences from then on. Further, the students went on to plan curriculum and lessons with me over the ensuing eighteen months, as well as coevaluating lessons. The student-generated statement is as follows:

> Good teaching and learning involves a variety of new and exciting ideas for classroom activities. Where possible, activities should be hands-on, creative and set in different environments. At the beginning of a unit, students should set goals to be accomplished by the end of that unit. Where possible, students should be given choices because everyone has different interests and learning abilities. Students need to be respected and treated as individuals.

The changes in the class were extraordinary—within a few weeks, behavior had totally turned around, previously disaffected students were now engaged with their learning, they developed ownership of their learning and an understanding of both the teaching and learning process and how they learned. Lessons were so much more productive—and fun—for all, a very supportive class culture developed and academic results improved.

I have continued the process with subsequent classes with similar success, and other teachers have adopted elements of the process in their classes. Problems have arisen, however, particularly with colleagues who are more wary or skeptical of the power of student voice. This has required me to reflect on my personal leadership style and also on my relationships with both colleagues and the principal. This can be both confronting and complex, but seems to me to be part and parcel of the process of mature school leadership, including teacher leadership.

As I reflect on my thirty years of teaching I see myself now as both a specialist teacher and also a teacher leader, continuously honing my skills and building on the foundations of co-teacher leaders who preceded me.

SNAPSHOT TWO: WHISTLEROCK ELEMENTARY SCHOOL

Whistlerock Elementary School is a school of 650 students in the western suburbs of a large modern metropolis. When the longstanding principal and a number of experienced teachers left about five years ago, external reviews indicated that it declined into a serious stalemate, characterized by lack of direction, loss of community support, and seriously diminished staff morale.

This regression was substantially overcome, however, over the next three years, through implementation of an approach to school leadership that involved the principal, deputy principal, and teacher leaders working in unison but with individual roles and functions. In the space of three years, a revitalized school vision was created—*Individual Paths, United Journey*—and a coherent pedagogical framework was developed by the teachers. Through a dominantly teacher-led development over a period of almost a year, a Whistlerock Literacy Strategy was created out of the pedagogical framework. The Strategy was distinguished by six principles, each of which has been expanded into classroom resources and techniques. The six principles are as follows:

- Every Whistlerock teacher is a teacher of literacy.
- Whistlerock literacy pedagogy is multifaceted, in recognition of the numerous ways that individual students acquire language and communication skills.
- Teachers of literacy must be highly knowledgeable about literacy, literacy development, and literacy teaching.
- Teaching literacy should be characterized by regular diagnosis of students' individual needs, progress, difficulties, and accomplishments.
- Early intervention, with expert advice and support, is critical at all stages of students' literacy development.
- Student achievement data from standardized tests should be used thoughtfully and judiciously to ensure that students and their community are represented with dignity.

We asked the deputy principal, Simon, to explain Whistlerock's transformation, and to reflect on the nature of Whistlerock leadership.

The principal set the stage by taking a strong stance and insisting that we had to lift ourselves out of a rut. He challenged us to undertake a formal process of school revitalization with a well-known university consulting group and he took personal responsibility for coordinating the development of a new school vision. He also challenged us to think beyond traditional leadership models and to encompass both teachers and community members.

My role concentrated on moving the revitalization process along, coordinating timeframes and resources (both financial and human) and articulating an understanding of how we could make changes work, engage the community, and provide stability throughout the change process.

Particular aspects of the revitalization process were driven by Cathy. She is a very well respected teacher with credibility in relation to innovative and proven pedagogy, as opposed to formal management. This difference proved to be pivotal—Cathy's combination of enthusiastic and energetic personality, sophisticated pedagogical capabilities, and well-known task orientation extended the skill set of the school administration in ways that proved to be very important. But she also possesses leadership skills that became apparent only as the Literacy Project unfolded—the ability to draw from a range of people-management skills at varying times, depending on the requirements of the situation; the capacity to draw together the various threads, concepts, ideas, and opinions of staff and synthesize them into creative new ideas; the capacity to see through rhetoric and jargon to find authentic meaning to then share with colleagues; and a talent for encouraging colleagues to reflect on the school's vision and values in the context of their everyday work. It was these capabilities that enabled our teachers to not only create something new and powerful in the form of a Literacy Strategy but also to see for themselves how it was being done.

As a result, the notion of all staff being potential leaders in their own right is now acknowledged, actively encouraged, and celebrated at Whistlerock. While Cathy remains the key teacher leader at our school, all staff now contribute to areas of school operations traditionally the domain of "management"—including provisioning, staffing, and curriculum formulation.

Our Model of Literacy Leadership at Whistlerock is captured in the analogy of a water mill. The waterwheel is constituted of our pedagogical principles (the frame) and our vision and values (the spokes in the water wheel). The leadership capabilities of our professional staff—administrators and teachers—drive the waterwheel and can be likened to a constantly recycling flow of water. We all feel very happy with this analogy as an explanation of how we go about our leadership work.

In hindsight, I would say that Larry, our principal, has been primarily responsible for the development of our shared and collectively owned school vision. As Deputy Principal, I have perhaps done most to manage the school revitalization process. I continue to be the coordinator of resource allocation processes, community links, classroom support systems, curriculum cohesion, and professional learning activities. Cathy's role is one that neither Larry nor I could do justice to—enabling teachers to uncover their personal pedagogy, continuously refining the Whistlerock Pedagogy and Literacy Strategy, and linking our work as a school to credible international educational theory and practice. Pedagogical implementation at Whistlerock is now consistent and collectively owned. The results are apparent when the outcomes of our system survey results from 2003 are compared with those of 2007. Staff morale has improved greatly; community perceptions of the school have become far more positive; and students' attitudes toward school, and engagement with school activities, have also shown marked improvement. Also, gains have been made at both ends of the learning spectrum in several areas of student achievement. For the period ahead, student achievement for the full spectrum of students will be our main focus, with Cathy's pedagogical leadership a fundamental cog in our leadership waterwheel.

PROBING THE WORK OF TEACHER LEADERS: AN EXHILARATING ENDEAVOR

Our work since 2002 in several hundred schools has confirmed for us the ongoing appropriateness of the basic definition of teacher leadership that emerged from our first research efforts over a decade ago (Crowther &

Olsen, 1997, p. 12). The definition that we now work with, and which follows, represents a minor variation of our original statement:

> Teacher leadership is essentially an ethical stance that is based on
> views of both a better world and the power of teachers to shape
> meaning systems. It manifests in new forms of understanding and
> practice that contribute to school success and to the quality of life
> of the community in the long term.

But our recent research and school-based consultancy initiatives, combined with insights from authoritative researchers such as Murphy,
Katzenmeyer and Moller, Smyllie, Barth, Durrant, Katyal and Evers, and
Mujis and Harris, have produced a depth in understanding regarding the
dynamics of teacher leadership that we did not have a half decade ago.

Thus, in reviewing the six snapshots that are included in this edition of
Developing Teacher Leaders, we encourage you to look for evidence of the
recent claims of the theorists and researchers to whom we have referred. You
will find, for example, that Barth's claims about democracy in action and
Durrant's assertions regarding the vital role of teacher leaders in successful
schoolwide revitalization are indeed apparent in the case study snapshots.

The two snapshots that are included in this chapter illustrate the key features of our definition of teacher leadership. The featured teacher leaders
involved their professional communities in the construction of significant
new educational knowledge that inspired confidence in teachers, students,
and parents, and laid the foundations for heightened aspirations and
enhanced levels of student achievement. In effect, the sketches offer what we
regard as a glimpse of the futuristic social transformation advocated by
reformists like Drucker (1994), Beare (2001), and Hargreaves (2003).

Many teachers, of course, do not meet all of the formidable requirements of either our definition or our Teachers as Leaders Framework.
There are good reasons why some teachers may not seek to link their work
to the dynamics of leadership. For example, they may choose to pursue
subject matter specialization, research, or a range of other challenging
occupational avenues that do not necessarily lead to teacher leadership as
we define it. Moreover, some teachers who exert leadership at a certain
juncture in their careers, or in a particular educational context, may not
choose to do so at another time or in another context.

As Table 1.1 indicates, the capabilities required to exercise influence on
professional processes of learning, on pedagogical enhancement, and on
community agencies are very complex. It is unrealistic to assume that all
teachers have the energy, confidence, or experience to engage influentially
at all points in their work lives. Finally, our research suggests that teacher
leadership occurs most readily in supportive organizational environments. But environments that support and nurture teacher leadership are
not endemic to many schools. Regrettably, teacher leadership development programs such as the CLASS Plan in Chapter 6 have historically not
been readily available to most practicing and prospective teacher leaders.

Despite these drawbacks, there are far more classroom teachers who meet the demanding requirements of our definition and framework than is generally assumed. These individuals and collegial groups have, for the most part, been overlooked in the development of leadership theory in recent decades, and have been largely bypassed in the development of educational policy for schools. These oversights have cost us all dearly. They have inhibited educational reform and helped to marginalize the teaching profession. Fortunately, we now know that teacher leadership exists in its own right, and that the "sleeping giant" that Katzenmeyer and Moller observed to be rousing in 1996 has now awakened. Its image is discernible, its movement palpable. These developments we regard with enthusiasm because we believe they will dramatically reshape the school workplace, the status of the teaching profession, and the place of schools within communities. We confidently predict that the "I'm just a teacher" syndrome that came to characterize self-concept in the teaching profession worldwide in recent decades is now well on the way to becoming a historical anachronism.

THE FRAMEWORK IN ACTION

Thus, in analyzing the six elements of the framework, keep in mind that it presents an idealized image of how teacher leaders exercise influence in their school communities. In a sense, the framework is a hypothetical portrait, because no one teacher leader whom we observed fulfills the entirety of the sixteen descriptors that are associated with it. Yet all the teacher leaders whom we studied exhibited each of the six elements in some way, at some time, in their work. In this regard, the observation of Daniel Goleman and his associates regarding the presence of nineteen emotional intelligence (EI) "competencies"/"capabilities" in highly effective leaders is illuminating:

> Interestingly, no leader we've encountered, no matter how outstanding, has strengths across the board in every one of the EI competencies. Highly effective leaders typically exhibit a critical mass of strength in a half dozen or so EI competencies. (Goleman, Boyatzis, & McKee, 2002, p. 38)

Element One: Teacher Leaders Convey Conviction About a Better World

Cambridge (UK) University scholar David Frost and his "leadership for learning" research team have contributed what we regard as a very helpful dimension to the educational literature with their assertion that school renewal and revitalization should be inspired by a moral purpose that is underpinned by democratic values (Frost, 2006, p. 19). Frost's stance is reminiscent of the position of classical educational leadership theorist William Foster to the effect that responsible educational leadership should encompass "a striving for the ideal in schooling. As such, idealism offers hope and optimism" (as cited in Lindle, 2004, p. 170).

The critical importance of Element One in the work of teacher leaders is also particularly well summed up in Terry Wrigley's (2003) concept of "hope":

> Teaching is a profession of hope. We are driven by desires—for our students to discover a taste for learning, a feel for justice and care for each other. We aspire to turn children into thoughtful, creative and concerned citizens. Inspirational teachers are motivated by their dreams of a better world. (p. 1)

Wrigley makes clear that he does not live in a Pollyanna world. He goes on to say that

> By hope, I do not mean a rosy optimism, an emotional inner glow. I mean a grounded hope which arises out of a full recognition of material and social needs and possibilities. As educators, we need a hope which dares to confront our troubled world. (p. 6)

The teacher leaders with whom we have worked, including those in the Greenhills and Whistlerock snapshots, have invariably placed high value on forms of moral purpose and have seen themselves as responsible agents of hope and optimism in their schools, communities, and further afield.

At Greenhills, preparing students for a better future provided the motivation for the teacher leaders—Lisa, Nancy, and Andrew. They understood the generally severe disadvantage of students' backgrounds and felt responsible for preparing students for the world of work. Lisa explained, "As teachers, we can help these kids realize that they can do anything that kids in advantaged high schools can do. Getting confidence is the key step for students in making the break." Five years later, at the same school, Andrew told us that his personal engagement with the teaching profession to create images of a "better world" for students had changed his professional life:

> I acquired a strong belief in the transformative power of student voice to make a real difference in classrooms, to students' lives and for the school as a whole. I am often startled by their insights and honesty and commitment to learning. I can say that student leadership is a very natural extension of teacher leadership and parallel leadership.

At Whistlerock, it was a perception that the school was not functioning adequately to meet students' literacy needs that motivated Cathy to accept the challenge of her principal and deputy principal to engage in a long-term process of school revitalization. Her belief, and theirs, that disadvantaged contextual factors should not be allowed to impose shortcomings on students' futures, but rather should be challenged through teachers' professional action, provided the starting point in her journey to becoming a recognized teacher leader and the school's journey toward heightened literacy outcomes as well as staff morale and community attitudes.

In summary, we have been struck by the clarity of the values aspects of these teachers' lives, and also by their sense of confidence regarding the power of schools and the teaching profession to shape lives.

Element Two: Teacher Leaders
Facilitate Communities of Learning

The idea that schools can be communities of learning where significant knowledge is created to enhance students' lives is relatively new. Sergiovanni explained it clearly in 1994 when he said about a California school in which he was working:

> In their self-driven research processes, participants came to us openly to discuss their hopes and dreams. Through this process, we understood there were shared common values around which we could begin to imagine a more ideal school. (p. xi)

Just a year later, Newmann and Wehlage's (1995) large scale research established that the dual concepts of collective responsibility and authentic pedagogy constitute a vehicle for enabling schools to significantly (though not completely) overcome the impacts of sociocultural-economic disadvantage on student achievement in literacy, numeracy, and other subjects. In so doing, the University of Wisconsin researchers provided insights that enabled educators worldwide to challenge the debilitating assertion of the 1966 *Coleman Report* that "schools don't affect students' life chances." The Newmann and Wehlage (1995) research revealed that

> the most successful schools were those that used restructuring tools to help them function as professional communities. That is, they found a way to channel staff and student efforts toward a clear, commonly shared purpose for student learning; they created opportunities for teachers to collaborate and help one another achieve the purpose; and teachers in these schools took collective— not just individual—responsibility for student learning. Schools with strong professional communities were better able to offer authentic pedagogy and were more effective in promoting student achievement. (p. 3)

The key to the challenge of how to create shared pedagogical principles out of the diverse background experiences, curriculum responsibilities, and values of a school staff remains poorly understood in the school development literature. Our experience suggests that many teacher leaders do, however, possess that talent and almost all have a deep interest in acquiring it. We have coined the term "schoolwide pedagogy" to describe this complex and elusive concept and have defined it as follows:

> Agreed principles of teaching, learning and assessment that enable the members of the school's professional community to work collectively towards the enhancement of priority school outcomes. (Leadership Research Institute, 2007, p. 1)

Our experience in schools such as Whistlerock, where teacher leaders such as Cathy have successfully facilitated the development and implementation of schoolwide pedagogical constructs, leads us to propose that the process requires deep pedagogical knowledge, well-developed listening skills (in particular a capacity to identify potentially powerful ideas, thoughts, and imagery in colleagues' descriptions), an outstanding ability to verbalize synthesized meaning and solicit feedback, and perhaps a degree of serendipity. It also requires a certain form of professional altruism that has been captured by Moller and Pankake (2006) as follows:

> Most of the teachers who learn and begin to lead believe they are taking on these responsibilities to help their colleagues. Cross and Miller (2003) found . . . that these teacher leaders "believe their own kinship with teachers—as teachers themselves—uniquely qualifies them to help." (p. 168)

At Greenhills, Andrew's ingenious extension of the concept of schoolwide pedagogy to incorporate an element of student voice highlights a subtlety of teacher leadership as an emerging leadership construct—when schoolwide pedagogical practices are the focus, the professional stakes may be very high for individual teachers. Andrew's encouragement of student voice through the development of a student-created pedagogical framework invoked emotions within the teaching staff and a contestation for power within the professional community that, if not managed carefully, could have been destructive for all concerned. The implications for teacher leaders and principals of this aspect of teacher leadership are very important, and are explored in our analysis of parallel leadership in Chapter 3, and also in some of the exercises in our CLASS Plan in Chapter 6.

Element Three: Teacher Leaders
Strive for Pedagogical Excellence

The role and importance of personal pedagogical excellence in teacher leadership has a contested history. Murphy's recent treatise indicates that early models of teacher leadership made but limited reference to teaching and learning processes (Murphy, 2005, pp. 70–71) and that some recent frameworks continue to indicate a fairly minimal priority for pedagogical quality (pp. 70–71). Most recent authorities, however, tend to take the view articulated by Odell (1997), that "One cannot be an effective teacher leader if one is not first an accomplished teacher" (p. 122).

Our research affirms Odell's position. We know of no instances where teacher leaders have enjoyed sustained success without being able to model pedagogical excellence. This conclusion is evident in the Greenhills and Whistlerock snapshots where Andrew and Cathy, as well as their colleagues and principals, viewed their teaching capabilities as prerequisite to their leadership capabilities.

Authenticity in teaching, learning, and assessment practices took on a number of meanings in our snapshots. At Whistlerock, it was Cathy's recognized expertise as a literacy teacher that provided the impetus for development of the Whistlerock Pedagogical Framework and Literacy Strategy. At Greenhills, Andrew's initiative in enabling a difficult cohort of students to generate a definition of high quality teaching practices had the effect of modifying students' behaviors. What followed for Andrew was a process of self-interrogation that led to changes in his professional demeanor, interpersonal relationships, and career opportunities. At Minnemanka Senior High School (Snapshot Four) principal Jane Richards described a similar outcome from her teacher leaders' search for personal pedagogical meaning:

> It was very revealing, therefore, when teachers reflected on *Minnemanka teaching is . . .* and students reflected on *Minnemanka learning is . . .* But of most significance was that those teachers who had begun to see themselves as leaders used these exercises to create explanatory frameworks that would hopefully lead to better teacher-student understanding, interaction and relationships. That, I believe, is now happening.

Based on professional experiences such as these, we have recently developed a five-question pedagogical scaffold that appears to us to define how teacher leaders might approach challenges associated with the third element of the Teachers as Leaders Framework. The five questions that comprise the scaffold are the following:

- What are your core values, hopes, and aspirations for the future?
- What is your special gift for teaching? How do you use it?
- What authoritative educational philosophy guides your work?
- How do you enhance your school's pedagogy through your professional learning and sharing?
- How do you contribute to your whole-school workplace? (Leadership Research Institute, p. 10)

This is a daunting set of criteria in that it extends the boundaries of classroom practitionership in multiple directions—deep personal reflection and analysis, engagement with colleagues in shared learning, creation of new forms of pedagogical meaning, and explicit contributions to quality of life in the workplace. We have observed that teacher leaders find the scaffold helpful in understanding the depth of their lives as teachers. We have also found that, in implementing it with professional cohorts, they acquire professional satisfaction. Finally, one teacher leader who contributed to the creation of the five-question scaffold shared with us the following philosophical stance that she had identified to guide her teaching:

> The mediocre teacher tells
> The good teacher explains
> The superior teacher demonstrates
> The great teacher inspires.
>
> —William Arthur Ward

This teacher explained to us how she is now attempting to integrate her dual roles of pedagogical role model and teacher leader:

> I can't justify being a role model for my colleagues if I don't feel truly excited by teaching. So I have to work incessantly on being an inspiring teacher. But there is no point in inspiring my own students if what I do gets lost in the school. So I feel that my colleagues across the school have to learn from me at the same time as I learn from them.

Element Four: Teacher Leaders Confront Barriers in the School's Culture and Structures

The notion that schools are essentially bureaucratic organizations that have a clear responsibility to ensure orderliness, stability, and coherence in their core operations is a pervasive theme in much educational administration and leadership literature, perhaps most notably in the work of Hoy and Miskel (1991). As these authorities stated in one of the earlier editions of their classic educational administration text:

> When teachers join a school organisation, they accept the formal authority relation. They agree within certain limits to follow directives that administrators issue. (p. 78)

But what should responsible teachers do when they encounter practical or ethical constraints that diminish the work of their school? Such constraints are well-documented in recent educational literature, as for example in the recent work of Youitt (2004), who has classified them using four subheadings:

(1) teacher culture, (2) school structures, (3) school cultures, and (4) micropolitics. Our own research complements the perspective of Boles and Troen (1996, p. 48 as cited in Murphy, 2005, p. 69)—responsible professionals do not turn a blind eye when they perceive that barriers are diminishing the integrity of their school. To the contrary, they are inclined to challenge the status quo.

This proclivity is evident in the two snapshots in this chapter. When Lisa approached the Greenhills principal to ask for one more chance for a highly disruptive student who was threatened with exclusion, she epitomized the social justice orientation of Greenhills teacher leaders and their preparedness to extend ideals into social action. This orientation included a wide range of activities, including provision of basic food and laundry services for needy students. The principal summed up the advocacy role of teacher leaders as follows: "I regard the teachers here as the guardians of the culture. They take personal responsibility for managing projects that fit the school's vision."

At Whistlerock, Cathy's decision was perhaps easier because her principal had invited the teaching staff to challenge the culture of mediocrity that he perceived to be negatively influencing students' achievements. But in opting to test her capabilities as a leader, Cathy nevertheless had to make a personal decision that confronted the existing mores of the school. In so doing, she demonstrated several leadership qualities, including preparedness to take a calculated risk, standing up for a disenfranchised student cohort, and exerting substantial energy to acquire new professional skills.

These examples capture the essence of "teaching against the grain" that some theorists (e.g., Boomer, 1985, p. 20) have articulated as fundamental in projecting images of teacher leadership. They manifest conviction, courage, and strategic skill that might not be expected of most teachers and, thus, might be generally discouraged. They are, however, essential to teacher leadership as we envision it in a rapidly maturing profession.

Element Five: Teacher Leaders Translate Ideas Into Sustainable Systems of Action

Every framework for teacher leadership with which we are familiar draws attention to the importance of a management function. Durrant (2004) has captured the essential reason for this emphasis—school-based leadership cannot be separated from the stimulation and successful execution of processes of change, and sustained change is not possible without definitive development planning and strategic action planning. Some authorities have in fact located the organizational and management aspect of teacher leadership at the center of their models and definitions. O'Connor and Boles (1996), for example, are cited by Murphy (p. 69) as conceptualizing teacher leadership around seven key competencies that are substantially management-oriented:

- understanding of politics, power, and authority
- skill in managing interpersonal relationships

- communication skills
- understanding of group dynamics
- presentation skills
- organization skills
- ability to change

At both Greenhills and Whistlerock, the teacher leaders whom we observed demonstrated well-developed competencies such as these. In both instances, they translated their concern into direct actions that contributed to the implementation and sustainability of their innovations. Thus at Whistlerock, Cathy mobilized staff development processes, with the support of her deputy principal, and also worked closely with an external consulting agency. At Greenhills, teachers managed all aspects of the Aspirations program, including curriculum, community service, publicity, and budget. In creating and sustaining productive relationships with school administrators and with external constituencies, and in using the Aspirations program to enrich the self-concepts of a disadvantaged community, these teachers set in motion programs that were still in effect seven years later and in fact had evolved into new, highly sophisticated reform processes.

Element Six: Teacher Leaders Nurture a Culture of Success

Noted leadership theorist Warren Bennis has observed that leadership is about optimism because pervasive optimism carries people through tough times (1999). It is therefore probably no surprise that the highly successful teacher leaders with whom we have worked have tended to exude optimism and a "can do" attitude that is contagious. Expressions such as *Success breeds success; We can achieve the extraordinary; There are no limits to what is possible for our school*; or *Let's dream the impossible dream* tend to be associated with the work of these professionals. Messages such as these tend to have the effect of encouraging individuals—teachers, students, administrators, parents—to focus on the positive aspects of events and experiences, to heighten goals because success is achievable, and to encourage others to emphasize their capabilities rather than their perceived limits.

One might ask—can optimism be learned? We believe, with Seligman (1998), that it can. Hoy and Smith (2007) quote Seligman as arguing that optimism matters as much in leadership as talent or motivation, but optimism has an added advantage because it can be learned and enhanced. Thus, at Greenhills, the teacher leaders collectively emphasized a "We can do anything" attitude. This had a demonstrable impact on students' self-esteem and achievements. Even seemingly insignificant achievements were held up as evidence that all students can achieve beyond normal expectations when they are encouraged and recognized. The Greenhills principal provided us bemusedly with this example: "Even a student taking a cow to the Greenhills fair can provide a basis for building confidence. These fairs bore me silly except for what I can do for the school just by being there."

At Whistlerock, the principal and teacher leaders determined to attack the absence of enthusiasm, purpose, and vitality that they observed in their school through a comprehensive revitalization process. The vision that they subsequently created—*Individual Paths, United Journey*—seemed to them to capture the imagination of their school community and they then proceeded, substantially through Cathy's leadership, to develop a literacy framework that resulted in a united professional effort (and that, after two years, had contributed to enhanced school outcomes). Contagion was certainly a feature of the Whistlerock process.

Amid the disillusionment and anxiety that invariably creep into our lives, success may be hard to recognize and equally hard for many of us to acknowledge. But leaders routinely recognize and acknowledge success. Teacher leaders do so to enhance confidence, induce high expectations, and extend horizons for their students. In the process, as new values, visions, and pedagogical principles are generated and publicly articulated, the uncertainty of the emerging knowledge-based society becomes not a threat but a promise for a better future.

CONCLUSIONS

In this chapter, we have presented a definition of teacher leadership and a related framework that derives from our own extensive research in diverse school settings but is consistent with the outcomes of significant scholarly thinking that has emerged since the first edition of *Developing Teacher Leaders* was published six years ago (2002). We regard this definition and framework as confirmation of a capacity for professional leadership that had previously been obscured in the educational literature and also in most professional development programs for practicing and aspiring educational leaders.

In the eyes of their colleagues, principals, and communities, the teacher leaders whom we studied had remarkable impacts on their schools and communities. The Teachers as Leaders Framework provides what we have found to be a very helpful explanatory model of these so-called ordinary people doing what are clearly extraordinary things. We assert that while the Framework does not yet have the recognition or status that is associated with a fully developed, formal teacher leadership role, it has served important purposes in enabling us to explore and understand the dynamics of successful school revitalization. It also seems to us to be well-suited to a postindustrial world where hierarchy in organizational relationships will decrease in importance, and the capacity to help communities enhance their quality of life through the creation of new knowledge will increasingly become a priority.

2

Five Premises to Guide
Revitalization of the
Teaching Profession

Internationally, this is a "golden age" of school leadership (Leithwood &
Day, 2007, p. 1). Educational reformers widely agree that school leader-
ship is central to the success of their reforms. Governments around the
world are devoting unparalleled resources to the development of school
leaders. . . . And the international research community has, at long last,
produced a sufficient body of empirical evidence of high quality to per-
suade even the most skeptical that school leadership matters.

—Bill Mulford
(2007, p. 1)

SUSTAINING THE REFORM AGENDA

It is our view that Mulford's assertion of a new "golden age" of educational
leadership is justified on two grounds. First, the past decade has indeed
seen the creation of profound new insights regarding the ways that leadership underpins sustained school success. Second, new constructions have
emerged during that time regarding the nature of successful school-based

leadership itself—constructions that acknowledge the vital role of the school principal but reach beyond the principalship to incorporate teacher leaders. Thus, we predict that the current golden age will metamorphose during the next decade to incorporate a new era for the teaching profession, one in which teacher leadership is a driving force.

In introducing this chapter in our first edition in 2002, we made reference to a powerful metaphor, Katzenmeyer and Moller's sleeping giant. We wrote:

> There are . . . no guarantees that Katzenmeyer and Moller's sleeping giant will rouse just because there is a need for it or because we think it should. One cannot take for granted that teacher leadership will, through natural evolutionary processes, become ingrained in our collective consciousness and thus realize its potential. To the contrary, the challenge confronting the education community in further exploring the meaning of teacher leadership and ensuring its applications in schools is massive. (2002, pp. 17–18)

Now, six years later, we believe that the paradigm of teacher leadership has in fact changed. What we see now is a more mature teaching profession, one that is possessed of a clearer sense of its own significance in twenty-first-century society and also of rapidly developing skills for school capacity-building.

It would therefore be expected that the "premises to guide revitalization of the teaching profession" that we proposed in 2002 will have evolved somewhat in the interim. That is indeed the case. The differences are outlined in Table 2.1.

Thus, in this chapter, we confidently propose five premises that we believe are supportable on the basis of our own and related international research and that, viewed together, constitute a compelling rationale for a new professionalism for teachers worldwide. Before discussing these five premises, it may be helpful to reflect on another case study in which the well-being of a school and its wider community has been dramatically enhanced by teachers' leadership.

SNAPSHOT THREE: ADAMS SECONDARY COLLEGE

Adams Secondary College is a medium size Grade 7–12 school in a low socioeconomic area within a large city. It was designated by system supervisors in 2004 as achieving unsatisfactory levels of student outcomes, particularly in literacy and numeracy. The principal and staff were challenged to resolve this problem with the threat of either closure or amalgamation with one or more other schools also presented as plausible alternatives.

Table 2.1   A Summary of Changes in "Premises to Guide Revitalization of the Teaching Profession" From First Edition (2002) to Second Edition (2008)

Premise	2002	2009	Explanation
Premise One	Teacher leadership exists; it is real.	Teacher leadership is a conceptual and practical entity in its own right.	The 2002 Premise One was presented as a declaration of discovery; 2009 Premise One is presented as one of established substance.
Premise Two	Teacher leadership is grounded in authoritative theory.	No change.	This premise remains unchanged (although the authoritative theory in which teacher leadership is grounded has evolved somewhat).
Premise Three	Teacher leadership is distinctive.	Teacher leadership is integrally linked to individual and schoolwide pedagogical excellence.	In 2002 we took the position that teacher leadership manifests an emphasis on teaching and learning processes that distinguishes it from other forms of educational and noneducational leadership. Our research since 2002 has extended and refined our knowledge of the pedagogical processes that are associated with successful teacher leadership.
Premise Four	Teacher leadership is diverse.	Teacher leadership is versatile and adaptive.	Our 2002 Premise Four emphasized the diversity of teacher leadership that we had observed in a range of practical situations. The new Premise Four extends that understanding to include both conceptual variations and the enhanced capabilities that we have observed in teacher leaders as processes of school improvement have taken hold.
Premise Five	Teacher leadership can be nurtured.	The development and sustainability of teacher leadership is inseparable from strong principalship and supportive systemic frameworks.	We have retained the basic intent of our 2002 Premise Five but refined it to reflect our own and recent international research findings regarding the integral importance of the principalship, systemic support systems, and university faculties of education in nurturing concepts and processes associated with teacher leadership.

Nancy Riggs, a teacher at Adams at the time of this ultimatum, and one of the teacher leaders who emerged during the ensuing three years, tells her story. It reveals in practical terms the five underlying premises of a revitalized teaching profession as we describe them in this chapter. A synthesis of the changed dynamics and outcomes of Adams Secondary College during the period 2004–06 is reflected in Figure B.1, Appendix B.

Our school was no different from many schools searching for a way forward and experiencing continuous frustration and wasted effort. The school had begun a myriad of worthwhile teaching and learning programs but never really completed them. The recommendation of the principal to commit to yet another school improvement, as part of a cluster arrangement with a national School Leadership Institute, naturally raised eyebrows, questions, and cynicism.

But we were determined to do something very different, beginning with endorsement of a set of five operational principles that I drew from the School Leadership Institute and that emphasized the central importance of teachers as professional leaders:

- Teachers individually and collectively are the key to enhanced student outcomes.
- Success breeds success.
- "No blame" should characterize all professional dialogue.
- Professional learning is the key to school-level revitalization.
- Alignment of the school's strategic direction, pedagogy, and support systems is a collective responsibility.

My own role in the Adams Revitalization Project began as a purely voluntary one. As an experienced and proud professional, I was not prepared to accept many of the negatives that surrounded our students, staff, and community. I felt a burning desire to do something to correct them. But I did not view myself as a "leader" in any way, shape, or form when the project began. As it unfolded and evolved I certainly came to do so, however, and I now believe that leadership in its many guises was central to the successes that we have begun to enjoy as a school.

Indeed, three years later (September, 2007) the results of Adams College's *Staff Opinion Survey, 2007* indicate a profound change in almost every aspect of our school's ethos and operations. (See Appendix B for indicative details.) There has been a huge upward movement from that of two years ago on a wide range of specific indicators: individual and school morale, supportive leadership, role clarity, professional interaction, participative decision making, goal congruence, appraisal and recognition, professional growth, curriculum coordination, and effective discipline policy. At the same time, staff perceptions of excessive work loads, individual distress, and school distress have dropped noticeably. Overall, statistics show that we have moved from well below to well above state averages on items such as these. As I reflect on our journey, I can identify what I regard as a number of watershed moments.

The first was the joint examination of survey data by the teaching staff and administrators, resulting in creation of statements of *Driving Forces* and *Preventing Forces at Adams Secondary College*. Particularly shattering to teachers was the revelation that a perception on the part of many staff that "the kids really didn't want to learn and some of them can't be taught anyway" had become ingrained over time in the consciousness of students, with teachers blamed by students for the problem. It was at this juncture that I volunteered to assume a Teacher Leader role with the project. It was a level of responsibility that exceeded anything that I had ever done previously.

The revitalization team (i.e., the principal and a volunteer team of teachers, ranging at different times from four to twelve members) concentrated on the concept of no blame in seeking to address this highly negative mindset. This sat well with staff who had felt for some years, rightly or wrongly, that they had been blamed for the lack of student academic performance. So the project team conducted a number of staff "professional conversations" without the principal or other administrators in attendance. Very frank comments were aired. These conversations gave us the opportunity to talk as a school, rather than as individuals, about what really mattered to us—*knowing and understanding our students*.

Another watershed moment occurred when staff voted for an additional meeting once a week that was totally devoted to the revitalization process. There was growing goodwill, so much so that the regular hour-long meetings stretched in some cases to twice the allocated time. Meetings were no longer information dissemination sessions but workshops and discussion groups where each staff member was heard. The terms "collective responsibility" and "shared leadership" were increasingly used in conversation. The physical layout of the staffroom was changed from tables grouped separately to their being all together. A longstanding tradition of "This is my chair" slowly faded and staff began to move to sit next to different colleagues.

A third watershed moment occurred when staff members were examining data about what made Adams College students unique. We quickly agreed that our students came from a clearly disadvantaged base, they lacked confidence in their own abilities, and had limited aspirations beyond school. Many months were spent throwing around thoughts and slogans as we tackled our visioning process. The original Adams College slogan of *Embracing Opportunities for Success* was eventually replaced by what we regarded (others of course may disagree) as a far more focused and student-centered vision and values:

Adams College Vision:
Be Brave, Lead, Succeed

Adams College Values:
Perseverance, Respect, Positive Attitude

This stage was supported by two whole-school professional development programs run by external specialists:

- Ramon Lewis' *Building Positive Student Relationships*
- Darryn Cruise's *Facilitating Student Engagement*

Following these explorations, I extended my role in the revitalization team and worked with the Leadership Institute consultants to lead our staff through an analysis of their successful teaching practices relating to the Adams College vision and values. I also facilitated an activity that resulted in the following pedagogical framework (Box 2.1):

Box 2.1   The Adams College Pedagogical Framework

- Catering for individual needs by knowing students personally.
- Creating positive learning environments that have clear expectations for active student engagement.
- Nurturing a culture of respect in which successful relationships are established and sustained.
- Providing diverse community experiences to build confident individuals who are able to interact positively with their world.
- Building foundational knowledge to encourage student confidence to think deeply.
- Employing explicit assessment tasks to encourage reflection and self-evaluation.

One might ask: When teachers have experienced professional growth, and have come to appreciate their leadership capabilities, what benefits are transferable?

First, the enhanced confidence, clarified focus, and heightened expectations of teachers rub off on students, leading to important changes in how students see their school and themselves. These changes are reflected in our school survey data (as evidenced in Appendix B, Figure B.1).

Second, Adams College is now part of a Regional Redevelopment Project, which is rationalizing the number of sites where education is offered in the region and examining the best way of delivering education to the next generation of students. Our staff and school community overwhelming made the very significant decision a few months ago to contribute to the regeneration of educational delivery in the North Hapsburg District by agreeing to merge with another school of similar makeup to ours. In so doing, we will access new facilities—something that we believe will give our students and community a sense of creating a new identity.

I think often about what has made this experience different. I do not believe that the transformation of Adams College would have been possible without multiple forms of leadership as well as new professional learning processes. My professional life has been changed forever because I have experienced teacher leadership firsthand. I now have skills and confidence to work with a range of educational challenges that I did not previously have. I feel a sense of accomplishment that I had not thought possible and I now know that leadership in very distinctive forms is part of our twenty-first-century profession.

Case studies such as Adams College stand as testimony that where successful school reform is in place, teachers play essential leader roles. Their leadership work is centered on their own professional practice but extends to schoolwide teaching, learning, and assessment practices as well as to community and system dynamics. Thus, teacher leaders exercise influence well beyond their individual classrooms. They demonstrate how knowledge—in the form of school visions, values, and pedagogical frameworks—can be created and what new knowledge looks like. They are, as may be inferred from the statement by Drucker (1994) with which we opened the preface to this book, core knowledge workers, who have the potential to give the emerging knowledge society its character and its leadership.

FIVE PREMISES TO GUIDE THE DEVELOPMENT OF THE PROFESSION

The five premises that follow encapsulate the theoretical foundations on which our Teachers as Leaders Framework (Table 1.1) is based. The premises comprise an integral part of this book. Taken together, they constitute an unequivocal stance that teacher leadership is perhaps the most fundamental ingredient of successful school reform. It is also the key to the esteemed future that we believe to be on the horizon for the teaching profession.

We present these premises for the consideration primarily of practicing teachers, but also for educators who function in a range of professional venues—professional development agencies, policy development forums, preservice teacher education programs, and principals' development and certification processes.

Premise One: Teacher Leadership Is a Conceptual and Practical Entity in Its Own Right

Teacher leadership is more than a promising concept with potential for future positive effects. It is observable in many schools now, and it can be described in clear terms. By any standards for judging, teacher leadership is no longer an interesting hypothetical possibility or even a credible opportunity. It is a conceptual and practical entity in its own right.

The Teachers as Leaders Framework is based on the work of classroom teachers who compelled attention because of their powerful ideas-in-action. As researchers, we documented these actions, described and analyzed their dynamics, and translated them into concepts that made sense to the teachers, their colleagues, and their principals.

Thus the framework captures, in generalized form, the essence of the professional lives of many classroom teachers at particular junctures. Situations we observed and documented varied from largely individual ideas-in-action to mainly collective ideas-in-action. At Adams, for example, Nancy Riggs, a teacher leader, her principal, and colleagues confronted, head-on, a "failing school" label and school and community disillusionment and apathy. In the relatively short space of two to three years, the school became a dynamic source of pride for the community and a model for regional school renewal. The six elements of the Teachers as Leaders

Framework are all readily identifiable in the work of Nancy as an individual professional and to a lesser extent in the work of Nancy in collaboration with her colleagues.

Our own quite definitive viewpoint about teacher leadership as a conceptual and practical reality is shared by credible international authorities. Joseph Murphy's outstanding recent treatise, *Connecting Teacher Leadership and School Improvement*, provides particularly compelling documentation. Murphy's analysis lends support to five insights that have emerged from our research regarding the recent evolution of teacher leadership into a clearly identifiable and professionally defensible entity:

- While there is no particular set of human characteristics that can be used to define teacher leadership, it is nevertheless very much a human construct. It cannot be reduced to a set of generic standards. Rather, the work of successful teacher leaders invariably reflects a combination of significant professional values and processes on the one hand, and distinctive personal convictions and capabilities on the other.
- Being perceived as an effective teacher practitioner is fundamental and prerequisite to the capacity to influence other teachers, as well as school administrators, in their work.
- A capacity for visioning, and for big picture explanation and projectioning, is important in processes of engaging colleagues in meaningful school development.
- Teacher leadership has a strong management function (our research suggests that this aspect of teacher leadership poses no major challenge to most teachers, whose everyday work requires complex management capabilities).
- Enhanced school improvement is inseparable from a teacher leadership component. Teacher leadership flourishes when a significant school need provides a focus for teachers' developmental work and when senior administrators (usually the principal) present project opportunities and facilitate leadership skill development.

As would be expected, a number of emphatic definitions of teacher leadership are now emerging in the educational literature. It is our view that Wasley's observation in 1991 that "clearly the whole issue of defining teacher leadership is problematic" (as cited in Murphy, p. 11) is no longer valid. Consider the following recent definitions, and note their confident assertiveness as well as their dual emphasis on pedagogy and professional influence:

- York-Barr and Duke: The process by which teachers, individually or collectively, influence their colleagues, principals, and other members of school communities to improve teaching and learning practices with the aim of increased student learning and achievement (2004, pp. 287–88).

- Katzenmeyer and Moller: Teachers who are leaders lead within and beyond the classroom, identify with and contribute to a community of teacher learners and leaders, and influence others toward improved educational practice (2001, p. 5).
- Miller et al.: Teacher leadership generally refers to actions by teachers outside their classrooms that involve an explicit or implicit responsibility to provide professional development to their colleagues, to influence their communities' or districts' policies, or to act as adjunct staff to support changes in classroom practices among teachers (2000, p. 4).
- Youitt: Teachers who are leaders lead learning by embracing new methods of teaching and learning. They understand the importance of the relationship between teachers and students (and their families). These teachers also frequently engage the use of new technologies in their teaching, and understand the need for resourcing flexibility to support educational innovation (2007, p. 1).

And, of course, our own definition:

- Teacher leadership is essentially an ethical stance that is based on views of both a better world and the power of teachers to shape meaning systems. It manifests in new forms of understanding and practice that contribute to school success and to the quality of life of the community in the long term (2009).

The teacher leader in Snapshot Three (Nancy Riggs) and, indeed, all of the teacher leaders that are contained in snapshots in this book meet the requirements of all four definitions of teacher leadership that we have presented, as well as the requirements of our own. In essence, a growing community of international scholars shares the view that teacher leadership now possesses identifiable conceptual qualities as well as an established role in practical processes of sustained school improvement. Teacher leadership is unquestionably an idea whose time has come.

Premise Two: Teacher Leadership Is Grounded in Authoritative Theory

In our search for a new professionalism for teachers—one that honors teaching as a profession and teachers' work as fundamental in postindustrial learning communities—we investigated the literature on educational leadership. We found that, until very recently, there has been a striking lack of recognition of teachers as either potential or actual leaders in schools.

A quick look at the history of educational leadership theory reveals just why past concepts offer little support for new forms of leadership. Educational leadership is firmly grounded in ideas about authority that stem from Weber's notion of legitimate power (Mayer, 1943). Weber, with his focus on hierarchical coordination in bureaucracies, noted that authority constituted the right to command, to instruct, to order, and to exercise sanctions in support of such commands. To early management theorists, the role of prescribed authority was basic. Pioneer theorists like Katz and Kahn (1966), for example, observed that "the management sub-system in every organization and the structure of authority are inseparable" (p. 203). In other words, a structure of official persons who have the right to command was regarded as essential to conditions of order, coordinated effort, and goal attainment. Karpinski and Lugg (2006) have traced how the "cult of efficiency" (as cited in Callahan, 1962) that derived from this mindset created a "one size fits all" approach to U.S. educational administration that denied the diversity of schools, their communities, and democracy (pp. 279–280). Bates (1983) summed up this ideological perspective on educational administration, and his perception of its immense impact on teachers' professional lives, when he stated:

> Educational administration is a technology of control. . . . The concepts, the theories, and the organizing systems are a clear indication of a preoccupation with control that is endemic to the occupation. (p. 8)

It follows that the development of theories of leadership that encompass teacher leaders, and that promote individuality, community, and democracy, may therefore be somewhat at odds with some traditional areas of educational leadership theory. It also follows, we assert, that the development of theories of teacher leadership will, in the next decade, undoubtedly challenge dominant features of the broad field of educational administration.

Regarding theories of leadership, we briefly consider four well-known approaches to contemporary educational leadership and the place that teacher leadership occupies in each. We discuss them briefly here as transformational, strategic, educative, and organizationwide.

Transformational leadership emphasizes the significance of the person and personal traits in bringing about social and cultural change. To Avolio and Bass (1988), whose pioneering research was instrumental in developing transformational approaches to leadership, leaders are individuals who "motivate followers to work for transcendental goals instead of immediate self-interest, and for achievement and self actualization instead of safety and security" (p. 33). Transformational leadership, with its associated concepts of charisma and inspiration, has frequently been proposed as the most appropriate leadership approach for school principals and as the prerogative of principals (Leithwood, 1994). Consistent with this line of thinking is a recent British study by Day (2000, p. 117) that concluded that effective principals are transformative and require the ability to engage reflectively in a much more complex, broader range of contexts than do teachers.

Until recently, little space appears to have been allowed for significant teacher leadership in the transformational approach. Very recently, however, authorities such as Hallinger (2003) have noted that transformational leadership models are beginning to conceptualize leadership as an organizational and collective, as opposed to individual, entity. The traditional equation of transformational leadership with the "hero paradigm" (Gronn, 2003) is a concept that would seem to us to have limited relevance in the work of professional school communities in the twenty-first century, and may therefore now be abating. Indeed, Kouzes and Posner's five types of behavior that are asserted to be features of transformational leadership appear to us to apply in the work of teacher leaders: challenging the process; inspiring a shared vision; enabling others to act; modeling the way; and encouraging the heart (2002, p. 45). "Behaviors" such as these are particularly apparent in those elements of our Teachers as Leaders Framework that imply the articulation of positive futures, recognition and development of personal "gifts," contribution to an image of teaching as a profession that makes a difference, and nurturing of a school culture of success.

In summary, it appears that transformational leadership theory represents an approach to leadership that has limited historical association with teachers, but may now be evolving into forms that have the potential to explain some aspects of teacher leaders' work.

Strategic leadership, as the term clearly implies, emphasizes systematic, rational management in leaders' roles. Hambrick (1989) suggests that it involves aligning the organization with anticipated external forces—technological developments, market trends, regulatory constraints, competitors' actions, and so on. Like Hambrick, Caldwell (1992) has advocated a leadership function that is primarily strategic as the most appropriate approach for principals in self-managing schools:

> The principal must be able to develop and implement a cyclical process of goal-setting, need identification, priority setting, policy making, planning, budgeting, implementing and evaluating in a manner which provides for the appropriate involvement of staff and community, including parents and students as relevant. The complexity of the process in respect to the numbers of actors indicates a capacity to manage conflict. (pp. 16–17)

Strategic processes such as those identified by Caldwell are undoubtedly central to the work of school principals. But what meaning, if any, do they have in the work of highly effective nonadministrator educational leaders? Lieberman, Saxl, and Miles (1988, p. 153), in one of the earliest conceptual frameworks for teacher leadership, proposed six "skill domains" that bear some resemblance to the elements of Caldwell's strategic principalship:

- building trust and rapport
- organizational diagnosis
- dealing with the process
- using resources
- managing the work
- building skills and confidence in others

The fifth element of our Teachers as Leaders Framework—translating ideas into sustainable systems of action—clearly incorporates such "skill domains."

Another relevant line of thinking is offered by Hoy and Smith (2007). To them, successful school strategists place a particular value on the concept of "influence." Hoy and Smith propose ten principles that are intended primarily for principals seeking to expand their school-based and community influence. Most, if not all, have relevance in the six elements of our Teachers as Leaders Framework:

- the principle of attraction
- the principle of reciprocity
- the principle of colleagueship
- the principle of commitment
- the principle of demonstrated expertise
- the principle of priority for scarce resources
- the principle of trust
- the principle of fairness
- the principle of self-efficacy
- the principle of optimism

Any consideration of the potential significance and relevance of strategic leadership in teacher leaders' work might profitably take into account principles of influence such as these. All are clearly discernible in the work of Nancy Riggs at Adams College and also in other snapshots throughout this book.

Thus, we conclude that while strategic leadership in education has evolved primarily with the principalship in mind, it is apparent that it is an essential element of teacher leaders' work.

The essential meaning of educative leadership, appropriately labeled "advocacy" leadership by teacher leaders in snapshot schools Greenhills and Adams, is well-captured in the words of activist leadership pioneer William Foster: "to develop, challenge and liberate human souls" (as cited in Lindle, 2004, p. 169). Following Foster's lead, Duignan and

Macpherson (1992) coined the phrase "educative leadership" and defined it as follows:

> Educative leadership . . . must closely respond to the cultural context, be critically aware of the long-term practices of participants in educational processes, and when action is proposed, justify ends and processes using an educative philosophy . . . . Hence, educative leadership implies a responsible involvement in the politics of organization. (pp. 3–4)

Bates also affirms the importance of educative leadership as "culture building" within complex values contexts when he says that it "involves the making and articulating of choices, the location of oneself within the cultural struggles of the times as much in the cultural battles of the school as in the wider society" (1983, p. 19).

MacBeath has asserted the critical importance of this leadership approach in contemporary communities and Western society and provocatively labeled it "subversive." He has described it pointedly and eloquently:

> Subversive leadership is intellectual, moral and political. . . . It cannot accept children being shortchanged whether by government policies, by teachers unaccountable for their actions, or by young people who settle for the mediocre. . . . Subversive leadership is intolerant, not in a bullish or confrontative sense, neither personalized nor necessarily even direct, but implicit in the fostering of a climate in which critical inquiry is simply the way we do things around here. (2006b, p. 7)

Implicit in MacBeath's challenge, and that of Foster and Bates, is the view that, if education is to create human emancipation or liberation, it will be unlikely to do so solely through the influence of school administrators. Historically, it has been assumed that it is the school principal who has most opportunity to exercise leadership of this type (see, for example, Rizvi, 1992, pp. 137, 163). But with the evolution of teacher leadership frameworks over the past decade that assumption has changed dramatically. Thus, our Teachers as Leaders Framework emphasizes an "educative" or "advocacy" function through the articulation of clear value positions relating to a "better world," professional learning as a consciousness-raising process, confronting of barriers to just educational practices and student well-being, and encouragement of self-respect in students' communities.

Without evidence of teachers as educative leaders, there is little prospect of the creation of a new paradigm for the teaching profession that is grounded in principles of justice or global sustainability. But our research leads us to conclude that a vision for emancipatory educational leadership is indeed eminently realistic.

The concept of leadership as an organizationwide process has a range of applications in recent literature. Examples include leadership of the many (Lakomski, 1995), multiple-role leadership (Limerick, Cunnington, & Crowther, 1998), distributed leadership (Handy, 1996), collective intelligence (Heifetz & Laurie, 1997), community of leaders (Senge, 1997), and coleadership (Heenan & Bennis, 1999). Concepts like these—recognizing, as they do, that today's leaders can come from many places and assume many forms—are in fact increasingly significant in management and organizational literature.

Leadership as an organizationwide quality resonates strongly with the notion of teachers as leaders. We say this for two reasons. First, it implies the existence of leadership capabilities throughout organizations and centers leadership attention away from positional authority and onto core organizational processes. Pounder, Ogawa, and Adams (1995) explain this approach to leadership as it relates to a school:

> The concept of leadership as an organizational quality suggests that the total amount of leadership found in schools will have a positive relationship to their performance. Furthermore, it suggests that all members of schools—including principals, teachers, staff members, and parents—can lead and thus affect the performance of their schools. (p. 567)

The second reason for regarding organizationwide leadership as inseparable from emerging constructions of teacher leadership relates to contemporary concerns regarding the ongoing development and refinement of democratic processes in Western societies. Mulford has noted recently that while Western democracies tend to have explicit national statements that affirm the importance of their schools in nurturing democratic processes and institutions, it is difficult to see mature manifestations of "deep" democracy in the workings of their schools (2004, pp. 635–36).

Among Mulford's conclusions is that if schools are in fact to nurture "deep" democracy, they must become professional learning organizations, with students, teachers, and leaders bound by relationships that are grounded in trust, collaboration, shared mission, risk taking, and ongoing professional learning. It follows that recognition and implementation of the concept of teacher leadership, through schoolwide leadership processes, is fundamental to the enhancement of democratic values in the development of future citizens. Miller provided the following helpful illumination of how a new image of the teaching profession might contribute to this end:

> When teachers (feel) valued as members of a coherent community, and empowered as decision-makers, they (are) able to empower their students by offering them choices and by including them in decisions affecting their own instruction. (as cited in Murphy, 2005, p. 56)

The second element of our Teachers as Leaders Framework—facilitates communities of learning—is intended to represent a response to the concerns for schoolwide professional learning and democratic development that analysts such as Mulford have articulated. Moreover, our construction of parallel leadership (Chapter 3) as a particular manifestation of organizationwide leadership represents a specification of leadership functions that are grounded in overt values of mutual trust, shared purpose, and allowance for individuality—central premises of democratic theory and practice. Parallel leadership is also linked to complex processes of knowledge creation in ways that are not featured in other constructions of leadership.

Thus, parallel leadership as we define it recognizes the need for educational organizations to show the way in advancing the cause of twenty-first-century knowledge societies as well as democratic theory, thinking, and practice.

In summary, while three of the four approaches to school leadership that we have reviewed were each developed with the principalship most clearly in mind, and the fourth (leadership as an organizationwide quality) did not specify teacher leadership, all four have obvious meaning in our Teachers as Leaders Framework. The teacher leaders who feature in our snapshots projected into the future and generated visionary ideals and explanatory frameworks; they designed and negotiated plans across levels, systems, discipline areas, and governance bodies; they advocated for marginalized groups and demonstrated deep-rooted concern for social justice; and they engaged collaboratively with other leaders across diverse groups to empower communities and to create novel solutions to long-standing problems. In so doing, they manifested all four forms of educational leadership that we have used as benchmarks for legitimate leadership action.

As a final critique of the place of teacher leadership in the changing world of leadership theory, we briefly consider the links of the Teachers as Leaders Framework with the concept of emotional intelligence that Goleman (1998) has asserted to be the "sine qua non for leadership" (p. 93). Goleman, Boyatzis, and McKee (2002) have recently described the link between emotional intelligence and leadership this way:

> This emotional task of the leader is *primal*—that is, first—in two senses: It is both the original and the most important act of leadership. . . . In the modern organization, this primordial emotional task—though by now largely invisible—remains foremost among the many jobs of leadership: driving the collective emotions in a positive direction and clearing the smog created by toxic emotions. The key, of course, to making primal leadership work to everyone's advantage lies in the leadership competencies of *emotional intelligence:* how leaders handle themselves and their relationships (pp. 5–6).

Goleman, Boyatzis, and McKee justify this assertion through reference to two emotional intelligence "domains," four "competencies," and twenty "capabilities" (p. 39):

Personal competence domain: how we manage ourselves, comprising four *Self-awareness* capabilities and six *Self-management* capabilities.

Social competence domain: how we manage relationships, comprising three *Social awareness* capabilities and seven *Relationship management* capabilities.

The conclusions from our analysis are presented in Figure 2.1, in the matching of Goleman's two domains and associated competencies and capabilities of emotional intelligence with the six elements and sixteen descriptors of the Teachers as Leaders Framework. It is apparent from Figure 2.1 that the main tenets of teacher leadership coincide with core principles of emotional intelligence.

Figure 2.1   The Intersection of the Sixteen Teacher Leadership Descriptors and Goleman's EI Domains, Competencies and Capabilities

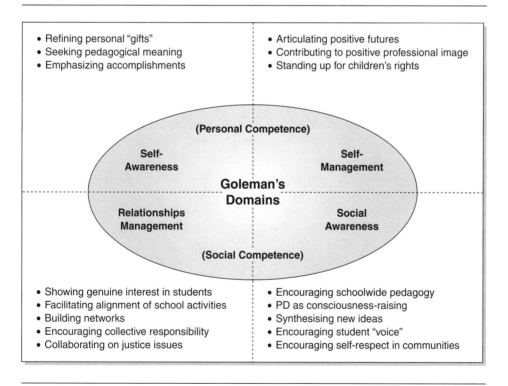

It follows from our discussion of Premise Two that educational leadership is rapidly evolving into new forms, forms that are responsive to the very diverse and challenging needs of democratic societies, of

knowledge-generating organizations, and of futuristic concerns for a sustainable world. Among the compelling and exciting developments of the past decade, teacher leadership stands tall, if not supreme. It is largely for this reason that we concur with Peter Drucker's (1994) projection of the teaching profession as a "leading class" in postindustrial societies.

Premise Three: Teacher Leadership Is Integrally Linked to Pedagogical Excellence

Educational research of the past decade has asserted the fundamental importance of pedagogical quality in determining the educational achievement of children and youth. However, the nature of teachers' work in creating and sustaining pedagogical quality has undertaken a profound shift in meaning during that time.

Following the publication in 1966 of both the Coleman report in the United States and the Plowden report in the UK, and the assertion of those reports that schools don't fundamentally affect children's life chances, the importance of teaching as a profession, and of pedagogical excellence, came under serious question worldwide. Then, during the "effectiveness" movement of the late 1980s and early 1990s, many frameworks for educational excellence identified factors such as school philosophy, the principal, parents, prescriptive curricula, and school organization as at least as important in influencing school outcomes as was teachers' work. Little wonder that the image and status of the teaching profession declined significantly during the three decades that followed the Coleman and Plowden reports.

This mindset was challenged in 1995 with the publication of a report that contained the findings of Newmann and Wehlage's paradigm-breaking research at the University of Wisconsin–Madison's Center on Organization and Restructuring of Schools. These researchers concluded from their nationwide studies that when classroom teaching is "authentic" (i.e., it is developed and owned by a school's professional community), and when teachers as a school staff assume "collective responsibility" for school standards and students' well-being, the effects of cultural, social, and economic disadvantage can be substantially overcome (though not totally, since, after all, students attend school for just a limited portion of their lives).

Influenced heavily by Newmann and Wehlage's research, we asserted in the first edition of our book in 2002 that generation of "authentic" approaches to teaching, learning, and assessment should be regarded as central to constructs of school-based leadership, particularly teacher leadership. We noted at that time:

> Essential to such development is schoolwide understanding of the diversity of teaching approaches within a school. . . . Appreciating this diversity requires illumination of teachers' philosophies, dreams, and aspirations. It also requires identifying the common ground of teachers' classroom successes across subject areas, teaching levels, age, experience, and gender. (p. 29)

In our 2002 edition we also postulated the process through which we believed teacher leadership manifests in school practices that bring about schoolwide improvements in student outcomes. We introduced a construct that we called "schoolwide pedagogy," and in an earlier version of the explanatory framework that is contained in Figure 3.1 (Chapter 3), we presented what we regarded as the place of this construct in successful school capacity-building. Since that time, we have explored the work of successful teachers further and have generated a three-dimensional image of pedagogical excellence that we believe is suited to twenty-first-century teacher professionalism. The three dimensions, as outlined diagrammatically in Figure 2.2, are as follows:

Dimension one: Personal pedagogy—the "gifts," talents, values, and specialized expertise that shape and define the work of teachers as individual professionals.

Dimension two: Schoolwide pedagogy—a school's agreed approach to teaching and/or learning, derived from consideration of the school's vision, the particular values and needs of students, and analysis of the most successful practices of teachers.

Dimension three: Authoritative pedagogy—established theories and rationales for outstanding teaching, learning, and assessment.

Our recent research has disclosed that teacher leaders invariably have a deep interest in becoming "three-dimensional professionals," and also in facilitating the spread of three-dimensional pedagogical practice in their workplaces.

In addition to our own ongoing research, two forms of inquiry over the past half decade, taken together, affirm the importance of the complex relationship between individual classroom quality, schoolwide pedagogical practices, and teacher leadership as the essential determiner of successful school outcomes.

First, Elmore (2000) and Lambert (2003) are among the researchers who have asserted that overall school outcomes are determined significantly by the efficacy of schoolwide approaches to pedagogical enhancement. Second, leadership that includes teachers has increasingly been recognized as fundamental to the creation of meaningful schoolwide pedagogical processes (Hord, 2004, pp. 1–4; Mulford, 2007, p. 16; Harris, 2004, p. 1; Leithwood & Jantzi, 2000, pp. 115–17). McKeever (2003) has recently summed up this rapidly emerging insight with a succinctness and definitiveness that we endorse:

Teacher leadership is vital to the improvement of student achievement. (as cited in Murphy, 2005, p. 61)

We hasten to add that we do not negate, question, or undervalue the importance of principals and other school administrators in systematic

Figure 2.2   Three-Dimensional Pedagogy (3-DP)

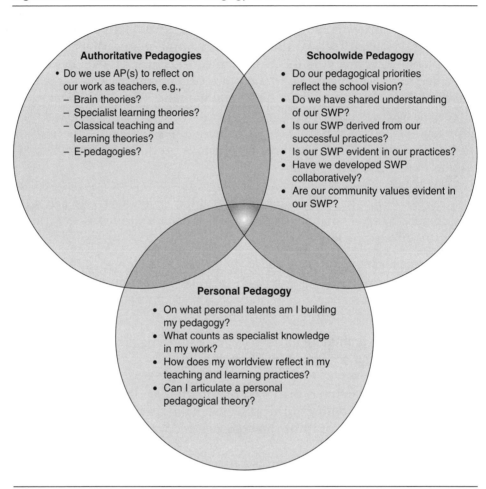

Authoritative Pedagogies
- Do we use AP(s) to reflect on our work as teachers, e.g.,
  - Brain theories?
  - Specialist learning theories?
  - Classical teaching and learning theories?
  - E-pedagogies?

Schoolwide Pedagogy
- Do our pedagogical priorities reflect the school vision?
- Do we have shared understanding of our SWP?
- Is our SWP derived from our successful practices?
- Is our SWP evident in our practices?
- Have we developed SWP collaboratively?
- Are our community values evident in our SWP?

Personal Pedagogy
- On what personal talents am I building my pedagogy?
- What counts as specialist knowledge in my work?
- How does my worldview reflect in my teaching and learning practices?
- Can I articulate a personal pedagogical theory?

SOURCE: Printed with approval of Frank Crowther, representing Frank Crowther and Dorothy Andrews, Leadership Research Institute, University of Southern Queensland.

efforts to improve school outcomes. As will be seen in Chapter 4, sustained school success without effective principalship is virtually impossible, in our view. But our research suggests that it is unlikely that administrators or external consultants, however capable, can manage the complex and sensitive process of developing schoolwide approaches to teaching and learning without the proactive and explicit engagement of teacher leaders. In case studies such as those that are contained in the Adams and Johnsonvale snapshots, where schoolwide pedagogical principles were developed and implemented in ways that impacted on student achievement levels, practicing teachers led initiatives to collect exemplars of pedagogical practice that reflected the school's vision and values, to synthesize core pedagogical concepts implicit in those exemplars and then to facilitate their transposition into strategies for school-wide application. Given the dominantly egalitarian culture of teaching as a profession (see the section on culture-building in Chapter 3) we doubt that highly sensitive and subtle processes such as these can be successfully undertaken in most schools by administrators, consultants, or other individuals who are not highly credible classroom practitioners.

In summary, excellence in pedagogy is now widely recognized as essential to school success. But "excellent pedagogy" is more than an individual construct; it impacts on student achievement most effectively when it is understood and practiced as a combination of individual and shared understandings, talents, and strategies. The implications for the twenty-first-century teaching profession are clear—to achieve the sort of synergistic outcomes for students that are associated with this new construction of pedagogy requires the exercise of a new school-based leadership function, one that must incorporate recognition of teachers as leaders. Herein lies the essence of our confidence in the changed image that we envision for the emerging teaching profession.

Premise Four: Teacher Leadership Is Versatile and Adaptive

The notion that leadership is as varied as the range of practicing leaders and the contexts in which they operate is well-ingrained in educational leadership thought. Indeed, some of the first major developments in educational leadership research almost a half century ago were premised on insights that emphasized the importance of "contingency" variables over generic leadership attributes and processes (Hersey & Blanchard, 1969; House, 1971; Kahn, 1956; Stogdill, 1974).

At the core of such thinking was that leaders should be able to change their style (i.e., how they lead) in line with what is required to achieve effective outcomes in a given context. Thus, in early educational leadership research, Hersey and Blanchard (1969) matched leadership styles and the maturity of "followers" while House matched styles with subordinates' characteristics. More recently, Hooijberg and DiTomaso (1996) have focused on matching leadership styles and organizational diversity and Hogan et al. (1988) have reopened the question of leadership for task, where task is regarded as complex and varied.

Needless to say, the construct of teacher leadership has not yet been subjected to research interrogation where "contingencies" associated with task, relationships, and context are the focus. But such research is starting. Hipp's (2004) analysis of ways in which teacher leadership varies in relation to the "maturity" of the school development challenge is outstanding in this regard (p. 55 ff). Hipp's finding is particularly significant, in our view, because it highlights that, as school development processes evolve, and new developmental needs emerge, different forms of leadership may be required.

The variable and adaptive aspect of teacher leadership is particularly apparent in the Greenhills (Chapter 1) and Minnemanka (Chapter 4) snapshots. Teachers in these case studies who rose to the occasion to colead (with the principal) processes of organizational diagnosis and visioning did not necessarily continue as leaders during processes of pedagogical development that required synergistic thinking and creativity. When community-building was the emphasis, particularly with indigenous or minority groups, other teacher leaders with relevant skills and convictions sometimes emerged. We can conclude only that teacher leadership as we have observed it is a remarkably versatile construct. Fortunately, the diversity of leadership talents within the teaching profession, it seems to us, is such that different responses are possible to the ever-changing demands of schools as workplaces.

Also of importance is that the characteristics of teachers who have entered the profession in the past half decade are different in some important respects from those of previous generations of teachers, namely Generation X and Baby Boomers. Prominent social commentator and futurist Bernard Salt (2006) has described the Y Generation as follows, highlighting the need for school-based leadership approaches to be sensitive to generational values and life experiences:

> Generation Y do not fear the future. . . . They have never experienced a depression. They think the world is happy and rich all the time.

In somewhat similar vein, a national American commentator concluded recently as follows:

> Generation Y has been pampered, nurtured and programmed. . . . They are both high-performance and high-maintenance. (Armour, 2005, p. 4)

Based on analyses such as these, we conclude that young teachers, as well as students in our schools today, are increasingly characterized by features such as the following:

- technologically connected
- economically inexperienced
- lifestyle-oriented
- upholding respect and loyalty as traits to be earned
- socially conscious and concerned
- focused on short-term goals

As Generation Y begins to impact more upon communities and the world of work, new forms of educational leadership in general, and teacher leadership in particular, must surely be encouraged to evolve, morph, and mutate. Indeed, case studies of the work of teacher leaders at Greenhills and Minnemanka, as examples, would suggest that a degree of morphing is already occurring in the way that teacher leaders adjust their actions to suit the changing characteristics of both contexts and students.

Moreover, our case studies make clear that teacher leaders may be found in both advantaged and disadvantaged schools; in denominational, private, and public schools; at all grade and year levels; and across all subjects and disciplines. The teacher leaders with whom we have worked reflect a wide range of dispositions, political allegiances, religious affiliations, personalities, ages, and other characteristics. Teacher leaders as individuals have in some cases preferred classical approaches to teaching and learning while in other cases their natural inclinations have been technological, futuristic, or humanistic.

We have observed that teacher leadership in communities beset by violence, apathy, and disillusionment is quite different in its value orientation, as well as its practice, from teacher leadership in schools with a large proportion of students who are privileged materialistically, culturally, and socially. In the former, teacher leadership has often involved action to uplift students' capacity to engage confidently with the broader world. In the latter, it has been more likely to entail sensitizing students to critical problems confronting the world and encouraging them to reflect on possible ways of addressing those problems in contexts quite different from their own. In both instances, barriers invariably have to be confronted, trust established, networks created, and successes celebrated. How these actions are approached and undertaken might be very different in different situations and with different individual teacher leaders.

It goes without saying, therefore, that attempts to identify teacher leaders in advance of observing them and working with them in their contexts has been, in our experience, unsuccessful. We tend to resist the popular view that teacher leadership can be defined by identifiable personal or professional attributes. Profiles of teacher leadership such as the following, which were very helpful a decade ago, may now have served their purpose:

> The composite teacher leader is warm, dependable, and self-effacing with a genuine commitment to the work of colleagues and the school. She has well-honed interpersonal skills which are exercised with individuals and groups of colleagues, as well as with students. In addition, the teacher leader possesses the technical skills required for program improvement and uses them in concert with a broad knowledge base about education policy, subject matter, the local community and the school's students. (Leithwood, Jantzi, Ryan, & Steinbach, 1997, pp. 23–24)

Although attempts such as this to conceptualize teacher leadership highlight the human dimension of school-based leadership, they can be criticized on the same grounds that behavioral and trait approaches to leadership have been criticized for many years—they deny the capabilities of individuals whose characteristics and talents lie in areas other than those identified. Recent constructions of teacher leadership, by contrast, tend to be more reflective of individual capabilities and convictions than of personality factors and more focused on the dynamics of school-based pedagogical enhancement than on prescribed technical skills.

It follows from this brief analysis of the variability of teacher leadership that we believe that it is both unrealistic and unhelpful to suggest that all teachers are leaders. We believe that all teachers are *potential* leaders, but to suggest that all teachers *are* leaders at a particular point in time and in all situations defies considerations of context, power relations, personal characteristics, individual circumstances, and human nature. We have no doubt that, as further defensible formulations of teacher leadership are generated and begin to affect school practice, teacher leadership will expand in both theory and application. At this time, however, it is more instructive to recognize that teacher leadership is a highly demanding educational construct that, while it is rapidly developing deep professional meaning, remains the prerogative of a critical mass, rather than the totality, of practicing teachers.

Premise Five: The Development and Sustainability of Teacher Leadership Is Inseparable From Strong Principalship and Supportive Systemic Frameworks

In the 2002 edition of *Developing Teacher Leaders* we drew attention to the interdependence of teacher leaders and their principals. We said:

> Where we have seen teacher leadership begin to flourish, principals have actively supported it or, at least, encouraged it. System-wide policies in these schools have also supported teacher leaders, and external mentors have provided encouragement and helped to clarify teacher leader and administrator leader roles. We believe that it is possible for teacher leadership to exist without the support of administrators. But its outcomes will not be as positive as when such leadership is accepted and encouraged. (p. 33)

Our position has evolved somewhat since that time, illuminated by our own experience and international research. While we know of some situations in which teacher leaders have exercised successful leadership in the absence of strong principalship, and others in which teacher leaders have successfully overcome very negative barriers in their schools without principals' support, we know of no evidence to support the view that teacher leadership can either flourish or be sustained indefinitely in the absence of strong support systems, particularly from principals or other senior administrators.

These sentiments have also been articulated recently by other observers, as noted in Murphy's recent (2005) treatise:

> The principal, it seems, has a disproportionate influence upon teacher leadership—for better or worse. (Barth, 2001, as cited in Murphy, p. 128)

> Principals play a key role in developing teacher leadership. (Buckner & McDowell, 2000, as cited in Murphy, p. 129)

> The role of the principal is paramount in creating the infrastructures to support these roles. (Childs-Bowen, 2000, as cited in Murphy, p. 136)

> It is a paradox of teacher leadership that it requires administrative leadership to be effective. (Smyllie et al., 2002, as cited in Murphy, p. 136)

> Where teacher leadership thrives, administrators make teacher leadership a priority and take risks to provide teacher leaders what they need to succeed. (Katzenmeyer & Moller, 2001, as cited in Murphy, p. 137)

Olivier and Hipp (2006) have drawn on Lambert's (2003) research to conclude that formal training in facilitative leadership is essential for prospective as well as practicing teacher leaders. They cite Fullan's (2005) "long lever of leadership" to demonstrate just how teacher leadership can be developed:

> Lead leaders are creating intensive opportunities for new leaders to learn in context—job-embedded learning that is specific to the organization and is learned on the job through mentoring and related opportunities to engage in reflective practice, working with others on significant school and district priorities. (Olivier & Hipp, p. 507)

Our experience supports the views of Olivier and Hipp and Fullan. The CLASS Plan that comprises Chapter 6 has been created as a direct response to our recognition of the need for comprehensive leader development programs for teachers. Our experience suggests that one particularly important exercise for principals to encourage, and experience with their teachers, involves identification of barriers to teacher leadership within the profession as well as the school. Table 2.2 contains the outcomes of analysis in schools in which we have worked (see also Chapter 6 CLASS Exercise 7).

Table 2.2   Overcoming Barriers to Teacher Leadership

Barriers to Leadership	Ways to Overcome the Barriers
"I'm just a teacher" mindset	Draw attention to ways in which teachers exhibit leadership in school activities and processes
Lack of confidence	Ask teachers to take a lead role where they will be comfortable
Unclear understanding of the concept	Engage in professional dialogue and analysis, using the Teachers as Leaders Framework and snapshots
"I just want to teach" mindset	Explore three-dimensional pedagogy and its links to the Teachers as Leaders Framework
No time for development	Highlight developmental opportunities in daily operations
System that expects only principals to be leaders	Encourage mentoring from teacher leader (TL) models
Possible encouragement of rabble rousers	Insist that the school's vision and values be used as a guide to action
Belief that too many cooks spoil the broth	Discuss how to make $1 + 1 = 3$
No rewards for extra effort	Highlight intrinsic reward systems
Open to abuse by manipulators	Make projects transparent and accountable
Previous failures with lead teachers	Create new labels, without attached baggage
Language that reinforces teachers as subordinates ("bosses" and "staff")	Devise lists of appropriate and inappropriate language
Not taught in preservice education	Make sure that beginning teachers become aware of TL and its relevance for their careers
Peer pressure	Reiterate that TL is voluntary but a commitment to school success should be obligatory
Lack of principal support	Ask the principal to explore (and critique) metastrategic leadership concepts

Thus, the past half decade has been characterized by a significant research emphasis on the teacher leader/principal relationship. But our own research and development has led to a further conclusion—that potential teacher leaders gain immense benefits from external relationships that reinforce the importance of their work while also enabling them to enrich and clarify their roles. Two strategies stand out in our experience—university-based critical friends and cluster opportunities for collaborative sharing and problem-solving. In all case study snapshots that are used in this book, the teacher leaders had ongoing access to both of these forms of network resources.

A number of recent international research initiatives support our conclusions in this regard. For example, Firestone et al. (2005) have concluded recently that "Districts *can* play a key role in supporting instructional reform . . . (if they) cope with numerous pathways through which teaching and learning can be influenced" (p. 414). Rusch (2005) has noted that school districts have the potential to both encourage and inhibit school improvement (p. 87). Our experience supports Rusch's contention that networks that are created for district purposes and managed by district officers may inhibit professional growth while networks that emerge from shared collegial need and are led by teacher leaders have the potential to be exceptionally powerful in their effects.

As a concrete example, we have observed quite remarkable differences in the effects of two forms of district-initiated professional learning activity. In the first, teachers were asked by supervisors to share pedagogical success stories to enable the supervisors and a task force of teacher colleagues to develop formal "District Standards for Pedagogical Best Practices." In the latter, teachers were asked to share how they enabled their school to progress its distinctive vision and in so doing contribute to enhanced school-based pedagogy. Our observation has been that teachers frequently resist the competitive, "show, tell, and judge" mindset of the former activity but engage creatively with the professional problem-solving mindset of the latter. It is easy to envision enhanced teacher professionalism emerging from the latter activity and very difficult to imagine such an outcome from the former.

It is a fundamental premise of this book that the continued evolution of teacher leadership is universally beneficial. It follows that responsibility for generating mature new leadership hybrids for teachers is the responsibility of the educator profession in its entirety—particularly teachers themselves, but also their principals, district supervisors, and university researchers and scholars.

CONCLUSIONS

Teacher leadership is now a conceptual and practical reality, it is grounded in authoritative theory, it is integrally linked to pedagogical excellence, it has qualities of versatility and adaptiveness, and it is interdependent with strong principalship and external support systems. One can only conclude that teacher leadership is an essential and highly credible component of schooling in the early part of the new century and that its impacts on the future shape of the teaching profession specifically, and schooling more generally, will be profound.

Furthermore, in this chapter we have introduced the construct of three-dimensional pedagogy and presented it as integral to teacher leadership, but also as sufficient in its own right to provide a rationale for advanced forms of twenty-first-century teacher professionalism. Moreover, we have demonstrated that our Framework for Teacher Leadership is consistent with four established theories of educational leadership and also with principles of emotional intelligence. In essence, we believe that teacher leadership has achieved maturity as a professional construct. The potential now exists for the teaching profession to reach for new levels of influence and esteem and for schools to confidently accept challenges that have not been within reach in most Western nations in modern educational history.

3

Building School Capacity Through Parallel Leadership

Simply put, new and different working relationships need to be established between teachers and administrators in order for any new leadership role to make a positive and lasting contribution to the improvement of teaching and learning in a given setting.

—Patricia Wasley (as cited in Sherrill, 1999, p. 57)

Our concept of parallel leadership derives from research of the past decade into educational leadership as a shared or distributed professional responsibility, but it differs in two important regards from most conceptions of distributed leadership. First, it proposes that the leadership of principals and teachers in school reform varies in form and method but is similar in significance. Second, it articulates an inextricable link between school-based leadership and the enhancement of educational outcomes and also presents a model to explain the dynamics of that link.

As recently as a decade ago, Hallinger and Heck (1996) described the relationship between school leadership and school improvement as a "black box" mystery: "The process by which administrators achieve an impact is hidden in a so-called black box. A relationship is empirically tested, but the findings reveal little about how leadership operates" (p. 8). Only when school leadership is construed as a "parallel" relationship between competent principals and competent teacher leaders, in our view, will the mystery of the black box be revealed. In Chapter 3 we pry the lid of Hallinger and Heck's box open and explore its contents.

SNAPSHOT FOUR: JOHNSONVALE ELEMENTARY SCHOOL

We're already seriously overloaded. Why take on something extra?

Why fix it if it isn't broken?

These two well-worn questions pose serious challenges for responsible educators in many schools, for it cannot be denied that the range of curriculum and structural innovations that schools have been asked to address in recent years has been very extensive. At the same time, accountability demands, particularly in relation to student learning outcomes, have increased.

Over a four year period, the principal and staff of Johnsonvale Elementary School engaged in a process that enabled them to reject external demands that did not complement their agreed vision and increasingly focus their attention on students' learning outcomes, particularly in literacy. As a result of their efforts, some (but not all) aspects of student literacy improved beyond their expectations. Additionally, staff morale improved and students' perceptions of their school experiences changed for the better. But, in the process, they experienced a journey that could be described as unpredictable, uncertain, and full of surprises. The one common factor in their journey, the one variable that seems to underpin their success, is that of parallel leadership between the principal, Patrick Hay, and a number of teacher leaders, but most notably the school librarian, Gayle Shower.

This is the Johnsonvale story, as it was explained it to us in a report by Gayle, Patrick, and two other teachers.

Our school, Johnsonvale Elementary School, is a large K–7 school located in the center of a small city. The school community mainly draws on students from established local residential areas as well as drawing some students from further afield.

In the late 1990s, it was decided by the school staff and school board that a key issue for our school was the lack of consistency in relation to behavior management. However, there were other areas of concern. Most notably, our literacy results indicated room for serious improvement in the areas of writing and reading comprehension.

At this point the principal and council agreed to identify a school facilitator to identify, initiate, and coordinate a suitable school development process. It was also decided at this early stage that the serious involvement and leadership of the principal would be critical, as would the leadership of a representative Project Management Team. Volunteers were called for, and ten staff accepted. This step in hindsight seems to have been the right one.

Basically, our three year journey followed four stages:

Diagnosis (2000)

We obtained diagnostic survey instruments from a highly reputable educational consulting agency. The results of the surveys revealed that Johnsonvale was strongly supported by all three stakeholder groups—staff, parents, students—and was widely regarded as achieving very sound outcomes for students. But concerns were also identified by the Project Management Team and ratified by the staff:

- the lack of a vision that provided the school community with inspiration and purpose
- teachers' concern that school planning processes were not sufficiently inclusive
- a shared concern of students and teachers that physical infrastructures were inhibiting effective teaching and learning
- highly individualized (indeed, balkanized) teaching approaches, and a lack of reinforcement and consistency across the grade levels, particularly for low-achieving students.

Envisioning (2001–2003)

After more than a year of brainstorming, debating, and voting, a very simple five-word vision statement was decided upon as our image of how we wanted to see ourselves and be seen by the outside world:

Together We Achieve the Extraordinary

Following the adoption of our vision statement, we turned our attention to the analysis of our teaching and learning practices. We determined to address the area of written literacy, which had been a concern for the school community for several years. We undertook an audit of the uses that were being made of various strategies in our classrooms. Four focus questions guided our professional conversations:

- What do you do in your classroom that is most effective?
- What makes it so effective for you?
- What educational thinking supports your strategies?
- How do these strategies bring the Johnsonvale vision alive?

After much debate, the Johnsonvale Learning Framework was finalized:

Together

- We Cooperate.
- We Communicate.
- We Support.

We Achieve

- We Are ALL Learners.
- We Are Responsible.
- We Are Adaptable.

The Extraordinary

- We Take Risks.
- We Celebrate Success.
- We Strive for Excellence.

Actioning (2004–2005)

Once we had finalized our Johnsonvale Learning Framework, we were faced with further complex questions:

- How should we apply it in aspects of Johnsonvale's daily work?
- How specific should our applications be?
- How should we manage these processes to ensure that they are maximally effective?
- How might we apply them in a schoolwide literacy approach?

Our explorations led us to an innovative Literacy Cycle that seemed to reflect both our Vision and our Learning Framework. It was distinctive in that it promoted oral literacy as a precedent to written literacy. In so doing, it targeted five major student skill areas: higher order thinking, cooperative student research, individualized diagnosis of progress, oral communications, and extensive experiences in guided writing.

Teachers agreed to use the nine broad principles of the Learning Framework as a guide in their teaching, and to emphasize the five skill areas of the Literacy Cycle. They were encouraged to keep work samples to show growth, or otherwise, in children's writing. We also decided that teachers should be encouraged to maintain reflective journals in which they recorded their personal experiences with the Literacy Cycle. Our staff professional development for the next two years centered on the experiences of our staff with the Framework and the Literacy Cycle. We also brought in consultants to assist us with the refinement of strategies and the ongoing analysis of student data.

In year three of the project (early 2004), we decided to measure the midterm impacts of our involvement with the Literacy Cycle. To do this, we readministered the original school surveys and implemented a series of strategies to measure students'

Table 3.1 Literacy Developments, Preproject and Midproject, for Students Involved in the Literacy Cycle

Current Grade 5 students	N	Relative change in literacy achievement
Lower Band	26	All students showed improvement beyond the norm.
Middle Band	25	5 students showed improvement beyond the norm.
		9 students showed predictable improvement.
		11 students showed less improvement than was expected.
Upper Band	15	5 students showed predictable improvement.
		10 students showed less improvement than was expected.
Current Grade 7 students	N	Relative change in literacy achievement
Lower Band	13	9 students showed improvement beyond the norm.
		4 students showed predictable improvement.
Middle Band	30	4 students showed improvement beyond the norm.
		20 students showed predictable improvement.
		6 students showed less improvement than was expected.
Upper Band	12	1 student showed improvement beyond the norm.
		11 students showed less improvement than was expected.

literacy levels. The results of the readministered surveys revealed that, overall, Johnsonvale was perceived by its stakeholders as having consolidated its image as a highly successful school during the three-year renewal process.

The data that are contained in Table 3.1 are literacy-specific and are based on the results of a standardized testing program conducted annually by the State Education Department.

In interpreting the data contained in Table 3.1, the following comments were offered by the School Renewal Project Team as midproject conclusions:

- The Literacy Cycle seems to empower many of the boys, which is encouraging.
- We are doing very well in the lower and middle bands ... but we seem not to be so good at extending the brighter students in our classes ... As teachers are still mastering the Cycle, some may be focused on targeting the below average and average students within their classes, thereby not catering adequately for above-average students.
- In the case of the Grade 5 Middle Band, 8 of the 11 students whose achievement dropped were in the same class, where the teacher had not agreed to follow the Literacy Cycle in its intended form.

Thus, it would appear that our creation of a school vision and schoolwide learning framework, and transposition into a schoolwide literacy approach, has been associated with a number of improvements in student achievement in a designated area of school priority (written literacy) as well as some question marks in this same learning area. Of particular note is that the standardized test results suggest that major gains in written literacy have been made by students of lower ability (particularly among boys) but high-achieving girls have not improved at the same rate. We have considered these issues and are taking steps to address them, through modifications to the five strategies of the Literacy Cycle.

Professional Reflections (2006)

We have considered the question of Leadership as it relates to our work over the past several years, particularly the way that it has enabled us to work toward enhanced student outcomes in Literacy. Our individual thoughts are as follows:

Gayle Shower (Facilitator)

- Parallel leadership is the central concept—the principal has stepped outside the safety zone and teachers have had opportunities to acquire leadership skills that enable them to influence others and engage confidently with different audiences.
- External consultants have helped us deal with the key issue of pedagogy.
- It will take a long time to achieve our aspirations, but we feel in charge of the process.

Patrick Hay (Johnsonvale principal)

- Gayle (facilitator) has emphasized the centrality of teaching and learning, and this has enabled us to get to the point where Literacy is our focus.
- We have found the Literacy Cycle rationale to be very convincing and have also found that it complements our Learning Framework and Vision very nicely.
- As a school we are now able to say, "If a new idea from outside doesn't fit our vision and Framework, consider rejecting it." That has helped us get a sense of control over what we do.
- Our vision has been important to our success. People have come to accept that you can do extraordinary things without anxiety if you go about it with purpose, trust, and optimism.

Shauna Paul, Mark Cranston, Cathy Lincoln (Johnsonvale teachers)

- The principal and project facilitator were both passionate about the overall project. They saw it as a way of enabling teachers to overcome interpersonal barriers and to share their professional successes and questions.
- Not everyone got involved initially. Those who did so tended to be the teachers who were most passionate about their work. A critical mass of us created new images and symbols that changed how we think about ourselves. This has rubbed off over time on the doubters and noninvolved.

Fred Ryan, external consultant

- Parallel leadership has been a constant feature of the Johnsonvale Project. The principal's role has been classic metastrategy. Teacher leadership has taken a range of forms, but has featured the facilitator and other school management team (SMT) members on an ongoing basis.
- The use of data (student literacy achievement in particular) has enabled the facilitator, principal, and SMT to search for enhanced coherence in the school and to take deliberate steps to enhance student outcomes.
- The confidence and enthusiasm of the principal and facilitator have rubbed off and created a sense of self-belief for other teachers, and also students and parents.

Conclusion

We began this snapshot with the question, *Why fix it if it isn't broken?*

The Johnsonvale experience shows that, even when a school is achieving satisfactory results, there is immense educational merit and professional reward to be gained from seeking new goals. It of course takes courage and a degree of bravado to create and publicly articulate a vision that includes a term such as "extraordinary." It also takes professional trust and resilience to commit to a developmental process that has no prescribed endpoint. Furthermore, it takes deep commitment to confront disappointing results in a midterm review and to then make significant adjustments in complex processes. But that is what happened, and continues to happen at Johnsonvale, largely as a result of parallel leadership in action.

DEFINING PARALLEL LEADERSHIP

Parallel leadership, as we define it, is a process whereby teacher leaders and their principals engage in collective action to build school capacity. It embodies three distinct qualities—mutual trust, shared purpose, and allowance for individual expression.

Conceptually, the power of parallel leadership resides in its connection to the emerging constructs of organizational capacity (King & Newmann, 2000), collective intelligence (Heifetz & Laurie, 1997; Nash, 2005) and educational capital (Hargreaves, 2001). As such, it has potential relevance for a wide range of postindustrial organizations, but it is most appropriate to schools, where the creation of new meaning from teaching and learning—primarily for students, but also for communities, cultures, and societies—constitutes the core business.

One of our main research foci has been on ways that parallel leadership might spur changes leading to enhanced student outcomes. Our conclusions point to the importance of three intersecting processes—namely holistic professional learning, distinctive culture-building, and schoolwide pedagogical development—that appear to us to depend upon parallel leadership if they are to be achieved either singly or in combination. This chapter focuses on the critical role of parallel leadership in activating these foundational processes, in developing them simultaneously, and transposing them into enhanced school capacity.

THREE ESSENTIAL CHARACTERISTICS OF PARALLEL LEADERSHIP

Our definition of parallel leadership contains explicit reference to three distinctive underpinning qualities: *mutualism, a sense of shared purpose,* and *allowance for individual expression.* All three qualities are very apparent in the relationship of the principal Patrick Hay, and teacher leader, Gayle Shower, in the Johnsonvale snapshot.

Mutual Trust

Mutual trust, as we have observed it, embodies values such as dignity and respect as well as care and nurturing. It resembles what Bryk and Schneider (as cited in Fleming & Leo, 2000) refer to as relational trust:

> Relational trust creates an environment where individuals share a moral commitment to act in the interests of the collectivity, and this ethical basis for individual action constitutes a moral resource that the institution can draw on to initiate and sustain change. (p. 4)

For teachers, the issue of relatedness has long-standing significance. Building on the work of Lortie (1975), numerous researchers have illuminated ways that teachers have found the isolation of their work not only alienating but also very difficult to redress. Hargreaves (1994) asserted that the establishment of trust is central to the restructuring of school systems that strive to enter a postmodern paradigm:

> The challenge is of building confidence and connectedness among teachers who may not know each other quite so well, by investing mutual trust in complementary expertise—without this also leading to burgeoning bureaucracy. (p. 254)

Bryk and Schneider (2002) have drawn on both scholarly research and their own experiences in schools to propose that what they call "relational trust" comprises a "dynamic interplay among four considerations: respect, competence, personal regard for others, and integrity. . . . A serious deficiency on any one criterion can be sufficient to undermine a discernment of trust for the overall relationship" (p. 23). In a somewhat similar vein, Elmore (2005) has recently argued that trust is a compound of respect, personal regard, competence, and personal integrity (p. 20).

From these researchers and others, we know that both staff and students benefit from the presence of mature professional learning communities where trust is nurtured, practiced, and valued. Teachers are less isolated, share in the collective responsibility for student success, and have higher morale and lower absenteeism. Students in such schools also tend to have greater academic gains, and there are smaller achievement gaps between students of different backgrounds (King & Newmann, 2000; Newmann & Wehlage, 1995).

The Johnsonvale sketch provides a clear demonstration of how mutualistic relationships across the school community, but particularly in the critical interplay of principal and teacher leaders, make such gains in student improvement a concrete possibility, not just a vague hope. Specifically, the strategic role of the principal and the pedagogical expertise of the key teacher leader at Johnsonvale were regarded as equally important, effective, and dependable in shaping and implementing an ambitious innovation. The result of their parallel leadership in action was the generation of an inspiring vision and ingenious literacy approach, a willingness to acknowledge and support a wide spectrum of ideas, a high level of integrity in all school operations, and a capacity to acknowledge deficiencies in student achievement and work collectively toward their resolution.

A Sense of Shared Purpose

Also noticeable in the Johnsonvale snapshot—and in all of our case studies where parallel leadership has flourished—is a sense of shared purpose. The ultimate effect at Johnsonvale was an alignment between the school's stated vision and teachers' preferred approaches to teaching, learning, and assessment.

The alignment that evolved at Johnsonvale had its origins in the school's visioning process. The Johnsonvale experience illustrates the complexity of successful school visioning as captured by authorities such as Licata and Harper:

A robust school vision is perceived by teachers as relatively high in dramatic content. Such a school vision dramatizes the discrepancy between the challenges facing a school in the present and a more desirable future. The sharing of a robust school vision probably arouses teachers and others to ongoing action in accomplishing that future. (2001, p. 8)

In the Johnsonvale case study, the "high dramatic content" of the "extraordinary" vision would not have been regarded by many Johnsonvale teachers as either realistic or helpful if it had not been for the obvious shared purpose of the principal and key teacher leader. Because of their demonstrated commitment to a daunting moral challenge—enabling a somewhat tired and apathetic community to see itself as able to achieve outstanding levels of student outcomes—teachers engaged increasingly with the revitalization process and looked for ways to reflect the school's vision in their teaching practices. While difficulties were encountered in the short term—including disappointing literacy results for academically talented female students—they became designers of their own professional roles, proposing and implementing pedagogical adjustments to the school's literacy approach.

Thus, "shared purpose" began at Johnsonvale through a manifestation of parallel leadership but, over time, became a pervasive feature of the school's culture and operations. The Johnsonvale experience lends support to Cowan's (2006) explanation of how collaboration enables enhanced organizational success:

> . . . in high performing schools and districts, collaboration fosters a clear sense of shared purpose and helps to define roles and responsibilities. Teachers readily share and solve problems. . . . Interactions of this nature strengthen instructional program coherence and can thus lead to increased student achievement. (p. 602)

Allowance for Individual Expression

The third characteristic that we discerned in our research case studies—allowance for individual expression—may appear, at first glance, to fly in the face of much recent thinking about school reform.

Principal-teacher leader relationships in our case studies allowed for, even encouraged, a high degree of individual expression and action. This phenomenon may appear to be inconsistent with recent emphases on teamwork, collegiality, and collaboration in educational workplaces. But in case studies such as the Johnsonvale snapshot, the two key leaders had strong individual convictions and assertive dispositions as well as a well-developed capacity to accommodate the values and circumstances of others. Thus, successful shared leadership as we observed it was associated with recognition of strong, skilled, autonomous individuals and with collaboration among them rather than with consensus.

Hargreaves's (1994) distinction between individualism, which connotes isolation and solitude, and individuality, which connotes personal independence and self-realization, is one that we have found very helpful in reaching this conclusion. What we observed as individual expression and action is more akin to individuality than to individualism. At

Johnsonvale, for example, Gayle and Patrick were publicly acknowledged as the initiators of the innovative literacy initiative but undertook fundamentally different responsibilities in its design, implementation, and evaluation. Patrick was later recognized nationally with an Outstanding Principal award for his metastrategic successes—visioning, aligning, culture-building, alliancing, and nurturing of teacher leaders—while Gayle was recognized as the key professional in the development of the school's pedagogical framework and literacy successes.

On the basis of our research to date, we are inclined to agree with Limerick, Cunnington, and Crowther (1998) that collective processes that serve to obscure individuality are more likely to contribute to the perpetuation of questionable practices on the part of both principals and teachers than are processes that recognize individual action and the legitimacy of dissent. We have also seen evidence to support the view that "teamwork" without acknowledgment of individuality can be open to managerial manipulation and control by principals—a suspicion that has been well captured by a number of authors including Wilkins and Ouchi (1983, as cited in Sinclair, 1995, p. 48) and Hargreaves (1994).

The demands on principals to accept and accommodate teacher leaders who may be workplace agitators are obvious if the legitimacy of the concept of individual expression is accepted. A number of authorities, including Boomer (1985), who has applauded "teaching against the grain" (p. 20); Shor and Freire (1987), who espouse teaching for liberation; and Gutierrez, Rymes, and Larson (1995), who speak of teachers searching for the "third space," have noted the importance of allowing for discrepant voices in facilitating creative organizational problem solving. The effects of individuality may sometimes be too much for some principals to accommodate, but principals in our case studies recognized its value and gave it considerable opportunity to materialize constructively.

The three qualities that underpin parallel leadership—mutual trust, shared purpose, and allowance for individual expression—are equally important. All three qualities are required if teacher leadership is to flourish. They are also essential in relationships between teacher leaders and their principals if the complex processes that enable school capacity-building to transpire—namely, holistic professional learning, distinctive culture-building—and schoolwide pedagogical development—are to achieve practical meaning.

PARALLELISM IN THE SCIENCES, ARTS, AND HUMANITIES

In advancing parallelism as a professionally appropriate approach to school-based leadership, we acknowledge, first of all, its dictionary definition: "agreement in direction, tendency or character" (Macquarie Library,

1998, p. 1560). Essential to our developmental work, however, have been the rich and complex meanings of this concept in a number of fields of cultural and intellectual endeavor.

Consider, for example, the field of *music,* where parallelism connotes the harmony derived when two independent parts or voices within a musical texture move up or down by the same distance in tandem (e.g., parallel fifths). In *language,* parallelism is well known. For example, analogies allow new meaning to be constructed through correspondence between two different concepts. In the world of *mathematics,* parallelism refers to forces that mirror each other. Parallel lines, for example, sustain their individual identities while maintaining a common direction and an unwavering distance from each other. In *computer science,* parallel processing refers to the management of complex data through systems that operate in a complementary fashion. Finally, consider the discipline of *philosophy,* in particular metaphysics, where parallelism connotes a doctrine of mind and body interacting synchronistically while remaining independent.

Parallelism in these human endeavors suggests respect, harmony, direction, alignment, individual presence, and complementarity. The three specific qualities that we have attributed to parallel leadership—mutual trust, shared purpose, and allowance for individualism—are readily discernible in these broader constructs and have been generated from our research with them in mind.

As would be expected, the three specific qualities that define parallel leadership are also to be found in other manifestations of contemporary culture.

In sport, for example, the notion that "A champion team will always beat a team of champions" implies at least two of the three qualities that we attribute to parallelism in school leadership. In musical performance, the complex relationship between a conductor, orchestral heads, and specialist performers can be viewed as reflecting aspects of all three underpinning qualities of parallelism—mutualism, shared purpose, and allowance for individual expression. The same is true in other performing arts, perhaps particularly dance, where ballet, rock 'n' roll, line dancing, and a preindustrial war dance may each be regarded as demonstrating particular forms of parallelism and manifesting varying degrees of the qualities of mutualism, shared purpose, and individuality.

But the three qualities are, we think, more deeply meaningful in leadership for successful school-based reform than in other culture forms that we have explored. We therefore assert that parallel leadership is a distinctive educational construct that has the potential to decisively advance the cause of schools and the teaching profession in the twenty-first century.

HOW PARALLEL LEADERSHIP WORKS IN SCHOOLS

The key contention of this book is that, with mature teacher leadership, school improvement can become a deliberate process of design and accomplishment. But no matter how assertive or sophisticated it may be, teacher leadership cannot engender improvement on a sustained basis in and of itself—that is possible only through the dynamic interplay of effective teacher leadership and effective principalship in the process that we have designated parallelism.

In Phase Three of our decade-long research and development, we focused primarily on the dynamics that occur as schools engage successfully in revitalization and reform. As part of a national research endeavor into the dynamics of successful school reform, we traced the experiences of nine schools that initiated and managed processes resulting in documented evidence of enhanced student achievement in literacy or mathematics (Crowther, Hann, & McMaster, 2001).

Figure 3.1 shows the product of this research in conceptual terms while the Johnsonvale snapshot illustrates it in practical terms. In essence, to enhance a school's effectiveness necessitates a three-pronged strategy by a committed professional community over an extensive period of time (two years or more, in our case studies). That is, the school's professionals must engage in shared learning, focused reflection, and in-depth problem-solving (outer circle of Figure 3.1) while refining and deepening the school's culture and identity (middle circle) and simultaneously designing and implementing school-specific pedagogical principles and associated strategies (inner circle).

The daunting nature of this multifaceted challenge should not be underestimated. But it is within the capability of the modern teaching profession to achieve, so long as parallel leadership is used to guide school development and revitalization processes. Based on our association with school revitalization over the past decade, we know of very few, if any, instances where sustained improvement has been achieved without parallel leadership—possibly because visioning and culture-building without strong principal leadership invariably fail to produce teacher and community commitment and the creation of schoolwide pedagogical principles and frameworks without strong teacher leadership is invariably lacking in authenticity.

When these three constituent processes are activated and sustained, however, school-based capacity-building can occur. Specifically, as the three processes individually take shape, merge, and evolve, a school's teaching and learning activities become more focused, more coherent, more mutually reinforcing across classrooms and subjects, and less constrained by external distractions and internal disruptions. Expectations heighten—for teachers first, then students and parents—effort increases, and problem solving becomes more creative. The data from our most recent research, as outlined in Appendix B, indicate that enhancements in teacher morale, student engagement, and community attitudes follow.

Let us look briefly at the three constituent processes of our framework for successful school revitalization as they manifest in the Johnsonvale and other case studies.

Figure 3.1   Linking Parallel Leadership and Successful Capacity-Building

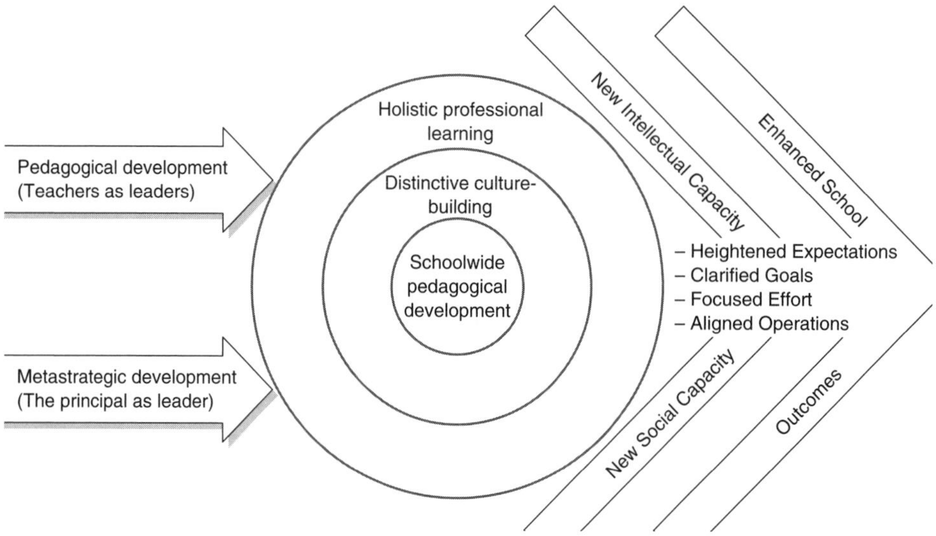

HOLISTIC PROFESSIONAL LEARNING

Our research-based observation in schools that successfully managed processes of revitalization was that professional learning invariably involves principals and teachers in comprehensive joint professional development activities. This feature of our research findings is reflected in the outer circle of Figure 3.1. It makes clear that the customary separation of principal development and teacher development was largely rejected in schools that we studied and replaced by ongoing joint inquiry that enhances the alignment of the school's vision with schoolwide approaches to teaching, learning, and assessment.

Johnsonvale School is one example where the principal (Pat) and a teacher leader (Gayle) worked in parallel to develop professional learning opportunities that fostered such schoolwide pedagogical approaches. Whereas Gayle coordinated inquiry into the school's approach to literacy at professional development sessions, Pat coordinated the visioning process and subsequently raised questions about how best to align the approach with the school's vision and promote the approach with students and parents.

Furthermore, both Pat and Gayle liaised with external consultants to ensure that a Literacy Cycle was adopted that reflected the Johnsonvale vision and pedagogical framework. Workshops that were conducted for the whole staff were designed by them in conjunction with the Project Management Team. Other members of the Project Management Team took responsibility for such diverse functions as project scribe, data collection and analysis, workshop organization, mentoring of new staff, project evaluation, conference presentations, and hospitality arrangements.

The Johnsonvale sketch appears to us to represent a clear example of the three features of a successful professional community that Newmann and Wehlage (1995, p. 30) identified through their internationally renowned research:

- Teachers pursue a clear shared purpose for all students' learning.
- Teachers engage in collaborative activity to achieve the purpose.
- Teachers take collective responsibility for student learning.

The emphasis of Johnsonvale's parallel leaders in bringing together teachers, administrators, and support staff in shared professional learning had one other powerful effect—it helped sustain focus and momentum in spite of changes in staff, while providing opportunities for new staff to engage with the school's Literacy Cycle innovation and contribute fresh ideas to it.

Shirley Hord's (1997) conclusion that successful professional learning communities are characterized by the following dimensions appears to have application in the Johnsonvale and other case studies included in this book:

- shared values and vision
- collective learning and application
- supportive and shared leadership
- supportive conditions
- shared personal practice
- an unwavering focus on student learning

Also evident in the Johnsonvale snapshot is that effective leadership, for both principals and teacher leaders, emphasizes inquiry into the professional task at hand rather than the expertise of individual leaders. As Spillane, Halverson, and Diamond (2001) have stated:

> The most notable trait of great leaders, certainly of great change leaders . . . is their quest for learning. They show an exceptional willingness to push themselves out of their comfort zones, even after they have achieved a great deal. (as cited in MacBeath, 2006b, p. 4)

It is perhaps for this reason that a recent analysis of research into the impacts of leadership on student outcomes has disclosed that by far the most significant leadership variable in engendering success is that of "Leadership that not only promotes, but directly participates with teachers in, formal or informal professional learning" (Robinson, 2007, p. 8). As Fred Ryan, a consultant to the Johnsonvale Project, concluded in his reflections on the Johnsonvale experience, "The confidence and enthusiasm of the principal and facilitator have rubbed off and created a sense of self-belief for other teachers, and also students and parents."

DISTINCTIVE CULTURE-BUILDING

The second process that our research has shown to be essential to successful school revitalization is culture-building. This finding from our research is reflected in the middle circle of Figure 3.1.

The multidimensional nature of "culture" seems to us to require that school-based leadership be approached as a shared leadership responsibility. Schein's (1992) cultural model (*artifacts, values, assumptions*) demonstrates the complexity of the concept and provides for us a very helpful framework that can be easily recognized in the snapshots in this book. At Greenhills, for example, *artifacts* (students' pride in wearing the school uniform, celebrations at school assemblies) were readily observable. *Espoused values* such as high expectations and positive community relationships were evident in the school's policy, strategic plan, and behavior-management plan. The *assumption* that socioeconomic disadvantage need be no barrier to success was reflected in statements like, "We can do anything," and "Every student has a gift." Moreover, in referring to the school's achievements and teachers' roles, the principal used terms like "the guardians of our culture." In so doing, he illustrated the integration of artifacts, values, and assumptions within the school and the importance of parallel leadership in linking all three entities to the school vision and to teachers' work.

A second important consideration in school culture-building relates to the culture of the teaching profession itself. Murphy (2005, p. 126) has pointed out some of the difficulties that educational researchers have postulated regarding a deeply entrenched professional concern for egalitarianism:

> When teachers do accept schoolwide leadership responsibilities, they often "seem reluctant to challenge the norms of professional equality" (Smyllie & Denny, 1989, as cited in Murphy, 2005, p. 126).

> And since in an egalitarian culture "the opinions of peers are important to teachers . . . negative comments . . . may stop their initiatives" (Moller & Katzenmeyer, 1996, as cited in Murphy, 2005, p. 126).

The key teacher leader at Johnsonvale made particular use of the "extraordinary" Johnsonvale vision as one mechanism for addressing the issue that Murphy, Smyllie and Denny, and Moller and Katzenmeyer have highlighted. Indeed, all of our case studies suggest that visioning activities can serve the purpose of encouraging teachers to think beyond their immediate contexts and to focus on what is possible rather than upon workplace or community-based constraints. Kelley and Finnegan (2003) have captured very precisely the essence of Johnsonvale's parallel leaders as culture builders, in our view, with their concept of teacher expectancy. Working from a definition that "Expectancy is the belief that individual effort will result in the achievement of specific goals" (p. 604) they conclude from their research that teacher expectancy for heightened student outcomes can be enhanced through specific actions: meaningful rewards, helpful feedback, lack of goal conflict, consideration of school level, and professional community (p. 623). In all of our case studies, a "Can do" school culture was indeed able to be fostered in teachers' work lives through the initiative of parallel leaders and actions such as those that Kelley and Finnegan have identified.

A third consideration for principals and teacher leaders is that of "cultural capital"—in particular, that young people growing up in areas of poverty frequently lack the "cultural capital" needed for success at school. This point has been argued by sociologists such as Bourdieu (see Wrigley, 2006, p. 69, for a brief analysis). The teacher leaders in our case studies invariably demonstrated the capacity to confront institutional and cultural barriers in support of students' well-being. To them, it seems, culture-building cannot be separated from the moral dimension of leadership (MacBeath, 2006b, p. 7).

This brief description of the political and moral dimension of school culture-building would not be complete without a mention of language. In our case studies of successful school reform, both principals and teachers tended to reject the language of hierarchy (e.g., "I'm just a teacher," "my superior," "my subordinates," "let's see what the boss wants," "just tell me what to do and I'll do it," "I came here for the express purpose of turning this school around," "my school staff"). We explore this notion in Chapter 6, CLASS Exercise 8.

Finally, the parallel leaders whom we observed building rich school cultures were concerned to create an identity that reflected their individual contexts and uniqueness. Sergiovanni (1998) has noted the importance of this subtle process:

> Schools with character have unique cultures. They know who they are and have developed a common understanding of their purposes. They celebrate their uniqueness as a powerful way to achieve their goals. (p. 88)

In the case studies that are included in this book, each school created a distinctive identity, one that reflected cultural qualities such as those articulated by Schein, Murphy, and MacBeath. Without parallel leadership we do not believe that the cultures that were created would have evolved as meaningfully as they did, nor do we believe that they would have been easily sustainable over time.

SCHOOLWIDE PEDAGOGICAL DEVELOPMENT

The third of the three intersecting processes that contribute to school capacity-building—a schoolwide approach to pedagogy—is reflected in the inner circle of Figure 3.1. This has emerged not only from our studies but also from other recent research, most notably the University of Wisconsin's Center on Organization and Restructuring of Schools (CORS) project. Newmann and Wehlage (1995) have described the CORS research into ways to use restructuring to elevate student learning:

> What kind of teaching promotes high quality learning? To address this issue, CORS developed teaching standards. . . . Our standards emphasize teaching that requires students to think, to develop in-depth understanding, and to apply academic learning to important, realistic problems . . . . We call this "authentic pedagogy." . . . Schools with strong professional communities were better able to offer authentic pedagogy and were more effective in promoting student achievement. (p. 3)

The CORS research has shown that where school reform is undertaken through collective responsibility and an agreed approach to teaching, learning, and assessment, it directly and significantly affects student achievement, especially for students from lower socioeconomic backgrounds. Peter Senge (as cited in O'Neill, 1995) provides a vivid image of the importance of the concepts of collective responsibility and schoolwide pedagogy:

> You cannot implement "learner-directed learning," for example, in one classroom and not others. It would drive the kids nuts, not to mention the stress on the individual teacher. (p. 21)

But how can the numerous individual pedagogical preferences of teachers be brought together into a schoolwide approach without inhibiting the natural talents of individual teachers? In our view, only through processes that fly squarely in the face of most school organizational practices of the past one hundred years. In our experience, successful schoolwide approaches to teaching, learning, and assessment develop when teacher leaders assume responsibility for identifying critical commonalities in the most successful teaching practices of themselves and their colleagues and then, in conjunction with their principals, aligning those synthesized practices with the school's vision and values. Herein, we believe, lies the most important and most challenging function of parallel leadership.

The schoolwide pedagogical frameworks that were developed at Johnsonvale, and other schools in our snapshots, provided a basis for teachers to reinforce each others' proven practices and to create heightened consistency in the learning experiences of students, particularly those experiencing academic difficulties. Implementation of the frameworks in question also enabled teachers to refine their individual pedagogical talents through focused professional dialogue with colleagues. Significantly, the impacts on teacher morale and professional esteem showed major improvement across the duration of the revitalization projects in question. Based on case studies such as these, we propose the following definition of the process of schoolwide pedagogical development:

> A schoolwide pedagogy is created when teachers engage as a professional community to synergize their personal teaching talents in relation to their school's distinctive vision. In so doing, they create the means for complementing and extending each other's successful practices and for building shared responsibility for the quality of their school's teaching, learning and assessment practices. (Leadership Research Institute, 2007)

In our experience, this essentially new educational construct, a synergistic adaptation of Newmann and Wehlage's concepts of "authentic pedagogy" and "collective professional responsibility," is most effectively developed when the process is led by teacher leaders working in close cooperation with their principals.

The three core processes that we have identified as central to school capacity-building—holistic professional learning, distinctive culture-building, and development of schoolwide pedagogy—are conceptually distinct but should be viewed as interrelated and developed conjointly. Each process requires both strong principalship—in relation to the school's metastrategic development—and strong teacher leadership—in relation to the school's pedagogical development—if it is to evolve in meaningful forms. When the three processes do in fact materialize, as Figure 3.1 indicates, the possibility of significant capacity-building is established.

THE DYNAMICS OF SCHOOL CAPACITY-BUILDING

We began this chapter by stating that we would endeavor to pry open the lid of Hallinger and Heck's (1996) black box of school reform and expose ways in which effective school-based leadership appears to contribute to enhanced student outcomes.

The results of our explorations are presented diagrammatically in Figure 3.1. Specifically, Figure 3.1 reveals that as processes of holistic professional learning, distinctive culture-building, and schoolwide pedagogical development take shape, merge, and evolve, a school increases its capacity to nurture a distinctive sense of identity and belonging, to engender coherence in its multifaceted operations, to concentrate effort on particularly meaningful pedagogical practices, and to reinforce student learning across classrooms, subjects, and year levels.

Snapshots such as Greenhills, Adams, and Johnsonvale reveal that the outcomes of the three central processes that are featured in Figure 3.1 can be described in terms of two forms of capital that have been proposed by David Hargreaves (2001)—intellectual and social. Newly created intellectual capital is evident in each of these snapshots in the form of a distinctive and inspiring school vision and an equally distinctive and educationally defensible pedagogical framework. Important social capital in the form of enhanced identity, mutual respect and constructive networks, is also readily apparent in the snapshots.

Our case studies further reveal that as significant intellectual and social capital is generated in a school, teachers are encouraged and enabled to elevate their goals, collectively and individually. Flow-on effects to students and communities occur. Educational effort becomes more skilled, although our research data (see Appendix B, Figure B.1) suggest that this is not necessarily resource-intensive. Positive changes in student outcomes, teacher morale, and parent attitudes begin to reveal themselves. Success breeds success and a spiral of ongoing successful achievement is established.

One might well ask, "Why has the mystery of the black box confounded educators for so long, when the secret seems to be relatively simple and obvious?" The answer to this question, in our view, is that two generations of leadership researchers have focused their attention too exclusively on the work of principals. Only when the integrity of teacher leadership is accepted, and dynamics of the relationship between teacher leaders and metastrategic principals understood, can the deep secrets of the black box be discerned. That day has arrived.

CONCLUSIONS

In this chapter, we drew on recent international developments in educational leadership, as well as on our research-based observations of teacher leaders and their principals at work, to describe a new educational concept—parallel leadership. We substantiated our claims about the integrity of this new concept by exploring its meanings in a number of fields of cultural and intellectual endeavor and by teasing out its underpinning values. Extending these analyses, we linked parallel leadership with processes that contribute to successful school reform and thus enhance a school's capacity to produce positive outcomes. Our diagram linking parallel leadership and successful school reform (Figure 3.1) represents a visual image of this very important linkage.

To conclude this chapter, we comment briefly upon five questions that are frequently directed to us regarding parallel leadership:

Question: Why not use a well-known term such as "shared leadership" rather than the new term, "parallel leadership"?

Our response: Parallel leadership should not be regarded as new language for the somewhat diffuse constructs of distributed and shared leadership. It manifests definitive leadership functions for both principals and teacher leaders. It also embodies a specific set of values that connect teacher leaders and principals in accountable and synergistic relationships. It contains specific meaning that is not explicit in generic terms such as "shared" and "distributed."

Question: Can parallel leadership incorporate parents and students?

Our response: Parallel leadership as we envision it can be extended to include a governance function for parents—perhaps a three-way form of parallelism. Also, in some of our case studies, parents and paraprofessionals assumed significant roles in both visioning activities and pedagogical analyses, and would undoubtedly be justified in seeing themselves as having exercising leadership. Indeed, in some of our case studies, cohorts of students successfully performed similar tasks. But, we regard teacher leadership as fundamental to the creation of schoolwide pedagogy and principal leadership as fundamental to processes of strategic development within a school. We doubt that these functions can, under most circumstances, be assumed by other groups, including parents and students.

Question: Is the exercise of parallel leadership guaranteed to enhance school outcomes?

Our response: Andy Hargreaves and Dean Fink (2006, p. 103) have provided a clear answer to this question—leadership, however it is construed, can be good, bad, or indifferent. It follows that leadership that is modeled on parallel relationships but is grounded superficially in the six elements of the Teachers as Leaders Framework (Chapter 1), the five functions of metastrategy (Chapter 4), and the values of shared purpose, mutual trust, and allowance for individual expression (this chapter) will be unlikely to transform a school significantly. We say this because such leadership would probably lack the intellect, conviction, or energy that is central to meaningful parallel leadership.

Question: Is parallel leadership a leadership "style"?

Our response: No, but the individuals who comprise a parallel leadership team will each have a preferred style (e.g., strategic, transformational, educative, democratic). The likelihood of creating a balanced overall leadership approach in a school will, we assert, be greater if parallel leadership is in place and a range of leadership styles can be drawn upon.

Question: How many variations of parallel leadership are there?

Our response: We have noted that major variances in parallel leadership occur when contextual influences are taken into account. This is evident in the six snapshots throughout the chapters of this book. The personalities of individual leaders will also give each parallel leadership team a distinctive quality. Thus, while the underlying tenets of parallelism remain deep-rooted and perhaps immutable, there are potentially as many variations of parallelism in practice as there are people and places.

4

New Roles for School Principals

The point to be underscored here is that for many principals, a personal transformation in leadership must accompany the quest to rebuild schooling to cultivate teacher leadership and efforts to nurture the growth of teacher leaders.

—Joseph Murphy
(2005, p. 132)

THE PRINCIPAL'S ROLE: CHANGE IS OVERDUE

Traditionally, school-based leadership has centered on the role of the principal. As shown in our review in Chapter 2 of four significant theories of educational leadership, it is difficult to separate the evolution of leadership concepts in education from principals' work.

In our view, any efforts to rethink the role of the principal in contemporary schooling should be undertaken in full cognizance of the competing values that have underpinned the history of educational administration as a field of academic study and professional practice. In particular, the evolution of the principalship has been shaped by two quite separate, but equally defensible, educational value systems. The first value system is associated with bureaucratic theory and the second with democratic theory.

Hoy and Sweetland (2001, p. 296) have noted the origins of bureaucratic theory in the work of Weber and the continuing importance of bureaucratic theory in educational management and leadership:

> Like it or not, schools are bureaucracies—they are structures with hierarchy of authority, division of labor, impersonality, objective standards, technical competence, and rules and regulations (Weber, 1947). The dark side reveals a bureaucracy that alienates, breeds dissatisfaction, hinders creativity, and demoralizes employees. The bright side shows a bureaucracy that guides behavior, clarifies responsibility, reduces stress, and enables individuals to feel and be more effective (Adler, 1999; Adler & Borys, 1996; Hoy & Miskel, 2001).

In our view, issues of clarity of purpose, accountability, and duty of care are as important today as they ever have been in schools, hence the importance of recognizing the place of bureaucratic theory in defining the role of the principal. But the theory of democracy in schooling, stemming largely from the work of Dewey, is equally important, for two reasons. First, as Mulford has stated recently:

> Evolving from the work of Dewey (1916), "deep" democracy involves respect for the work and dignity of individuals and their cultural traditions, reverence for and proactive facilitation of free and open inquiry and critique, recognition of interdependence in working for the common good, the responsibility of individuals to participate in free and open inquiry, and the importance of collective choices and actions in the interest of the common good. (2004, p. 639)

Mulford's contention is that schools have a special place in society in contributing to the recognition and ongoing refinement of democratic values and processes. Katzenmeyer and Moller (2001) extend this line of thinking to include consideration of leadership:

> A democratic community assumes that all participants are equal and contribute value through their participation. This matches our notion that all teachers should assume leadership roles within the school. (p. 27)

We assert that the construct of parallel leadership, with its grounding in values of shared purpose, mutual trust, and allowance for individual expression, and its links to enhanced organizational and community capacity-building, represents recognition of key principles associated with the advancement of democratic practice.

In our view, therefore, constructions of the principalship for the twenty-first century should recognize the dual traditions of bureaucratic and democratic theory in educational administration and the need to critique and refine these traditions on an ongoing basis. The concept of "metastrategic" leadership that we propose in this chapter is believed to be sensitive to emerging developments in both traditions.

Regarding the "bureaucratic" tradition, we acknowledge in particular Hoy and Sweetland's recent construct of "enabling bureaucracy" as an organization where systems of rules and regulations are imbued with trust (2001, p. 318). Regarding the "democratic" tradition, we have drawn from a range of international sources to integrate time-honored democratic values and processes with emerging concepts of justice. In the UK, Philip Woods's (2006, p. 329) notion of ethical rationality as the key democratic instrument in human progress and goodness, and as inseparable from the work of principals, seems to us to be fundamentally important. In Australia, Mulford (2004) has noted that the concept of professional learning organization represents a democratically-derived alternative to reliance on bureaucracy in the work of school leaders. In the United States, Catherine Marshall is but one of a growing number of authorities who have called for the enhanced recognition of principles of justice in the work of school leaders and of the need for educational leadership to expand its conceptual base:

> We need to advance new definitions of democracy and pluralism to elicit participation of historically disenfranchised and disenchanted communities . . . . But who will these leaders be? (2004, p. 8)

In our construct of metastrategic principalship, as outlined in this chapter, emerging meanings of both bureaucracy and democracy are core to our argument. Our construct comprises five functions:

- envisioning inspiring futures
- aligning key institutional elements (i.e., vision, stakeholder expectations, school infrastructures, pedagogical processes, and professional learning)
- enabling teacher leadership
- building synergistic alliances
- culture-building and identity generation

This five-part framework implies a somewhat new and expanded role for principals in successful school reform. It is a role that recognizes the expanding duty of care functions of educational managers at all levels; is linked logically, ethically, and professionally with emerging forms of teacher leadership; and is responsive to the growing reality of the school as a fundamental cog in networked communities. The metastrategic framework for principal leadership is, in our view, as exciting for principals as the Teachers as Leaders Framework is for teachers. It is a role that our recent experience suggests principals everywhere will welcome. We introduce it with a description of metastrategic principal leadership in action at Minnemanka Senior High School.

SNAPSHOT FIVE: MINNEMANKA
SENIOR HIGH SCHOOL

At a state educational conference in mid-2007 that featured Best Practices from a range of high schools, three teachers and several students from Minnemanka High School described how a two-year process of school development had impacted on the lives of the groups that they represented and on the overall culture of their school. They made the key point that successful school improvement is inseparable from the exercise of leadership at multiple levels, with one key level being that of the principal. We crosschecked the successes that were described by the conference presenters and concluded that the principal, Jane Richards, captured the essential qualities of metastrategic leadership as we envision it. We asked Jane to tell her story, which follows.

Our school development process is a journey and a story. We have been on our journey since 2005—this is our story.

When I came to Minnemanka six years ago the school surveys and local community told of a school that had lost its sense of identity. Neither the parents, students, nor staff had a strong sense of pride, a sense of joy, or a sense of purpose. While the school was not in crisis, we were asking ourselves—where to from here?

Although the school reform literature suggests many starting points are acceptable I believe a sense of pride and belonging are essential building blocks. So between 2001 and 2004 we set about dealing with what I call the externalities—communication with parents and the local community, celebrating successes, improving the physical environment, strengthening dress codes, improving twelfth grade academic results, reconnecting with the community, and valuing our history and traditions. For this part of our journey, as I took time to understand the school and its culture, I worked primarily as what I regard as a combination of strategic, transformational, and instructional leader.

In 2005 as we began to reach our goals in these areas I looked for a process that would facilitate, scaffold, and sustain ongoing school improvement but that would enable the school to work together to create a vision, to clearly articulate what our school stands for, to broaden the leadership base, and to align these directions with specific strategies for pedagogic improvement.

As a staff, based on my recommendation, we selected a school development process that appeared to us to best capture these priorities. I took personal responsibility for this decision and monitored the work of the external consultants closely during the ensuing two years. I also took the first internal step in our developmental journey by selecting an enthusiastic, highly credible classroom teacher as a Project Coordinator and creating a Project Management Team (PMT). The message I wanted to convey was that as principal I would introduce, support, and be a part of the change process and of the PMT but that the leadership and drive should come substantially from the teacher practitioner level. Teachers would be welcomed and nurtured as coleaders, complementing my responsibility for overall coordination of school functions and custodian of legal and ethical requirements.

The personal and professional growth and leadership of the coordinator, together with the corresponding growth of several of the fifteen volunteers of PMT, has been remarkable during this two year period.

They are a diverse group, some of whom I would not have thought would become school leaders. While it has not been my experience that all teachers at any one point in time want to take on leadership responsibilities, I have found that a sufficient number do want to do so, and have the potential capabilities to do so, to ensure that no school challenge should go ignored because of a lack of leadership resources. As tangible evidence of the successes of our own teacher leaders, I cite the progress made with the developmental project while I was on professional leave for a year—the process of finalizing our school's vision and values continued to evolve quite naturally during this time through teacher-led workshops and interactive sessions. I also believe that experience in this initiative, along with regular exposure to teacher leadership models, was very important in enabling our teachers to begin to see themselves individually and collectively from a leadership perspective.

The vision that was created—*Sharing Our Forest of Possibilities*—represented what I regarded as a powerful image for our school, which is located in flowing hills and a forested area. The roots and trunks of the trees symbolize our traditions and history and provide a strong foundation on which our school community's new vision and values can grow and flourish. Our values—*love of learning, respect, resilience, pride, and community*—have become a unifying theme across the school and a lens for teachers and students to explore their daily activities.

It was very revealing, therefore, when teachers reflected on *Minnemanka Teaching is . . .* and students reflected on *Minnemanka Learning is. . . .* The results were compiled into lists, and then categorized into themes. The similarities between the thinking of the two groups were found to greatly outweigh the differences. But of most significance was that those teachers who had begun to see themselves as leaders used these exercises to create explanatory frameworks that would hopefully lead to better teacher-student understanding, interaction, and relationships. That, I believe, is now happening.

The culminating point of our developmental process to date was a whole day of celebration as we launched our new vision and values. To acknowledge the connection to our past, the launch day included former students representing the five decades of our school history. This public affirmation has been a critical catalyst in my work in building and reinforcing school identity and culture. I have also found the vision and values to provide me with a very meaningful framework from which to ask whether new curriculum and technological proposals should be accepted or rejected, whether logistical aspects of the school's use of time and space should be adjusted, and how resource allocations should be made. The vision and values have also become a classroom charter, with staff using them as a reference point in their teaching and to illustrate an alignment of aspirations between students, staff, and parents. Our students have also come to see their school as a distinctive educational place, one that they are shaping, especially through their class contributions to our *Minnemanka Teaching is . . .* and *Minnemanka Learning is . . .* initiatives.

The progress we have made over the past two years has exceeded my expectations. A recent survey of parents, staff, and students has shown a significant turnaround in perceptions of the school and also growth in aspects of student engagement and attitudes. We have become a school of choice for many staff and families who talk of our sense of community and acknowledge the values we now publicly state.

Early in our process, I arranged for our teacher leaders to travel interstate to learn from similar projects in other contexts. More recently, I arranged for our teacher leaders, and also some students, to present our developmental work at significant educational conferences. It was gratifying on these occasions to hear teacher leaders talk about themselves as leaders. Our PMT will continue to lead and work with staff and students in the ongoing development of a schoolwide pedagogy. Our Project Coordinator has recently moved on from his position to take up a post at another school. A number of colleagues will quite easily take his place, something that I would not have thought possible just a year ago. The ripple effect of teacher leadership is a phenomenon that I do not yet pretend to understand very well. But it seems to me to be a very powerful force that will ensure that the dynamic new school culture that is evolving at Minnemanka will be self-sustaining.

THE PRINCIPAL'S FIVE METASTRATEGIC FUNCTIONS

Function One: Envisioning Inspiring Futures

According to Leithwood and Riehl (2005), the first function of educational leaders is that of establishing a shared vision and fostering the acceptance of group goals. Licata and Harper (2001) explain the importance of this function:

> Teachers who share a relatively robust school vision may be more likely to implement their imagined possibilities and less likely to be distracted by some of the more tedious routines and conflicts that tend to be part of everyday life in schools. (p. 5)

The envisioning function of metastrategy reflects this intent. It requires that the principal take an upfront and accountable role in the generation of an ethically defensible school vision and values statement; that he/she enroll staff, community, and, if possible, students in envisioning activities; and that whatever vision is created be inspirational, futuristic, educational, and reflective of the school's contextual features.

Vision statements such as the following, drawn from our case study schools, might be regarded as meeting these criteria in that each was developed within the school community, was widely endorsed, and provided a vehicle for shaping school-based pedagogical practices and enhancing school outcomes:

- Together we achieve the extraordinary.
- Be brave; lead; succeed.
- Individual paths; united journey.
- Sharing our forest of possibilities.

But not all professed school visions in fact meet such criteria. A statement such as *We are the heart and soul of our community* could be said to fall short on ethical grounds (it could be a put-down to other local schools). A statement such as *We aspire to provide a quality education* might be regarded as aspiring only to achieve what is required of schools by law (and therefore might not be regarded as inspirational). A statement such as *Labor Omnia Vincit* may well have been an appropriate vision statement in an earlier industrial era but does not seem suited to the realities of a delicately-poised political and ecological world in which "work" is but one dimension and "conquering" has dubious connotations.

Thus, the envisioning function of the principal's role requires moral courage, intellectual ingenuity, and well-developed collaborative capabilities. It could be said to constitute an important duty of care responsibility since the values that it represents commit the school to definitive courses of action and responsibility. In Snapshot Five, Principal Jane Richards demonstrated her preparedness to accept this challenging function of the twenty-first-century principalship when she said:

The vision that was created—*Sharing Our Forest of Possibilities*—represented what I regarded as a powerful image for our school, which is located in flowing hills and a forested area. The roots and trunks of the trees symbolize our traditions and history and provide a strong foundation on which our school community's new vision and values can grow and flourish. Our values—love of learning, respect, resilience, pride, and community—have become a unifying theme across the school and a lens for teachers and students to explore their daily activities.

Jane's words and actions show that she personally endorsed the values explicit in her school's vision and used them to guide her daily work. She also went to considerable lengths to ensure that her schoolwide envisioning initiative was extended by teachers (and also students) into pedagogical development that permeated multiple dimensions of school life. Through her envisioning efforts, she generated a sense of inspired effort and also facilitated enhanced organizational alignment, cultural cohesiveness, and pedagogical clarity.

Function Two: Aligning Key Institutional Elements

The concept of organizational alignment is not new. Indeed, it was more than sixty years ago that renowned theorist Peter Drucker wrote that "An institution is like a tune; it is not constituted by individual sounds but by the relations between them" (1946, p. 26). What is new is the insight that, without strategic alignment, any change activity may not be effective—and may actually be detrimental to an organization's sustainability (Leppitt, 2006, p. 214).

Alignment (or congruence, or integration, or fit) in schools occurs when distinct elements of the school's organization are brought into a relationship where they are mutually reinforcing. It is our view, based on the conceptual research initiatives of Schneider et al. (2003), Voss, Cable, and Voss (2006), Hitt and Ireland (2002), Goold and Campbell (2002), Leana and Pil (2006), and Dunbar and Starbuck (2006), that when organizations are "aligned" internally and externally they develop enhanced identity, effectiveness, and value-adding capability. Thus, when the following elements of the school are all clearly in evidence in a school's operations, and philosophically interrelated, school outcomes are postulated to be high:

- the school's vision and values
- the expectations and aspirations of the school's various communities
- the school's infrastructures (particularly use of space, time, curricula, technologies)
- the school's priority pedagogical practices
- the school's professional learning strategies

Each of these five elements is evident in Snapshot Five. Not so explicit is principal Jane Richards' thoughtfully-devised and carefully-executed quality-assurance system, encompassing brainstorming, collaboration, trust, coordination, evaluation, and celebration to ensure that the five elements develop synchronistically. In so doing, teachers' work lives are reduced in intensity and the basis is established for coherent goals, shared responsibility, heightened expectations, and schoolwide professional learning—some of the essentials of capacity-building. Harris (2004, p. 1) has recently summed up the impacts of the alignment function of metastrategy as it manifests in contexts such as Minnemanka as follows: Effective principals impact on the achievement levels of students through a "mediating" influence on the work conditions, functions, and practices of teacher leaders.

Function Three: Enabling Teacher Leadership

A major theme of this book is that, while evidence in support of teacher leadership is compelling, the educator professions have not yet reached the point of maturity where teacher leadership is a self-sustaining entity. Nor have education systems yet devised fully satisfactory ways of recognizing, nurturing, and promoting teacher leadership. It follows that efforts to enhance principles and processes of "deep" democracy through teacher-led professional learning communities (Mulford, 2004, p. 638) have not yet achieved their full potential.

The principalship, we believe, is the key vehicle in advancing the cause of teacher leadership—and hence of promoting the professional image of teachers, the cause of democracy, and the successful revitalization of schools. Fullan (2005) has noted the urgency of this challenge and promoted the concept of "proliferation of leadership" (p. 95) as a central function of principals while Murphy and Datnow (2003, as cited in Murphy, 2005, p. 137) have noted that principals occupy a central location in nurturing teacher leadership.

As if the challenges associated with developing leadership development are not sufficiently daunting to cause anxiety for many principals, Hargreaves (as cited in Hipp, 2006, p. 553) reminds us that "not all teacher leadership is better leadership. There is bad leadership in some corporate offices and government offices, and there is bad leadership among teachers" (Lipman-Blumen, 2004). Thus, the third function of the metastrategic principalship that we posit is one that will be both new and also very challenging to many principals.

In the snapshot of Minnemanka High School, Jane Richards shares some insights as to how she addressed this particular issue as part of an ongoing process of school revitalization:

> As tangible evidence of the successes of our own teacher leaders, I cite the progress made with the developmental project while I was on professional leave for a year. . . . I also believe that experience in this initiative, along with regular exposure to teacher leadership models, was very important in enabling our teachers to begin to see themselves individually and collectively from a leadership perspective. . . .
>
> The ripple effect of teacher-leadership is a phenomenon that I do not yet pretend to understand very well. But it seems to me to be a very powerful force that will ensure that the dynamic new school culture that is evolving at Minnemanka will be self-sustaining.

Other snapshots contain similar insights to demonstrate that direct intervention by principals to facilitate the growth of teacher leadership is not only a vital function of the principalship in evolving democratic contexts, it has the potential to enrich the work of principals themselves in very dynamic ways.

Function Four: Building Synergistic Alliances

Schools are frequently asserted to be the potential nucleus of the emerging knowledge society (Drucker, 1994). If so, the question of a new leadership function for school principals must be confronted. In our view, this question presupposes a definition of knowledge society that asserts a central role for schools. Our definition is as follows:

> Communities of people working together so that their collective intelligence results in creation of new knowledge that enhances their personal efficacy and their quality of life and enables them to contribute to a more sustainable and better world for others. (Crowther, 2003, p. 12)

This definition presumes that principals will be accomplished in demonstrating to their various communities how new knowledge, in the form of vision statements, values, and pedagogical frameworks, is created and also in linking that new knowledge to other community-building initiatives and community problem-solving processes. In most of the case studies that are represented in our snapshots, schools created significant new knowledge and took steps, at the initiation of the principal, to share the dynamics of their knowledge-generation processes, as well as the new knowledge itself, with their communities. In so doing, it is our view that they demonstrated the practical capacity to assume the significant role in a knowledge society that theorists such as Drucker have postulated as possible for twenty-first-century schools.

Three particular examples of productive alliances that we have observed in many schools are *consortia,* in which schools pool their resources to gain a benefit that they could not acquire alone; *joint ventures,* in which several schools pursue an opportunity that requires a special capacity from each; and *value chain partnerships,* in which organizations in different industries— say, education and tourism—with different but complementary skills, link their capabilities to create value for ultimate users. A particularly dynamic example of a *consortium* was described in Snapshot Three (Adams College), where teacher leader Nancy Riggs, encouraged by her principal, mobilized colleagues to contribute to a Regional Education Redevelopment Project. The net effect has been the creation of vastly improved facilities and educational resources for a disadvantaged student community.

In Snapshot Five, Jane Richards' work in network management involved creation of *joint venture* opportunities for both teachers and students to engage nationally with like-minded peers.

In all six of the case studies that are featured in our snapshots, principals took responsibility for developing and sustaining *value-chain partnerships* with university-based external consulting agencies. Jane Richards, principal of Minnemenka High School (Snapshot Five), described her value chain leadership function this way:

> As a staff, based on my recommendation, we selected a school development process that appeared to us to best capture (our) . . . priorities. I took personal responsibility for this decision and monitored the work of the external consultants closely during the ensuing two years.

Alliancing and networking are not new concepts. Indeed, they were primary characteristics of nineteenth-century business organization. What is new is the capacity of some institutions to disseminate meaningful new knowledge to their communities and to other organizations, thereby demonstrating to them some fundamental dynamics of a knowledge society. This aspect of alliancing, which we have labeled *synergistic,* seems particularly suited to twenty-first-century schools as we envision them and a core function of metastrategic principalship.

Function Five: Culture-Building and Identity Generation

As was outlined in Chapter 3, "identity" as a manifestation of culture-building has no reality other than the meaning that organizational members, and other observers, ascribe to it. It is a social construction that reflects values, aspirations, needs, and experiences. We also indicated in our analysis of culture-building in Chapter 3 that the complex, multidimensional nature of "culture" is such that responsibility for its development should be shared across a broad spectrum of the school community.

The various dimensions of school culture that have been identified by authorities such as Schein (1992)—*artifacts, values, assumptions,* for example—can indeed be managed and shaped, both constructively and negatively. Of particular relevance in this assertion is that, while student self-perception has long been widely regarded as one of the prime determinants of academic achievement, high expectations are not necessarily a feature of the culture and identity of many schools, particularly those in disadvantaged contexts. This implies, in our view, a duty of care role that is inseparable from the culture-building function of the twenty-first-century principalship.

The school principal who initiated and stood behind use of the term "extraordinary" in the school's vision statement (Johnsonvale) clearly accepted this responsibility. The same could be said of the Adams College principal's decision to use the provocative statement "be brave" in the Adams school vision, and also of the Greenhills principal's widespread use of the school "Success breeds success" motto. Principals at these schools recognized that school culture is influenced by a range of variables that impact on student well-being and that they can influence through their own actions—students' sense of efficacy, teachers' perceptions of students' sense of efficacy, and teachers' sense of their own efficacy.

The teachers and students in Snapshot Five who came to "see their school as a distinctive educational place, one that they are shaping, especially through their class contributions to our *Minnemanka Teaching is . . .* and *Minnemanka Learning is . . .* initiatives" did so substantially because their principal recognized the importance of a culture of active participation. When the principal stated that "A recent survey of parents, staff and students has shown a significant turnaround in perceptions of the school and also growth in aspects of student engagement and attitudinal achievement. We have become a school of choice for many staff and families," she was drawing attention to a relationship between culture-building, identity-generation, and school achievement that is, in our view, inseparable from the principal's leadership.

In the introduction to this chapter we stated that issues of clarity of purpose, accountability, and duty of care are as important today as they ever have been in schools. It is our view that the metastrategic function of distinctive culture-building, with its public assertion of definitive values as the basis for a school's core operations, and its ongoing analysis of the values dimension of school processes and activities, represents an important leadership response by responsible principals to these issues.

We believe that the five metastrategic functions provide a sound basis for principals aspiring to lead their schools in an era of major social and technological transformation. They are responsive to the challenges of both "enabling bureaucracy" and "deep democracy" that have been posited by authoritative educational observers as dominant in the daunting challenges to confront twenty-first-century schools. But none of the functions is easily realizable without shared leadership with teachers. Thus the fundamental question for the final section of this chapter becomes "What is the principal's role in enabling the development and maturation of teacher leadership?"

ENABLING TEACHER LEADERSHIP: SEVEN CHALLENGES FOR SCHOOL PRINCIPALS

In phase three of our research and development (Appendix B), we interviewed principals who had engaged successfully as metastrategic leaders and engendered heightened school success. From these interviews, we identified seven broad challenges that confronted them in their developmental work with teacher leaders.

Each challenge is described below, with illustrative quotations taken from the case study interviews. As becomes evident, the seven challenges are in some ways at considerable odds with time-honored views of the principalship. That said, our research suggests that the encouragement of teacher leadership is a function that most school principals embrace enthusiastically because of its potential to contribute to the maturation of the teaching profession, to school capacity-building, and to the effectiveness of their own roles.

Challenge One: Communicate Strategic Intent

A comment from a case study principal: "You have to build up in kids the notion that what they do is important. Our guiding philosophy here is, 'Students for the future and a future for our students.'"

A teacher leader's response: "I'd say, without a shadow of doubt, that he has a passionate attachment to what we are doing. He believes that we can make a difference. There's no passing the buck here, starting with the principal. Personal responsibility is always on show."

To encourage teacher leadership, principals need to be unambiguous about their strategic intent. If the principal's educational worldview is apparent through words and deeds, potential teacher leaders have a model for futuristic thinking about their workplace and can reflect, explore, and experiment with a sense of security. The principals we studied cultivated a clear sense of purpose in their schools and generated broad systems of action to support that purpose. They made their essential educational convictions explicit through their public and professional presentations. For example, the principal of Greenhills High reiterated the school motto—*Success breeds success*—on a regular basis in his descriptions of school projects. He also encouraged teachers and students to develop their own, personalized versions of that motto (the *We can do anything* motto of the student body originated in this way). The principal of West Town High (see Table B.1 in Appendix B), a school on the proverbial other side of the tracks, used the phrase "the hero within" to demonstrate his conviction that students from the school had unique talents that would enable them to achieve their aspirations in an exciting future world.

The explication of a clear statement of purpose enables teachers (and also parents and students) to understand and explain the values that guide the work of their principals. In our case studies, teachers understood and accepted that significant responsibilities went with the position of principal, including duty of care (stewardship of the students), trustee of public property and resources, and guardian of due process (or natural justice). They also knew that educational commitment, in and of itself, was valued. Thus the basis for deep professional respect was laid.

Principals who declare themselves in this way can, of course, be vulnerable if they do not manage dissonance skillfully, because their personal values are unlikely to suit all persons and all situations. But by making their views and patterns of action transparent, they demonstrate that visioning is an exciting and important school-based strategy for all leaders, both practicing and aspiring, whether they occupy formal or informal leader roles.

Challenge Two: Incorporate the Aspirations and Views of Others

A comment from a case study principal: "I have to ensure that when someone who is entrepreneurial comes up with a good idea, that idea can fit under the umbrella of the school vision. If it can, let's just see where it can go. Passion has to drive ideas or they lose momentum, so projects should be run by those who are most passionate."

A teacher leader's response: "She listens. She tries consciously to locate us in the context of where the school is going. I think it gives her a real buzz to see teachers developing new skills and getting recognition as leaders."

A fundamental characteristic of all six snapshots in this book is that when senior executives draw on the ideas and energy of colleagues from throughout their organizations, they not only engender more creative solutions but also build trust and commitment that they can call on in the future. In this way, the capacity-building potential of the organization is enhanced.

Principals in successful parallel leadership relationships act on this principle. They spend time and energy soliciting ideas and encouraging teachers and community members to view themselves as critically important in shaping the school's direction and values. As principals do this, potential teacher leaders gain important opportunities to clarify and refine their personal values. They also gain a sense of confidence to develop projects that they believe in but might otherwise not undertake. Thus the leadership potential of others, most notably teachers, is acknowledged, encouraged, and nurtured.

In one of our case study schools, the principal inherited a situation that was characterized by both conflict and atrophy. Her statement of strategic intent (*"to create a spiritual environment where everyone achieves success"*) struck a resonant chord in the school community and triggered a series of constructive, within-school programs and community volunteer initiatives. Within the short space of two years, her original vision had been modified significantly (*"to be a place where everyone has choices and everyone is responsible for what we achieve"*), and teacher leaders carried much of the responsibility for the ongoing development of the school. In the words of one young teacher, "Anyone here can lead. It's just a matter of having ideas that fit our school goals and following through."

In another case study, the principal made overt, significant adjustments to the school's vision when it became apparent that the one he had crafted did not do full justice to schoolwide teaching approaches that the staff had developed. One teacher, who was instrumental in establishing a nationally recognized literacy program at the school, asserted that "Peter (the principal) is a great communicator. The way he listens, we know that our ideas can go somewhere. It makes us eager to sort out our priorities and get on and do new things."

The enrichment of personal vision is, therefore, a complex and challenging process. It requires professional dialogue, reference to diverse value systems, careful listening, and, of course, an enthusiasm for enriching one's own professional values. It also requires skill in synthesizing messages that, in some cases, may be subtle or even unspoken. These proficiencies were not necessarily required in previous, less complex education systems, but they are essential in education systems where the generation of new knowledge is a key function.

Challenge Three: Pose Difficult-to-Answer Questions

A comment from a case study principal: "I might go around to the classrooms and ask the teachers questions like, 'What if . . . ?' and

'I wonder what . . . ?' It's not what I want but what can be done that matters. In the staffroom one day, I posed the question, 'What might a meaningful metaphor look like for this school?' Someone suggested that we all write our responses on the discussion board over a period of time, and out of that, we developed a metaphor together."

A teacher leader's response: "What he does is listen to the silences in people and drag out their ideas. If you are going to think outside the box, you have to believe that your ideas are going to be valued. That really happens here. No topic is taboo if kids' wellbeing is the motivation."

Individual expression is fundamental to teacher leadership and parallel leadership. It is a value that is grounded in respect for individuality and that implies a regard for questioning rather than inculcation and for consciousness raising rather than the imposition of dictates. Its significance for school leaders in a knowledge society is clear in Drucker's (as cited in Andersen Consulting Institute for Strategic Change, 1999) provocative, though simple, assertion that "Leaders of the future will be people who know how to ask rather than tell" (p. 2).

We observed this orientation to open-ended inquiry in our case studies when, for example, one principal invited staff members to create metaphors for the school's leadership, both as they experienced it and as they would like to experience it. A small group of teachers used the results to generate a whole-school leadership framework that encompassed the six elements of the Teachers as Leaders Framework (Chapter 1).

Posing difficult-to-answer questions makes clear to the professional community of the school, and also to the wider community, that taking an informed stance on an issue is valued. This will invariably include dialogue about a range of complex and unforeseeable matters relating to equity, justice, ecology, tolerance, and so on. It also means that the taken-for-granted practices of the workplace—including language, artifacts, slogans, and behaviors—are continuously open to challenge.

One might suppose that continuous critical analysis of this type would lead to unrestrained autonomous behavior, even anarchy. To the contrary, teachers in our case study schools responded enthusiastically to opportunities to uncover hidden values in their schools and to clarify their tacit beliefs regarding their work as teachers. One effect was the emergence of distinctive forms of teacher leadership, frequently involving professionals who had not previously seen themselves as leaders and who, in some cases, had been regarded as troublemakers or burrs under the saddle. In sum, principals who encourage questioning in this way lay the foundations for the emergence of a cadre of leaders who might otherwise remain obscured and for the creation of new insights and understandings that would not otherwise be possible.

Challenge Four: Make Space for Individual Innovation

A comment from a case study principal: "I tell people that I promote risk and, if something gets up to ninety percent and falls over, then I take the rap for that. If it goes well though, the teacher gets all the credit. Playing it safe and by the book might protect you as a principal, but it can lead to stultification of the school. In this current world, you either move forward or you decline in quality."

A teacher leader's response: "We often spend time at meetings just thinking up crazy ideas. Then we talk about 'How?' So you are constantly reminded of just how serious teaching is as a profession. You know that where there's a good idea to take the school forward, a way will be found to do it."

Potential teacher leaders (and a high proportion of practicing teacher leaders) are seldom, in our experience, aware of their leadership capabilities. Nor are they aware of the strength or nature of their individual leadership styles, in terms of personality type or natural gifts and talents. Thus, opportunities and encouragement to explore and express their talents in a relatively safe environment, both as individuals and in groups, are essential for their development and maturation. This is particularly so because the exercise of teacher leadership invariably involves confronting cultural, social, physical, professional, and psychological barriers. The political and personal skills that are required to overcome institutional obstacles appear to us to be most easily learned in environments where trust, security, and confidence are present.

Principals in our case studies recognized this need and indicated a sense of professional responsibility to respond to it. In one school where parallel leadership flourished, an administrator-adopted school code reminded teachers that assistance was available to address the following questions:

- How can we help remove obstacles in your way?
- How can we build on the positives in your innovation?
- How can we help you to create strong links between your work and the school's vision?

Our case studies revealed at least three broad ways in which principals encouraged innovative action and thus nurtured leadership. In several instances, principals identified individual teachers, or small groups of teachers, for leadership of priority school projects and then made themselves available as mentors. In other instances, they encouraged staff members to nominate colleagues to develop innovative ideas and, subsequently, accorded the nominees wide responsibility in following through on those ideas. In other situations, individual teachers proposed initiatives, usually focusing on innovative teaching and learning, and found their administrators not only supportive but forthcoming with advice as to how to overcome infrastructural barriers and to link the initiatives in question to the school vision.

Where potentially powerful ideas are identified early and supported through resource and infrastructure alignment, the likelihood increases that potential teacher leaders will look to innovation with confidence and enthusiasm. Thus, principals who make a point of making space for innovation serve several purposes at once. They enhance the alignment of key school processes—most notably, vision, teaching practices, and infrastructure; they broaden and deepen the leadership capacity of the school; and they enhance the stature of teachers. The net effect is the creation of change from within, one important hallmark of sustained school success.

Challenge Five: Know When to Step Back

A comment from a case study principal: "I have had to learn how to advance my own interests by stepping back. It's a subtle act of leadership and one you can learn easily by capitalizing on people's strengths. It helps you sustain what you have helped to create."

A teacher leader's response: "She has a habit of asking, 'Have you asked Joe or Mary what they think?' It's amazing how this brings quiet leaders out of the woodwork. She never assumes that she's the best at anything."

Teacher leadership is inseparable from the concept of empowerment, which is sometimes characterized as involvement in organizational decision making (Rice & Schneider, 1994). Because empowerment has been seen for several decades as critical to the creation of a learning organization (Argyris & Schon, 1979), it follows that principals who want to see their schools develop as learning organizations must empower their teachers in meaningful ways. In effect, they must know how and when to step back from their own leader roles and, in so doing, encourage teacher colleagues to step forward. This may present challenges in terms of ego disengagement and the learning of new skills regarding power sharing. But if potential teacher leaders are to be encouraged in their work, and if opportunities are to be created for them to further develop their leadership capabilities, then stepping back is a critically important strategy for a principal to adopt.

At most of the schools where we observed parallel leadership in place, shifts in curriculum and teaching practices were orchestrated by a school management team chaired by a teacher who received assistance from an external facilitator. Significantly, these teams did not answer to the principal; rather, the principal was usually a team member. This strategy served to provide important structural support for teachers undertaking significant leadership roles. It also demonstrated that power sharing among coprofessionals is important. Critically, it made explicit that teaching and learning were central to the school operations and should be managed by teachers. Potential teacher leaders invariably rose to the occasion when presented with this level of recognition, confidence, and trust.

In developing the capacity to step back, principals should keep in mind that leadership may be a less visible phenomenon when it is vested in several people instead of one. Individual leadership is undoubtedly easier to spot than distributed leadership. Our culture is laden with clichés about single leaders, such as "it's lonely at the top," "leading from the front," "down in the trenches," "a born leader," or "the buck stops here." All reflect an outmoded paradigm from an earlier, industrial era. New images of postindustrial forms of leadership are not yet incorporated into our thought processes or our vocabulary, although we have made a start. For example, one authoritative commentator observed that words and phrases such as *healing, please, common ground,* and *restorating* constitute a "language of potential" for leaders in service-oriented organizations (De Pree, 1997, p. 74). We suggest that "step to the back as the occasion requires" expresses the sort of leadership that should become part of everyday school practice, and, therefore, should also become part of our vocabulary.

Metaphors from both educational and noneducational settings can communicate that stepping back does not constitute an abrogation of leadership. It constitutes a mature professional stance. One case study school adopted the familiar metaphor of geese flying in v-formation (taking turns with the energy-sapping lead spot; maintaining alignment to maximize airlift; taking time out to look after injured, weak, or fallen cotravelers; honking from the rear to provide encouragement to those carrying the major burden) to express the form of shared leadership that they adopted. Another chose the concept of "swooping onto loose balls," a term used in some team sports, to illustrate that at their school any major problem that arose would preferably be addressed by the person closest to the scene of action.

Stepping back, with the sense of teacher empowerment that it implies, is fundamental to the development of parallel leadership. But it is also at odds with the dominant conceptions of the principalship that have been in place in most education systems for decades. It therefore poses a significant challenge for most principals.

Challenge Six: Create Opportunities From Perceived Difficulties

A comment from a case study principal: "In a complex place like a school, we can't always do everything right. But we can usually do the right thing. If we do the right thing and make a mistake, we can ask what went wrong and learn from the experience. I'm not saying we should go out of our way to make honest mistakes, but I am saying that honest mistakes can usually be used as valuable learning experiences."

A teacher leader's response: "The community was very politically divided at the time. His management of the different groups ensured that the feelings of animosity didn't spill over onto the playground. It was a learning experience for the whole community."

The following scenario from a case study school is an example of how one principal was able to transpose a difficult problem into an opportunity and, ultimately, into success. The principal at Palms School was faced with a difficult problem—how to persuade a number of alienated, homeless young people to attend school.

Some students, several from indigenous backgrounds, were causing serious disruption in the community, especially around shopping centers.

The principal had been subjected to considerable personal and professional attack and was faced with the choice of whether to leave the community, transfer blame for the problem somewhere else, or tackle it head on. Without the overt support of educational or social agencies, most of which had been quite hostile, he allocated funds and engaged a teacher who was considered, in some circles, an agitator because of her political involvements. She was known to have deep empathy for the youth group, as well as exceptional teaching talent.

Within a year, she successfully brought the group into her confidence and set up a shopping center point of contact. She worked on developing values associated with both indigenous and nonindigenous cultures and on building relationships with local merchants. Financial support was forthcoming as delinquency rates dropped, and political support followed. The project achieved national recognition and set a precedent that a number of other school communities followed. The teacher subsequently became a significant figure in representing alienated youth.

In schools where risk taking is encouraged and where leadership involves continuous journeys into the unknown, errors invariably will be made and problems created unknowingly. Our experience with schools in which parallel leadership has been in evidence is that errors and problems per se do not necessarily amount to obstacles or serious liabilities in the school's quest for excellence. To the contrary, where leadership is distributed and held together by trust and shared purpose, errors and difficulties can often be transposed into educational opportunities.

For this to occur, however, the principal's role must contain a distinctive culture-building dimension. An environment of "no blame"—in which processes, not people, are scrutinized when things go wrong—must be created. Outside influences and pressures that have the potential to become immutable constraints must be managed, and accountability must be viewed as "for us" rather than "for you."

One effect of an attitude that says, "We don't have problems, just opportunities," is that the efforts of agitators can more readily be turned to advantage. Another is that thinking outside the box is encouraged and problem solving assumes an intellectually provocative dimension. A third is that underlying institutional barriers are exposed, thereby heightening the level and authenticity of professional dialogue. As these strategies become part of the school's way of doing things, the potential for teacher leaders to express themselves and to assume responsibility is enhanced.

Challenge Seven: Build on Achievements to Create a Culture of Success

A comment from a case study principal: "You can have the greatest curriculum in the state, but unless you have a culture of hope, aspirations, recognition of successes, and directing kids towards success, then the whole thing can fall over."

A teacher leader's response: "Kids enroll here because they believe this school will give them a stamp. We don't need expensive PR. The principal goes out of his way to describe for them what that stamp looks like and how dynamic it is. Teachers feel that they are building something, and they look for ways to add to it."

For a range of complex reasons, the real achievements of many schools are not used to major advantage as often as they could be. Too few schools consider how they have influenced students' lives, or community well-being, in definitive and positive ways, and then proceed to provide documented evidence of their achievements. Many schools do not regard it as a high priority to generate a public image of a culture of success. In failing to do so, they undersell their contributions to the broader community and discourage initiative on the part of committed, energetic teachers and potential teacher leaders.

In pursuing this point in the schools we studied, we were told that some principals might be reluctant to emphasize positive achievements because, if achievements turn into negatives unexpectedly, they may cause embarrassment for the school, its staff, or the principal personally. We were told also that the teaching profession is not accustomed to a culture of overt promotion of its own achievements.

In our case studies of successful school reform, principals tended to regard the modeling of optimism for their school communities, and encouraging teachers to do the same, as an exciting professional responsibility. In one elementary school, a week-long project involved staff and students in analyzing the school's culture using these provocative questions:

What do we look like? What would we like to look like? What do we feel like? What would we like to feel like? What do we sound like? What would we like to sound like? What do we smell like? What would we like to smell like? What do we taste like? What would we like to taste like?

The exercise not only created a colorful depiction of the school but also sparked leadership action among a number of previously nonengaged teachers. With the impetus that the activity spawned, the character and ethos of the school evolved positively in a relatively brief period. The school eventually declared itself a "green school" in recognition of its ecological value base.

In one high school, department heads assumed responsibility for identifying and celebrating student achievements that grew out of the school's agreed-on approach to teaching and learning. The department heads in question viewed themselves—and became widely regarded by others—as guardians of the school culture, a critical link between the strategic and pedagogical functions of the school.

An emphasis on meaningful culture-building can provide potential teacher leaders with concrete experience in transposing their personal values into artifacts and symbols that enhance the school's distinctiveness and identity. In this way, powerful new forms of educational leadership can be tapped, and the image of the teaching profession enhanced.

SNAPSHOT SIX: ST. MONICA'S

We conclude this chapter with an account from a school principal, Terese Bushe, who sought to employ parallel leadership in her work as a newly arrived principal (2005) at a large Catholic elementary school in a middle class suburb in a large city. Terese had read the first edition of *Developing Teacher Leaders* and had spoken at some length to one of the authors, before deciding to rethink her role as principal to focus on metastrategy. She determined to place a particular emphasis on developing teacher leadership at St. Monica's, using materials from *Developing Teacher Leaders*.

The St. Monica's School Strategic Plan was in its last year, and our Catholic Education District was in the early stage of its new strategic plan. As the newly appointed principal to the school, I needed new ideas, energy, and direction to take the school forward to meet the special needs of students for the new century.

It was in this context that I decided to use a "metastrategic mental model" that I had begun to develop through my readings about parallel leadership and organizational alignment and through my professional contacts with educators who had used metastrategic processes successfully.

In line with a conviction that underpins my mental model—that every individual engaged in an educational challenge has an important talent, skill, or "gift" that can be aligned to the task—I made the decision to put an invitation to staff to join me in responding to the school's need for a new vision. The two staff members who took up the invitation initially recruited others, and more came on board once we began to make progress and teachers could see the value and momentum of our efforts.

Two years later, the benefits of my metastrategic journey are beginning to reveal themselves. We have a school vision in place, based on extensive parent and student contributions as well as staff proposals. We also have a clearly defined set of school values that the staff has developed out of our school's particular Catholic charism, combined with our perceptions of the needs of our Y Gen students. Finally, we are close to finalizing shared pedagogical principles that derive from analysis of our most successful teaching and learning practices—as described by both our teachers and students, and analyzed and conceptualized by our teacher leaders.

The blessing of our new school facilities took place toward the end of the school year. This occasion provided an ideal opportunity to launch our new vision in a very formal way, with the Bishop, senior Catholic Education office staff, political figures, parents, parishioners, students, and staff present. We were able to showcase not just our new facilities but the ingenious work of our teacher leaders and other staff.

As a basis for reflecting on my role in nurturing and emphasizing new forms of professional leadership at St. Monica's, I have used as my guide the seven Leadership Challenges outlined in the First Edition of *Developing Teacher Leaders: How Teacher Leadership Enhances School Success*. Not all of my efforts have been successful. But as I write this brief description, I am excited by my role as metastrategic leader, particularly in further encouraging teacher leadership.

Communicate Strategic Intent

Nurturing teacher leadership requires the principal to communicate both in word and action a strong belief in teacher leadership. I endeavor to demonstrate that our new vision provides a clear guide to me in my leadership role and can do the same for others who aspire to lead. I also encourage reflection on my role as principal, using the concept of metastrategy as a starting point. I find that teachers who are exploring their own leadership talents and capabilities are enthusiastic to respond to invitations to identify examples of leadership in my work and also to suggest other ways that I might engage metastrategically.

Incorporate the Aspirations of Others

Our staff is currently planning to explore a model where regular meeting time is set aside for looking at assessments. At these meetings, each staff working party will monitor the assessment for their area of responsibility. Guiding principles will be developed by each team. One of the hoped-for effects is a clearer sense of what our school aspires to in terms of student outcomes. Another is recognition of teachers' specialist pedagogical skills. Another is more indirect—teachers seeking to develop enhanced communication strategies in order to expand their influence as school leaders.

Finally, I have found real meaning in Covey's motto for creative leadership: "Seek first to understand, then to be understood."

Make Space for Individual Innovation

A kindergarten teacher spoke with me about trying a new approach to teaching mathematics in her classroom. I arranged for the district mathematics advisor to meet with her and provided release time for them to meet to explore ways that the approach might be relevant in a Catholic school with a large proportion of non-English speaking students. This teacher then worked with her grade partners to rewrite the kindergarten program. One of the grade partners moved to year one the following year and the program has now spread to that grade.

The experience of this teacher proved to be rather contagious. Another grade partner has now expressed her interest in developing the science program and support has been provided in the form of release time to attend appropriate in-services. My questions are always along similar lines in such instances:

- How might your proposal fit the St. Monica's vision and values?
- How do we know that this approach is educationally sound?
- How will the teaching approaches of your colleagues be affected?

Pose Difficult to Answer Questions

Throughout the visioning process and the development of enhanced teaching and learning, I have sought to ask questions that will extend teachers' thinking around important points that have not previously been raised. For example:

- How will the charism of the Sisters of Charity be incorporated in our vision for learning and our teaching strategies?
- What processes are in place to ensure that we have a vision for learning that really responds to the needs for Y Gen learners?
- How can we ensure our vision is presented in "child friendly" language and imagery?
- How can we use the Diocesan Learning Framework in developing our school-wide pedagogy?

The way I see it, whoever takes the time and exerts the effort to answer these questions gains esteem in the eyes of their colleagues and our external communities. Those persons begin to be perceived as leaders in their own right, and our school's approach to leadership broadened to include new people and new processes.

Know When to Step Back

While I am very much involved in the renewal process in our school, that involvement now looks different from traditional up-front involvement on the part of the principal.

Stepping back was important when community surveys were administered and analyzed early in the renewal process. By removing myself and other school administrators from the frontline at that time I encouraged staff to respond freely and openly. Teachers with a particular commitment to the well-being of the school became visible and led the process of conceptualizing survey outcomes. Some of these individuals have continued in, and heightened, their coordination roles throughout the two to three years of the process.

Create Opportunities Out of Perceived Difficulties

In late 2007, the third stage of the St. Monica's Building Project was completed. When embarking on the third stage, we were required to keep to the "footprint" of the original design. However, the internal fit-out could be changed in response to the need to create learning spaces that reflect the needs of learners in the twenty-first century. One significant change involved the use of glass to divide internal spaces. When teachers were allocated to classes for 2007, they were given the choice of working at another level if they were not comfortable with working in the new learning spaces. Those who chose to remain did so because they saw the physical design as both a challenge to their teaching routines and an opportunity to explore new strategies. Some began to modify their teaching practices, individually and collectively, almost immediately. These staff also began to see themselves as meeting specific criteria relating to entrepreneurial leadership.

Build on Achievements to Create a Culture of Success

Finally, I have learned that an emphasis on successes is very important at a time when teachers are frequently criticized in the media. External criticism, particularly if it is undeserved, is much easier for teachers to absorb if their workplace is positive and optimistic.

Teachers will also feel much more inclined to assume leadership roles if they see their vocation as a leading profession. Thus, our school successes are communicated through school newsletters and at weekly assemblies. Our regional consultants are briefed regularly and positive comments made by our external critical friends are communicated widely. This focus on success leads to a positive "can do" attitude and a sense that teachers' work is not only valued, but is at the core of creation of sustainable communities and the wider world.

CONCLUSIONS

If, as Katzenmeyer and Moller (2001) assert, teacher leadership is an idea whose time has come, the implications for school principals are considerable. Some principals will need to become accustomed to unfamiliar approaches to power sharing. Others, perhaps most, will need to achieve heightened understanding about relationships between school-based leadership and school outcomes. And they will need to acquire skills and expertise in developing both teacher leadership and parallel leadership.

In this chapter we have outlined the five characteristics of leadership that we believe are essential for successful twenty-first-century school principals:

- envisioning inspiring futures
- aligning key institutional elements (i.e., vision, stakeholder expectations, school infrastructures, pedagogical processes, and professional learning)
- enabling teacher leadership
- building synergistic alliances
- culture-building and identity generation

This framework implies a new role for principals, one that is suited to the demands of school leadership in a knowledge-based society. It is a role that highlights the central importance of the school as a generator of new knowledge and reinforces the image of teaching as a leading profession. The new role it assigns principals is as exciting as teacher leadership is for teachers. It is a role that we believe principals everywhere will welcome.

We have also focused our effort on seven challenges that principals with whom we worked, in seeking to develop teacher leadership and parallel leadership, confronted and turned to educational advantage. What emerges is new understanding of how principals might encourage and utilize teacher and parallel leadership. A summary is included in Table 4.1.

Table 4.1   Summary of the Principal's Role in Promoting Teacher Leadership

Communicate a clear strategic intent.

- Engage in futuristic thinking activities.
- Articulate and justify personal value positions on school-specific and other educational issues.

Incorporate the aspirations and ideas of others.

- Demonstrate confidence in teachers' contributions to school visioning and valuing processes.
- Explore with teachers the alignment between strategic goals and teaching and learning goals.

Pose difficult-to-answer questions.

- Adopt a motto such as "Leaders of the future will be people who know how to ask rather than tell."
- Heighten the level of professional dialogue and critique regarding "hidden" educational practices.

Make space for individual innovation.

- Create opportunities for individual entrepreneurship.
- Encourage identification and confrontation of institutional barriers to teacher leadership.

Know when to step back.

- Demonstrate trust in the concepts of teacher leadership and parallel leadership.
- Attest to the central place of teachers' pedagogical work in school planning and decision making.

Create opportunities out of perceived difficulties.

- Describe ways in which new knowledge has been created out of problem situations.
- Draw attention to examples of thinking outside the box.

Build on achievements to create a culture of success.

- Cite examples of "Success breeds success" in school initiatives.
- Explore with staff the concept of teachers as guardians of the school culture.

We do not presume to have uncovered all the subtleties or complexities associated with teacher leadership, parallel leadership, or the principal's role in nurturing these challenging constructs. But we believe we have uncovered sufficient insights to demonstrate the essential meanings associated with them. That done, we now move to Chapters 5 and 6 of *Developing Teacher Leaders,* where the concepts and processes that we have presented in Chapters 1 through 4 are transposed into a wide range of professional learning experiences.

5

Preparing for Teacher Leadership

During our decade-long association with significant teacher leadership initiatives in the United States, Australia, Singapore, and Sicily, we have reached new levels of understanding about the essence of teacher leadership and its indisputable relationship with enhanced school success. But that is only part of our story. We have also developed what we regard as clear insights about how to build new forms of leadership capacity in schools and the teaching profession.

In Chapter 6, we share the outcomes of our experiences with leadership development as it relates specifically to teachers. The exercises that are contained in the CLASS (Creating Leaders to Accelerate School Successes) Plan in Chapter 6 have been developed by us, trialed in a multitude of situations under our observation, and linked into an overall professional learning framework that we know from our experience to be both practical and also theoretically defensible. We have worked with the exercises in the CLASS Plan in three quite different settings—with school-based project leadership teams (comprising project facilitators and the principal), with clusters of cross-school leadership teams, and also with whole school staffs. Minor variations to the guidelines for the fifteen exercises will be required, depending on which of these three options best suits your particular circumstances. Of course, it is also possible to undertake most of the exercises on an individual basis, but the experience will probably be less interesting and the outcomes less tangible.

Before proceeding to the fifteen exercises that comprise Chapter 6, we briefly describe our purposes in preparing that chapter. Four questions provide the basis for this discussion:

- How have we gone about the process of developing successful teacher leadership in school workplaces?
- How do we justify, in educational and research terms, the approach to leadership development that we propose in Chapter 6?
- What are the essential features of the broad framework for leader development that is outlined in Chapter 6?
- What are the objectives of the fifteen individual exercises in Chapter 6 and how do they link to the key concepts that are contained in Chapters 1, 2, 3, and 4?

KEY QUESTIONS AND CONCEPTS UNDERPINNING THE CLASS PLAN

Question 1

How have we gone about the process of developing successful teacher leadership in school workplaces?

It is our contention that, where possible, efforts to develop teacher leadership ought to be undertaken in conjunction with a comprehensive and authoritative school improvement process. We say this for two reasons. First, we have found it difficult, if not impossible, to identify teacher leaders independent of engagement in a meaningful school-based challenge. We know of no instrument that can successfully identify prospective teacher leaders (we have attempted to develop several instruments ourselves, but have not been successful in developing one that has long term predictability). This of course is somewhat understandable, because teacher leadership is largely a values-based construct that is closely linked to contextual considerations. Indeed, we know from our decade of experience with teacher leadership that professionals who achieve outstanding feats of leadership in, for example, a context of indigenous cultural disadvantage, may have no particular interest in, or propensity for, developing and exercising leadership in a mainstream middle class educational context.

Second, the characteristics of teacher leadership that we and a number of other researchers across the globe have developed are substantially linked to engagement with school-based developmental processes. While we know that teacher leaders have strong personalities and other qualities, the fact remains that the teacher leaders whom we have seen grow and thrive do not fit any particular character or personality stereotype. Some are quiet and laidback, others exuberant. Some are spontaneous, others reflective. Some are highly analytical, others more inclined to right-brain creativity. Thus, the approach to leader development that we have grown to favor focuses on development of leadership of school-based processes rather than development of a particular set of values or personal characteristics.

We have learned most of what we know about teacher leadership from our work with the IDEAS Project, a school revitalization project that is managed through the Leadership Research Institute of the University of Southern Queensland and that has been implemented in about 350 public, Catholic, and independent schools in Australia. It has also been implemented successfully in schools in Singapore and Sicily. The IDEAS Project has been assessed by independent evaluators as highly successful in building teacher leadership and parallel leadership (Chesterton & Duignan, 2004). It has also been shown through independent research to contribute to enhanced teacher morale and satisfaction, as well as enhanced student efficacy and other outcomes (see Appendix B). Appendix A contains an overview of the IDEAS Project and Appendix B a synopsis of the five phases of research that underpin our constructs of teacher leadership, metastrategic principalship, and parallel leadership.

We believe that there are many highly successful school improvement and school revitalization initiatives in existence around the world that can be used to stimulate and nurture teacher leadership. Our experience with the IDEAS Project leads us to four definitive conclusions about the development of teacher leadership that are, we believe, generically applicable.

First, it should be voluntary. All of the schools in which we have worked in the IDEAS Project have contained one or more teachers who have been eager to explore their teacher leadership capabilities by undertaking the project facilitator role. We estimate that, on average, 10–30 percent of teachers at any one time have the personal interest and professional skills to explore and develop teacher leadership capabilities. Major factors that appear to determine the level of interest are (a) the degree of support from the principal for parallel leadership practices, (b) the practical appeal of the particular school development initiative that is proposed, and (c) the availability of highly credible external consultancy assistance and critique. Given the importance of factors such as these, we have invariably found it best to allow teachers to consider the opportunities and responsibilities that the IDEAS Project provides before offering to become involved, rather than attempt to seek out potential facilitators in advance.

Second, the development of teacher leadership is best approached as a team activity. We say this because school development initiatives such as the IDEAS Project require a range of leadership capabilities to successfully implement. Hence, it has usually been the case that teacher leadership in IDEAS Project schools has been a fluid construct, often involving teachers working in small teams and frequently changing membership as different stages of the process posed different challenges and opportunities. The most typical teacher leadership team composition during the implementation of the IDEAS Project has been as follows: (a) one to two teacher leaders have remained in formal facilitator positions throughout its duration and (b) from two to ten teachers (and in some cases paraprofessionals) have assumed key roles at particular stages of the project. In our experience, two functions are particularly important in any project team— overall coordination of both the school-based project and the leader development initiative, and recording of developmental events. However, there is no one best way, to our knowledge, of carrying out these essential tasks.

Some IDEAS Project school management teams have undertaken the CLASS Plan as a cross-school cluster initiative. In this way, a rich variety of school experiences and professional perspectives can be drawn upon in the completion of individual exercises. But because the data that are used in some exercises may require sensitivity to particular school circumstances, this option requires an additional degree of professional trust and consideration. In yet other instances, schoolwide staffs have chosen to undertake some or all of the fifteen exercises. This option has invariably led to new teacher leaders emerging at different junctures during the IDEAS Project, thereby increasing the leadership density of the school.

School development initiatives such as the IDEAS Project benefit immensely, we believe, if they are linked into an external professional agency. In the case of the IDEAS Project, the University of Southern Queensland's Leadership Research Institute provides trained academic staff members who are accomplished at working alongside teachers as critical friends, who possess the knowledge to clarify complex issues relating to teacher and parallel leadership, and who can assist in school-based data analysis and synergistic thinking. Such skill sets are not yet clearly articulated in the educational literature for one simple reason—teacher leadership is itself a relatively new and poorly understood concept.

Third, there are distinct conceptual understandings, processes, and skills associated with the development of mature teacher leadership. The fifteen exercises that follow in Chapter 6 are intended to enable school-based professionals to acquire this wide range of knowledge, skills, and values at the same time as they undertake a serious two to three year school development initiative.

Fourth, the development of teacher leadership capabilities is very often a professionally exhilarating experience and should therefore be approached with enthusiasm. We frequently hear IDEAS Project facilitators, for example, say that the experience of project facilitation has permanently changed their professional lives. We have heard experienced teachers state that it rekindled their professional interest and commitment when they had thought all they had left to look forward to was retirement and we have heard inexperienced teachers say that it has convinced them that they in fact made the right vocational choice. In essence, our experience is that the development of teacher leadership through programs such as the one that is outlined in the CLASS Plan in Chapter 6, undertaken in conjunction with a significant school improvement initiative, is extremely rewarding for participants.

The potential of teacher leadership to assist with the revitalization of schools and the enhancement of the teaching profession was established in Chapters 1 through 4, as was the need to seek comprehensive ways to stimulate, nurture, and refine it. The fifteen exercises in Chapter 6 represent our response to this priority concern. One needs to hear only bits of testimony from dedicated and competent professionals who have explored teacher leadership to feel this. A case in point is former Michigan Teacher of the Year Margaret Holtschlag, who spoke (see interview in Appendix C) of an interchange she had the day she was honored, along with other state teachers of the year, at the White House in Washington:

> I was having a conversation with one teacher who was fretting over not being worthy of being there that day—that there were so many others in her state that should be there instead of her. I pulled out my journal and read those six attributes of a teacher leader in the Teachers as Leaders Framework, Table 1.1, and she and I talked about how those qualities of leadership make a difference in making our schools a better learning place for our students.

Question 2

How do we justify, in educational and research terms, the approach to leadership development that we propose in Chapter 6?

The CLASS Plan that we have devised as a comprehensive approach to developing teacher leadership and parallel leadership reflects three features of significant international thinking about successful leader development, particularly in education.

First, we believe that professional learning occurs particularly effectively in the teaching profession when it involves a significant emphasis on a balance of individual and collective inquiry into practice. We endorse the view expressed by Tight (2000, p. 110) that action learning, experiential learning, and reflective practice are especially well-suited to educational leader development. The CLASS Plan, with its integration with school-based development initiatives, makes major use of each of these three approaches to professional learning.

Second, the six key points in Joseph Murphy's *General Framework for Professional Development* make eminently good sense to us as they apply to teacher leadership. Murphy's points are summarized here as follows:

- Participants' current paradigms should be seriously challenged by their professional learning experiences.
- Learning activities must be highly valued at the school by both participating teachers and the principal.
- Activities should be part of a long-term, carefully thought-out plan that involves regularly scheduled exercises.

- Continuous and intensive support over time is essential.
- Networks of support and judicious critique are important to ensure that insularity is avoided.
- A trusting context for learning is important in order to encourage risk taking and innovation (adapted from Murphy, 2005, pp. 146–48).

Each of the six features of Murphy's general framework is explicit in our CLASS Plan.

Finally, we strongly endorse Shirley Hord's contention that the concept of *professional learning communities*—in which principals, teachers, and other professional staff members lead and learn together to carry out a shared vision for student learning (Hord, 2003, p. xi)—is fundamental to educational enhancement. The fifteen exercises in the CLASS Plan in Chapter 6 involve a professional learning community of teachers and their principal in the joint exploration of ways to enhance their school's pedagogical practices at the same time as they develop and refine their professional leadership capabilities.

Thus, in summary, the CLASS Plan that follows in Chapter 6 reflects a range of authoritative international perspectives on school-based leader development.

Question 3

What are the essential features of the broad framework for leader development that is outlined in Chapter 6?

The fifteen exercises that are outlined in Chapter 6 comprise what we believe to be a comprehensive teacher leader development plan for either individual school project teams or cross-school clusters of project teams. Following is a brief overview of the Plan:

- **Title:** The CLASS Plan: Creating Leaders to Accelerate School Successes
- **Vision**: An ever-expanding cohort of teacher leaders who view themselves as shaping an advanced twenty-first-century profession and enhancing student successes in their schools.
- **Timeframe:** Two to three years
- **Program Components**:
  - *Component One:* Orientation to, and preparations for, the program (three exercises). *Note 1:* In our work in the IDEAS Project, Component One of the CLASS Plan has been implemented during the initiating and discovery stages. The three exercises that we propose have usually, in our experience, been spread over a period of two to four months. *Note 2:* Component One exercises

would most preferably involve all staff members, but would be coordinated by the teacher leadership team in its capacity as school development project management team.

o *Component Two:* Stimulating and nurturing teacher leadership capabilities (six exercises). *Note:* The six exercises that we propose will be of interest and relevance to most, if not all staff, not just those who have volunteered to facilitate the school development project. They may be completed in any sequence. A timeframe of twelve to eighteen months usually applies.

o *Component Three:* Developing parallel leadership relationships and strategies (three exercises). *Note 1:* The three exercises that we propose can be undertaken as soon as participants are familiar with the Teachers as Leaders Framework (Chapter 1) and the Functions of Metastrategic Principals (Chapter 4). *Note 2:* The three exercises that comprise Component Three are usually interspersed with Component Two exercises and implemented during the discovery, envisioning, and actioning phases of the IDEAS Project. A timeframe of twelve to eighteen months usually applies.

o *Component Four:* Sustaining teacher leadership into the future (three exercises). *Note 1:* The three exercises that are described have two distinct purposes—(i) to consolidate and extend what has been learned about, and achieved, with teacher leadership and parallel leadership and (ii) to provide vehicles for sustained focus on the school revitalization initiative that has been undertaken in conjunction with the leader development project. *Note 2:* These three exercises are usually undertaken by IDEAS Project participants during the sustaining phase of the project.

Question 4

What are the purposes of the fifteen individual exercises and how do they link to key concepts from Chapters 1, 2, 3, and 4?

In addressing this question, we pose key questions that are appropriate to each of the fifteen exercises in the CLASS Plan.

Orientation to, and Preparations for, the Program

CLASS Exercise 1: Group Portrait

Are you aware of your colleagues' backgrounds at your school? Their perceptions of how your school has developed and evolved over time? Their aspirations for your school's future?

We have found this activity to be very helpful as a launching pad for a school development initiative. It familiarizes staff with key features of the school's history and traditions and also the experiences and aspirations of colleagues as they commence an exciting journey of joint discovery and creativity.

CLASS Exercise 2: Readiness

How ready are you to commit to the development of teacher leadership and parallel leadership in your school?

CLASS Exercise 3: Assumptions

What assumptions do you and your colleagues hold regarding the construct of teacher leadership?

Having completed at least two orientation exercises such as these, you will now have clearer perceptions of distinctive features of your school, your own values, your preliminary insights regarding teacher leadership, and also the values and hopes of your colleagues. You will have now commenced an exciting journey of self-discovery and professional enhancement.

Stimulating and Nurturing Teacher Leadership Capabilities

CLASS Exercise 4: Me, a Future Teacher Leader

What do the six teacher leadership attributes (Table 1.1, Chapter 1) mean in real life school contexts?

This case study exercise provides participants with an opportunity to formulate speculative conceptions of what motivates teacher leaders and how they engage with their workplaces. It goes without saying that images of yourself as a teacher leader will be starting to take shape, albeit hazily.

Key reference: Teachers as Leaders Framework, Chapter 1.

CLASS Exercise 5: Imagining the Future

What are your personal convictions regarding "a better world"?

In this exercise you will be assisted to clarify your personal views about how to make the world a better place. In so doing, you will be investigating Teacher Leader Element 1 (Table 1.1, Chapter 1).

Key reference: Teachers as Leaders Framework, Chapter 1.

CLASS Exercise 6: 1+1=3

What is your talent for synergistic thinking?

There is no formula or textbook that can teach you how to engage with colleagues to make 1+1=3. But that talent—combining knowledge, insight, creativity, and serendipity to create new schoolwide insights and peda-gogical knowledge—is a quality of many highly successful teacher leaders (Teacher Leader Element 2). In this exercise you explore your talent for what we call synergy. You may well be very surprised—and pleased—with the outcome.

Key reference: Teachers as Leaders Framework, Chapter 1.

CLASS Exercise 7: Barriers

What barriers stand in the way of successful teacher leadership?

Certainly, we know that teacher leaders recognize and confront barri-ers with insight, diplomacy, and courage (Teacher Leader Element 4).

In this exercise you and your colleagues share your insights as well as your possible frustrations, but then proceed to create plausible solutions. Table 2.2 in Chapter 2 provides helpful data for use in this exercise.

Key reference: Teachers as Leaders Framework, Chapter 1.

CLASS Exercise 8: The Power of Language

How does the language that you and other staff members use promote or inhibit the potential for teacher leadership and/or parallel leadership in your school?

In completing this exercise you will be critiquing one of the more sub-tle aspects of school culture (Chapter 3) and you will be ensuring that you acquire some of the skills to engender a culture of success-oriented teacher leadership in your school (Teachers as Leaders Element 6).

Key reference: Teachers as Leaders Framework, Chapter 1.

CLASS Exercise 9: Creating a Personal Leadership Framework (PLF)

How do acclaimed theories of leadership apply in your emerging leadership profile?

The Leadership Wheel activity in which you will engage in this exercise has been used by several thousand teachers and principals to develop an understanding of the relevance of major theories of leadership in their value systems and professional activities.

This activity may take considerable time and may also frustrate you as you are asked to make difficult choices among a range of attractive alternatives. But we did not promise that becoming a teacher leader would be easy, just rewarding and illuminating.

Key reference: Five Premises to Guide Revitalization of the Teaching Profession, Chapter 2 (Premise 2).

Summary for Exercises to Stimulate and Nurture Leadership Capabilities

The six exercises in this section have all focused on the dynamics of teacher leadership. Having completed most or all of them, you will be in a good position to broaden your thinking to include the concept of "relatedness," particularly as it applies to the school principal.

Developing Parallel Leadership Relationships and Strategies

CLASS Exercise 10: Images of Parallelism in Workplaces

What does parallelism look like in real-life school situations?

In this exercise, you engage in analysis of two or more authentic case studies to generate metaphors of parallelism in practice. You then assess your metaphor against the values that our research has uncovered as the foundation of highly successful parallel leadership.

Key reference: Three Essential Characteristics of Parallel Leadership, Chapter 3.

CLASS Exercise 11: Leadership and the Arts

How can the arts be used to illuminate school leadership concepts?

In this exercise, you explore leadership as a reflection of culture—for example, in music, drama, sport, and literature. In so doing, you will learn very interesting things about yourself as well as the cultural element(s) that you focus upon.

Key reference: Parallelism in the Sciences, Arts, and Humanities, Chapter 3.

CLASS Exercise 12: Parallel Leadership in Diverse Scenarios

How might the dynamics of a school staff impact upon the application of parallel leadership in a school developmental process?

In this exercise, you explore the ways that human variables—the personalities, values, skills, and experiences of the principal and teacher leaders—might influence the development and implementation of a school development project.

Key reference: How Parallel Leadership Works in Schools, Chapter 3.

Sustaining Teacher Leadership Into the Future

CLASS Exercise 13: Linking Metastrategy and Teacher Leadership in Practice

What happens when the principal and teacher leaders come together to apply parallel leadership values and processes to resolve a real-life school challenge?

In this exercise the cumulative outcomes of the CLASS Plan to date are put to the test of practical usefulness.

Key references: Teachers as Leaders Framework, Chapter 1; Metastrategic Principalship Framework, Chapter 4; and Linking Parallel Leadership and Successful School Capacity-Building, Chapter 3.

CLASS Exercise 14: Staff Meeting

How might you apply your insights and capabilities regarding teacher leadership and parallel leadership to invigorate one of your school's essential functions (the staff meeting)?

Key reference: Chapter 1–4.

CLASS Exercise 15: Six Months Later and Beyond

Where to from here?

This exercise provides an opportunity for you and your colleagues to reflect on the impact of leadership development efforts on your school's revitalization processes. You then transfer your focus to the period ahead, and how you might extend your successes into possible future activities.

Key reference: Linking Parallel Leadership and Successful School Capacity-Building, Chapter 3.

Final Note: If you have completed a majority of the exercises in each of the four sections of the CLASS Plan, you are entitled to consider yourself well-prepared to represent the teaching profession in debates about, and analyses of, the concepts of teacher leadership and parallel leadership. You are also entitled to consider yourself well-prepared to undertake formal facilitation of a major school development initiative. We wish you well with the challenges and exciting professional times that lie ahead for you.

6

The *CLASS Plan*

COMPONENT ONE: ORIENTATION

CLASS Exercise 1: Group Portrait

Purpose. This exercise acquaints participants with each other's historical associations with their school and their aspirations for their school's future. It provides an initial basis of understanding for the development of trusting professional relationships.

This exercise is therefore best undertaken as a whole-staff activity at the commencement of a school development project. Project team members who implement it gain personal benefits associated with project facilitation, including management of group dynamics, presentation techniques, and synthesis of activity outcomes.

Rationale. The experiences and views of group members are significant resources for undertaking leadership initiatives in relation to successful school revitalization, renewal, and improvement. When organized and energized, these resources comprise a group's power to think creatively, generate shared purpose, and get things done. Therefore, a group has to become as well informed as possible about each other's experiences, views, strengths, and values. And, its members have to think about how to translate these assets into achievement of common goals. When this process of becoming acquainted takes place with care and respect, then trust—the basis of all positive action in organizations—can be built.

Time Considerations and Necessary Materials. The exercise is designed to unfold in two sessions, each of approximately one to one and a half hours. In total, the experience should consume anywhere from two to three hours, depending on how much depth participants seek to achieve. An overhead projector and transparencies or data projector are necessary materials.

Note 1: Our experience with Session One is that it is enhanced if participants are provided sufficient advance notice to enable them—particularly those of long-standing at the school—to collect artifacts to bring to the session to elucidate their descriptions.

Note 2: We have also found that the Session One exercise can be enriched by inviting a selection of previous members of staff whose contributions to the school are widely recognized to participate.

Session One Process

- Participants locate themselves in a horseshoe arrangement, positioning themselves so that everyone can see each other. At one end of the horseshoe is the person who has the longest association with the school. At the other end is the person with the shortest association. The facilitator locates himself/herself between the two ends of the horseshoe.
- The facilitator asks each person, beginning at the "longest association" end of the horseshoe, to address the following questions:
  o When did you arrive at the school?
  o What were your first impressions?
  o What is your most memorable experience here?
- Participants share their responses with the group. Generally speaking, a maximum of one minute per participant should be allowed for this exercise. Once it is completed, the facilitator might pose the following questions:
  o What patterns are identifiable in the school's evolution?
  o What surprises, if any, have come to light?
  o What phrases, images, or metaphors sum up the school's history to date?
- The facilitator should then be prepared to share his/her own thoughts on these questions with the participants, along with a statement that begins: "As we proceed into the future, we should be sure to build on the following distinctive features of our school's heritage and traditions. First, ... Second, ... What do you think?"

Session Two Process

- The same horseshoe format is used as was employed in Session One. This time, the emphasis in the questions is on participants' aspirations for the school and ways in which they might contribute most constructively to the school's development.

   o What do you hope our school might look like a decade from now?

   o How might your vision for the school's future be achieved?

   o In what ways would you see yourself as contributing over the next year or two?

- As responses are offered, the facilitator and other participants may probe a little to have their colleagues articulate values behind responses. For example, the first question above could be enriched with, "Why is this significant for you?" "How does that relate to what you consider important in teaching?"

- After participants address the set of questions, the group as a whole engages in a discussion that addresses the following questions:

   o What are our general observations about the character of this group?

   o Are we a heterogeneous or homogeneous group? In what ways? What strengths and/or limitations does this imply for us?

   o Are there shared or common points of view in the way we think about learning? About leadership? About diverse points of view?

- Based on the question and sharing sessions and the subsequent debriefings, the group composes a verbal portrait of itself, incorporating as many descriptors as possible. The facilitator might add other observations to give this initial portrait additional richness, contour, and color. Someone then writes the group portrait on a transparency so that everyone can discuss it.

- As participants conclude this exercise, they should record in their journals at least one significant observation drawn from the discussions.

CLASS Exercise 2: Readiness

Purpose. This activity provides an indication of participants' individual and collective perceptions of leadership and their readiness for teacher leadership and parallel leadership. It may profitably be undertaken as a whole-school staff, in a school-based project management team, or in a cross-school cluster.

Rationale. Self-knowledge is critical to the development of teacher leadership. It is essential for a group considering leadership initiatives to determine how much agreement there is in the room regarding the dimensions and dynamics of leadership. It is equally important for the group to be clear about differences of view. Through the Readiness exercise, group members build this picture of similarities and disparities from the ground up, from pairs to foursomes to the group as a whole.

Time Considerations and Necessary Materials. Completing the self-survey should take participants about thirty minutes. The complete exercise will likely consume about one and a half to two hours. Necessary materials include a data projector or an overhead projector and transparencies that can be written on, writing materials, a flip chart and markers, completed self-surveys, and the scoring protocol.

Self Survey to Assess Readiness for Leadership. Box 6.1 is a self-survey for each member of the group to complete individually.

Scoring Protocol for the Self-Survey. The scoring protocol is as follows:

- Count the number of times you chose *strongly disagree.*
- Multiply by -2, and write the number here (line 1):
- Count the number of times you chose *disagree.*
- Multiply by -1, and write the number here (line 2):
- Ignore the number of times you chose *no opinion* (line 3).
- Count the number of times you chose *agree.*
- Write the number here (line 4):
- Count the number of times you chose *strongly agree.*
- Multiply by 2, and write the number here (line 5):
- Write the total of these four numbers here (line 6):
  - ○ If the number on line 6 is between 21 and 30: Virtually all your attitudes, values, and beliefs align with the tenets of teacher leadership and parallel leadership.
  - ○ If the number on line 6 is between 11 and 20: The majority of your attitudes, values, and beliefs align with the tenets of teacher leadership and parallel leadership.
  - ○ If the number on line 6 is between 1 and 10: Some of your attitudes, values, and beliefs align with the tenets of teacher leadership and parallel leadership. Several don't.
  - ○ If the number on line 6 is less than 1: Few of your attitudes, values, and beliefs align with the tenets of teacher leadership and parallel leadership.

Process

- Participants complete the self-survey and calculate their individual results. Our experience suggests that the vast majority of participants will score in the 11–22 range, meaning that teacher leadership and parallel leadership have a reasonable degree of practical meaning and significance to them. Thus, as facilitator, you should feel confident in proceeding to the next stage of this exercise.
- If this exercise is completed by a whole-school staff, invite participants to submit to you, anonymously, a copy of their individual

(Continued on page 114)

Box 6.1   **Self-Survey of Preliminary Leadership Perceptions**

Respond to the Statements Below	Strongly Disagree	Disagree	No Opinion	Agree	Strongly Agree
Teaching is as important as any other profession.					
Part of being a teacher is influencing the educational ideas of other teachers, administrators, parents, and community leaders.					
Teachers should be recognized for trying new teaching strategies whether or not they succeed.					
Teachers should participate actively in educational policy making.					
Good teaching involves observing, and providing, feedback to fellow teachers.					
Administrators are a potential source of facilitative assistance for teachers.					

(continued)

Box 6.1   (Continued)

Respond to the Statements Below	Strongly Disagree	Disagree	No Opinion	Agree	Strongly Agree
Teachers are responsible for encouraging a schoolwide approach to teaching, learning, and assessment.					
Teachers can continue with classroom instruction and, at the same time, be school leaders.					
Teachers should allocate time to help plan schoolwide professional development activities.					
Teachers should know how organizations work and be effective at getting things done within them.					
Mentoring new teachers is part of the professional responsibility of a teacher.					

Respond to the Statements Below	Strongly Disagree	Disagree	No Opinion	Agree	Strongly Agree
An active role in decision making about instructional materials, allocation of learning resources, and student assignments is one of a teacher's responsibilities.					
An educational leader should convey optimism to students, colleagues, and parents.					
Teaching means standing up for all students, including those who are marginalized and disadvantaged.					
Teachers have knowledge and skills that can help their fellow teachers succeed with students, and these should be incorporated in professional development efforts.					

SOURCE: Adapted from a questionnaire created by Katzenmeyer and Moller (1996) and grounded in the six elements in the Teachers as Leaders Framework.

score sheets. Record on a tally sheet the distribution for each item on the survey. Then calculate the group score by ascertaining the total score and dividing it by the number of participants. If the exercise is completed by a small project team, participants should share their completed responses and collate findings collaboratively.

- In groups of four to six, participants identify the three to five items where there is most agreement within the school staff and the three to five where there is least agreement. They discuss possible reasons for the agreement and disagreement, and then present their hypotheses to the total group.
- Discussion among participants now focuses on the compiled results. For example, the group may take a closer look at those items on the survey that were marked *agree* or *strongly agree* on a number of the completed surveys.
- The facilitator might identify one item as a case in point (say, observing and providing feedback to fellow teachers, item 5 in Box 6.1), and the group could brainstorm about specific steps they can take to do this better, and record suggestions on the flip chart.
- The whole group, with the aid of the facilitator, composes a summary picture, graphically and/or verbally, of a school definition of leadership. This done, refer to our Teachers as Leaders Framework (Chapter 1) and our definition of parallel leadership (Chapter 3). As a final question, consider the similarities and differences between our definitions and your school's tentative definition.

Final Notes. Through this exercise, participants should form a clearer understanding of their collective thinking about leadership, including points of agreement and disagreement within the group. They should also generate ideas on how to take advantage of potential leadership opportunities and, finally, should identify initiatives that may assist in this respect. Teacher leaders should acknowledge that they will face difficult dilemmas as they assume leadership responsibilities. Several of these may come to the surface in the course of completing this exercise. Additional time might well be allocated for the whole group to discuss potential dilemmas, how they might have already manifested themselves in the functioning of the school, and how they can best be addressed. Participants can be confident, however, that succeeding exercises will provide more opportunities for discussion, creative thinking, and problem solving.

CLASS Exercise 3: Assumptions

Purpose. Participants examine their own and their colleagues' preliminary perspectives on teacher leadership. This exercise is intended primarily for either school-based project teams or cross-school clusters.

Rationale. Globally renowned organizational theorists, including Argyris (1993), Schein (1992), Schon (1953), and Senge (1992), argue that people seeking to achieve organizational change should uncover and examine the values and assumptions that guide their work. Only by examining their deeply held convictions on a continuing basis can individuals and the group effectively assess their actions and align them with changing goals and circumstances.

The analysis that participants complete in this exercise helps build the school's organizational learning capacity, which is essential if they are to improve teaching and learning schoolwide and develop a sense of empowered professionalism. In effect, teachers who become adept at the sort of analysis that this exercise calls for are taking the lead in forming professional learning communities within their schools.

Also, by working through the exercise, participants acquire an analytical tool that can be used to nurture shared understanding and trust in both the short and long term.

Time Considerations and Necessary Materials. The exercise can normally be completed in one hour. Necessary materials include a flip chart and markers, an overhead projector with blank transparencies that can be written on, and the Framework of Assumptions (Box 6.2).

Process

- Participants reflect on their current situation as encapsulated in the outcomes from previous exercises, including Group Portrait and Readiness. They discuss what they have learned about themselves and their work context. Together they agree on some rough characterizations of their work group, and post these as bullet points on flip chart sheets.
- The ten items in the Framework of Assumptions are then posted around the room on large sheets. Staff members mark a point on each continuum to indicate their perception on each Assumption. The following questions are suggested to help center the discussion that follows:
  - ○ What assumptions about leadership do we agree are reflected in our current context?
  - ○ What assumptions indicate a diversity of opinion?
  - ○ Are there assumptions that influence our present situation that are not shown in the Framework of Assumptions?
- A discussion follows about the effects that assumptions may have on the way people work together, and how assumptions might facilitate or impede progress as the group moves forward with its development. It is important here for participants to remind themselves of the unconscious nature of assumptions—often we are not aware of powerful assumptions that guide our actions, and we frequently have difficulty making our assumptions explicit.

Box 6.2   A Framework of Assumptions

Schools do not need teacher leadership.	◄—1—2—3—4—5—►	Schools need leadership from teachers.
Teacher leadership is distinctive.	◄—1—2—3—4—5—►	Teacher leadership is like other forms of leadership.
Teaching, learning, and assessment are the focus of teacher leadership.	◄—1—2—3—4—5—►	Organizational issues are the focus of teacher leadership.
Teacher leadership is enduring and sustainable.	◄—1—2—3—4—5—►	Teacher leadership is episodic and situational.
Teacher leaders are identifiable through scientific and personality analysis.	◄—1—2—3—4—5—►	Teacher leaders may emerge unexpectedly.
All teachers are potential leaders.	◄—1—2—3—4—5—►	Some teachers are potential leaders.
Teacher leadership can be nurtured.	◄—1—2—3—4—5—►	Teacher leadership is inherent.
Teacher leaders have pedagogical credibility.	◄—1—2—3—4—5—►	Teachers leaders do not need to have pedagogical credibility.
Teacher leaders work as individual professionals.	◄—1—2—3—4—5—►	Teacher leaders work as collaborative individuals.
Teacher leaders are popular with colleagues.	◄—1—2—3—4—5—►	Teacher leaders are seen as difficult by colleagues.

In closing, participants record in their journals a personal assumption about leadership in their school and the impact they believe it may have on the development of teacher leadership initiatives. Notes from this meeting are kept for examination as the group continues its work, identifies, and refines initiatives, and begins to implement them. Periodically (e.g., each semester or term), the group might revisit this material and refine it in light of new data emerging from the group's leadership development initiatives.

COMPONENT TWO: STIMULATING AND NURTURING TEACHER LEADERSHIP CAPABILITIES

Preamble. Now that the volunteer members of the CLASS Plan developmental group have generated introductory insights regarding their orientations to teacher leadership, conceptually and in practice, it is important to determine some logistics for engaging in the CLASS Plan:

- By whom will the exercises be organized and coordinated?
- How will a record of experiences be maintained by both individuals and the group?
- Where and when will the exercises be undertaken?
- What forms of external and/or critical friend assistance, if any, will be called upon?
- How might the implementation of the CLASS Plan be linked to a significant school-based developmental initiative?

While the dynamics of organization associated with the CLASS Plan can be varied at different junctures without detracting from the capacity of the Plan to achieve its goals, teacher leaders with whom we have worked have found it very beneficial to address each of these four questions before proceeding with Component Two exercises.

CLASS Exercise 4: Me, a Future Teacher Leader?

Purpose. This exercise provides the first formal opportunity in the CLASS Plan for prospective teacher leaders to explore the concept of teacher leadership and to reflect on the meanings of the six characteristics of teacher leadership in their professional lives. This exercise requires substantial individual reflection but additional benefits accrue if it is completed by a small group with shared interests and motivations.

Rationale. One of the exciting outcomes of research into teacher leadership is that it can be nurtured and developed. Teachers who aspire to become teacher leaders can usually do so, through personal growth and reflective action over time. This exercise provides a very important initial experience for aspiring teacher leaders—the opportunity to interrogate the Teachers as Leaders Framework that we present in Chapter 1 and to relate it to both real-life case studies and their own school situations.

Our experience with this exercise in schools is conclusive—teachers find the Teachers as Leaders Framework quite straightforward and gain considerable satisfaction from analysis of ways that it comes alive in their work environments. In so doing, many teachers are motivated to further explore and develop their own teacher leadership capabilities.

Time Considerations and Necessary Materials. This exercise usually takes about two hours. Participants will each require a copy of one of the snapshot case studies in Chapters 1 and 2 as well as a copy of the Teachers as Leaders Framework and an associated worksheet (Box 6.3). We suggest that you make multiple copies of the snapshot descriptions available and encourage participants to review them briefly and then choose the particular case study that most interests them.

Key reference. Teachers as Leaders Framework, Chapter 1.

Process

- Participants individually select a snapshot and peruse it for evidence of each of the six characteristics of teacher leadership. They note their key points on a worksheet that contains the six teacher leadership elements (i.e., convey convictions of a better world; facilitate communities of learning through organizationwide processes; strive for authenticity in pedagogical practices; confront barriers in the school's culture and structures; translate ideas into sustainable systems of action; nurture a culture of success).
- The next section of the workshop is usually best completed in groups of five or six. Participants share their analyses of each characteristic as they have observed it in their chosen snapshots. At this stage, they might make particular use of the sixteen detailed descriptors of the six elements that are contained in Table 1.1.
- On the same worksheet (Box 6.3), they then identify examples of each teacher leadership attribute that they have personally observed in their own school context.
- With a reasonable degree of shared understanding of the Teachers as Leaders Framework now established, ask participants to proceed to discuss its meanings in their own school context. In so doing, they should be as concrete as possible in their descriptions, but should also be reminded of the need for professional sensitivity (after all, their understandings of colleagues' work may be quite incomplete or formed through superficial assumptions). If each small group is able to identify one example of each characteristic in evidence in their work situation they will have achieved an important milestone.

Box 6.3   **Teacher Leadership Examples**

Teacher Leader Characteristics	Example From Snapshot	Example in Our School
Conveys convictions of a better world		
Facilitates communities of learning through organizationwide processes		
Strives for authenticity in pedagogical practices		
Confronts barriers in the school's culture and structures		
Translates ideas into sustainable systems of action		
Nurtures a culture of success		

- The third section of the workshop can be successfully undertaken as a total staff exercise. We suggest four guiding questions:
  - What have you tentatively concluded about teacher leadership from your analyses of the snapshots and your own professional context?
  - Which of the six teacher leadership capabilities do you think are most inherent in teaching as a profession? Why?
  - Which capability do you regard as most difficult for teachers to develop and practice in schools as they are currently structured and organized? Why?
  - How might heightened teacher leadership capabilities be nurtured and developed in your school? In the profession generally?
- The final section of the workshop involves individual reflection, although many teachers opt to approach it in conjunction with a trusted colleague. In this final activity, participants return to their worksheets and make notes regarding the implications of each characteristic for himself/herself. They should be reminded that it is possible to be a highly successful teacher leader without possessing all six characteristics, since successful teacher leadership is not entirely an individual enterprise. But aspiring teacher leaders should attempt to develop their capabilities within each characteristic. The next several exercises will contribute to that end.

CLASS Exercise 5: Imagining the Future

Purpose. This exercise is intended to enable participants to explore and clarify personal convictions regarding "a better world." It is intended for completion in a small group.

Rationale. Issues associated with values abound in education, and frequently create compelling professional challenges for teachers, individually and collectively. While some forms of educational leadership—particularly those relating to sound management practices—can perhaps be undertaken without cognizance of personal values, most forms of educational leadership are grounded in values and require that leaders know what they believe in, and why. In this exercise, prospective teacher leaders explore possible scenarios for "a better world," with a view to clarifying their own value commitments. Only when personal values are clearly understood can the values aspect of leadership be fully appreciated and implications for practice assessed.

There are many ways that teachers might explore their convictions, whether firmly entrenched, tentative, or hazy, regarding the future worlds of their students. In this exercise we have chosen as our starting point the distinctive characteristics of contemporary students, frequently referred to as Generation Y. In so doing, we recognize that some participants in this exercise will themselves be members of Gen Y (born since about 1985), others will belong to Gen X (born 1975–85), and yet others will be Baby Boomers. Each generation of teachers may be expected to have different perspectives regarding what constitutes a "better world" and what schools might do to facilitate that world. Additionally, of course, even within each generational group, wide variances in value convictions may be expected.

Time Considerations and Necessary Materials. This exercise is designed around a one and a half hour timeframe. It may be extended if you choose to gather and distribute readings about either value orientations or Gen Y. While we encourage you to use readings of your own choosing, the quotes that are included below have proven adequate to ensure a highly stimulating exercise and thoughtful outcome.

Process

- Ask participants to arrange their seating in a circle, so that all can see each other. After outlining the purpose of this session, use presentation slides to present the following three perspectives on Gen Y to workshop participants.
- *Perspective One:* "Unlike the generations that have gone before them, Gen Y has been pampered, nurtured and programmed with a slew of activities since they were toddlers, meaning they are both high-performance and high-maintenance. They also believe in their own worth" (Stephanie Armour, *USA Today* 11/6/2005).
- *Perspective Two:* "Generation Y do not fear the future. They have never experienced recession, they think the world is happy and rich all the time . . . Generation Y think money is an elastic concept. 'Gosh my mobile bill is a bit much this month (pause)—dad?' . . . Work is an important component of Gen Y's life but it is not the only component . . . " (Bernard Salt, Y the younger generation is so different, *The Australian*, November 15, 2006, *Newstext@newsltd .com.au).*
- *Perspective Three:* "Gen Y has clearly identifiable characteristics, including . . .
  - o racially and ethnically diverse
  - o independent because of divorce, daycares, single parents, latchkey parenting, and the technological revolution
  - o feel empowered, thanks to over-indulgent parents, have a sense of security, and are optimistic about the future" (General summary).
- Allocate fifteen minutes for participants to share their thoughts informally on two sets of questions:
  - o In your view, is Gen Y different from previous generations? If so, how is this difference captured in the various perspectives?
  - o To what extent do you see Gen Y characteristics reflected in your students?

- With the benefit of this consciousness-raising analysis, pose the following challenge for participants: Identify a student whom you are currently teaching. Get a clear mental image of this student as he/she now goes about his/her school life—motivations, talents, gifts, needs, disposition, attitudes, social demeanor, family and community support systems, and so on. Now project ahead ten years. What will this student need to acquire from his/her school experiences to ensure that he/she is well-equipped to manage the challenges that will likely present themselves in his/her life a decade from now?
- Encourage a free-flowing dialogue in which nobody speaks more than once and nobody criticizes another person's contribution. After fifteen minutes of dialogue, ask participants to discuss with one or more persons seated nearby the most commonly held views of the future that appear to be emerging. Extend this discussion to a whole-group dialogue and record the key understandings that emerge.
- Present a set of propositions such as those contained in Box 6.4. Ask participants to use these stimuli to clarify their own preferred futures for students.

There is no need to go further with this exercise at this time. Values clarification is an ongoing process and if participants have clarified their perceptions of the future as it relates to Gen Y, and if they have begun to identify one or more propositions that indicate how they personally might work toward that future, they will have made real progress in developing a defensible response to the first element of teacher leadership: *Conveys convictions about a better world.*

CLASS Exercise 6: 1 + 1 = 3

Purpose. This exercise simulates the experience of creating schoolwide pedagogical principles out of the successful teaching practices of staff members. The outcomes of this exercise will be determined in part by the dynamics of the group. Additional insights are to be derived by completing the exercise twice, with different group memberships.

Rationale. The second characteristic of teacher leaders, "Facilitating communities of learning through schoolwide processes," will be new to many readers and teacher leaders. It emanates from concepts of collective intelligence and synergistic thinking that are not yet well developed in educational literature. It involves engaging members of the school community—particularly teachers, and also students and parents where possible—in self-reflection and intensive dialogue to create new educational meaning that is not apparent in the experiences of individuals.

| Box 6.4 | Futuristic Projections |

Proposition One: Our most important challenge as an educational community is to

....

....

Implications:

Proposition Two: Our most important challenge as an educational community is to

....

....

Implications:

Proposition Three: Our most important challenge as an education community is to nurture self-esteem and equip our students to lead healthy, balanced personal lives.

Implications:

Proposition Four: Our most important challenge as an educational community is to strive for a world that is characterized by less poverty, disadvantage, and injustice.

Implications:

Proposition Five: Our most important challenge as an educational community is to shape thinking that will ensure the sustainability (ecological and human) of our planet.

Implications:

Proposition Six: Our most important challenge as an educational community is to nurture deep spiritual values and a sense of communal responsibility.

Implications:

Proposition Seven: Our most important challenge as an educational community is to ensure that our students enter the economic-political world with optimism and entrepreneurial confidence.

Implications:

Our experience suggests that synergistic thinking is largely an intellectual skill, just as logical analysis and coherent communication are largely intellectual skills. And, as with other intellectual skills, it can be developed through practice. In this exercise, participants try their hand at synergistic thinking. They do so through three steps—individual interrogation of data; focused listening to, and interpretation of, the thoughts of a cohort of colleagues; and postulation of explanatory frameworks. Some participants may find a natural affinity for these processes. If so, we challenge them to go a step further and attempt to transpose their explanatory framework into metaphorical imagery that is consistent with the particular metaphor of the Minnemanka school vision.

The creation of significant meaning out of people's life experiences is often an exceptionally complex task, and involves skills of "big picture" explanation that outstanding leaders invariably possess and use to great effect. It is, we think, perhaps the most challenging dimension of teacher leadership. Good luck!

Time Considerations and Necessary Materials. For practical purposes this exercise has a time allocation of one and a half hours. But it may be undertaken several times and may be extended if the members of the cohort so choose. The data for this exercise are contained in Table 6.1 and relate to Snapshot Five.

The teacher leaders at Minnemanka High in Snapshot Five used exercises entitled *Minnemanka Teaching is . . .* and *Minnemanka Learning is . . .* with staff (both teachers and paraprofessionals) and cohorts of students respectively to ascertain whether a set of Minnemanka Pedagogical Principles could be derived from their new school vision and values. The guidelines that they outlined on single page worksheets were simple:

- Describe a recent teaching/learning episode that you have undertaken that made our new school vision come alive in your classroom.
- In what ways did the episode reflect the school vision?
- What strategies made this teaching/learning episode so successful for you?
- If you were to revise what you experienced to enhance the link of this teaching/learning experience to your school's vision, what would you do? Describe the idealized teaching/learning experience as you envision it.

The hundreds of worksheets that were collected were perused by the teacher leaders. Their initial synthesis is contained in Table 6.1. A staff workshop was then convened by the teacher leaders and a small group of volunteer colleagues to attempt to generate a meaningful pedagogical framework out of the database contained in Table 6.1. This activity proved to be successful. In this exercise you simulate that experience.

Table 6.1   Minnemanka Pedagogical Worksheet

Minnemanka Senior High School	
Our Vision **Sharing Our Forest of Possibilities** Our Values **A love of learning** **Respect** for self, for others, our school, our world **Resilience:** Picking yourself up, turning over a new leaf, never giving up **Pride:** Celebrating and sharing our success **Reaching** out to the local and global community	
Students Say *We learn when we have . . .*	*Teachers Say* *For successful teaching . . .*
Fun activities and pleasant environment	Make learning relevant/interesting/exciting
Group-work interaction (interesting projects and games)	Cater for individual learning styles/multiple intelligences; flexibility
Lessons involving imagination and real choices	Practice inclusivity
Opportunity to learn in a lively atmosphere with some independence	Reflect on lessons and refine them
Enough discussion and some repetition for clarity	Use real life experiences and examples from other cultures, societies
Clear instructions, use of symbols, rhymes and tricks to aid memory	Encourage individualized learning/ choice/peer teaching/ownership of learning/student centered learning
Variety of learning: practical/listen/ read/observe/rote can help	Be enthusiastic, prepared, patient
We like teachers . . .	Provide clear instructions, structures, goals, and targets; scaffolding for big ideas
To be on time to class/prepared and organized/control the class	Create a safe environment so students can feel confident to contribute their ideas
To be cheerful not grumpy, strict but fun with a sense of humor	Use a variety of technologies; vary learning experiences

(continued)

Table 6.1   (Continued)

Minnemanka Senior High School

Our Vision
Sharing Our Forest of Possibilities
Our Values
A love of learning
Respect for self, for others, our school, our world
Resilience: Picking yourself up, turning over a new leaf, never giving up
Pride: Celebrating and sharing our success
Reaching out to the local and global community

Students Say We like teachers . . .	Teachers Say For successful teaching . . .
To tolerate some degree of joking if it is in good fun	Model preferred behaviors
To teach at a reasonable pace/listen and give some individual time	Use motivation/rewards/positive reinforcement/recognizing success
To explain why they teach the way they do	Include parents and community in student learning
To give course outlines and explain content	Encourage adventure in learning
To use a variety of teaching styles	Connect with prior knowledge
To teach relevant work (no word sleuths or "busy work," for example)	Create positive relationships with students
To show examples, use vis-aids, "model," tell stories and experiences	Modify curriculum to suit student needs

Process

- As individual group members, scan the two charts that are contained in Table 6.1. What pervasive concepts can you discern?
- Share your tentative concepts ("patterns") with group members.

In listening to the descriptions of others, note contributions that are unusual or surprising in some way, and also those that strike a familiar chord with your own descriptions. Note these items, including any creative phraseology that may be used to describe them. Note in particular language that relates to the "'forest" metaphor from the school vision (e.g., seeds, nature, planting, growing, lifelong, turning over a new leaf, sustainability, ecology, balance, beauty, natural, life-cycle, peacefulness, tranquility, navigating, and so on).

- Once all members have completed their comments, discuss as a group whether it seems most productive to attempt to develop a set of *Teaching* principles or *Learning* principles. (If you do not make this distinction the framework that you create will be for multiple audiences and may be virtually impossible to use professionally).
- Each group member in turn presents one pedagogical principle (see *Note 1*) that seems to him/her to be basic to the data. Continue until all recommendations have been presented. Record these for all to view. Discuss ways of categorizing until a finite (maximum of seven) set of principles has been determined. Adjust the record accordingly, using colored markers. In so doing, make maximum use of the distinctive language that you noted in Step Two.

Note 1: A pedagogical principle is defined as a broad teaching or learning strategy that is grounded in authoritative educational theory and that has potential application across a range of student developmental stages and subject areas. Examples include explicit instruction, real-life applications, e-learning, higher-order thinking, problem solving, risk taking, diagnostic analysis, individualized inquiry, modeling, engaged communications, positive feedback, self-assessment, prior learning, creative expression, etc.

- Adjust the emerging set of statements so that they show a clear link to the school vision and values.
- Discuss with group members ways in which you have experienced the creation of significant new pedagogical meaning for Minnemanka school (i.e., how you have enabled 1+1=3).
- Reflect on the process in which you have personally engaged. In metacognitive terms, how do you describe your approach as an individual to the creation of new pedagogical meaning? How does your approach compare with/differ from the approaches of others in the group? What have you learned about yourself from this experience? How might you use this self-knowledge in your future work as a teacher leader?

CLASS Exercise 7: Barriers

Purpose. Participants identify and come to terms with factors and forces that might prevent teacher leadership from germinating and proliferating in their schools and profession. In addition, participants are encouraged to explore how they might remove or circumvent these barriers in their quest for school revitalization and personal growth.

This exercise is best undertaken by whole-school staffs, although the project management team may wish to experience it for themselves before introducing it to other colleagues. It requires sensitivity in its execution if used as a whole-staff activity.

Rationale. Having completed the previous exercises, the group should be aware of members' core values and beliefs. They will perhaps have begun to envision school development initiatives that the group, or selected members, working together or individually, could undertake. With this grounding and self-confidence, the group can afford to stand back and assess barriers, both external and internal, in enabling teacher leadership to grow and sustain itself into the future.

Time Considerations and Necessary Materials. This exercise normally takes one to one and a half hours. Have on hand a flip chart and markers.

Process

- Participants begin by reviewing together the five Premises to Guide the Development of the Profession that were presented in Chapter 2. Initial discussion focuses on the following questions:
  - Is there agreement that teacher leadership is real? What, then, are the implications for us personally and for the school?
  - How is teacher leadership different from other forms of leadership, and do those differences show up in our school?
  - Teacher leadership develops differently in different contexts, so what form(s) might it take in our particular school?
- Having explored the premises and their bearing on the school, participants may have identified some barriers. In groups of three, they now brainstorm about barriers that stand in the way of making teacher leadership come alive in their school. Participants look at this issue from multiple angles (i.e., from the perspectives of teachers, principal, district and state administrators, parents, students). Groups record their responses on pages torn from a flip chart so they can be displayed later to the entire group.
- Participants discuss the following questions:
  - Do the identified barriers fall into categories? (Different colored markers might be used for separate categories.)
  - Which barriers do teachers appear to put in their own way?
  - Which (if any) are beyond teachers' control?
  - Which can be circumvented or ignored?
- As the discussion progresses, participants move from identifying barriers and characterizing them to focusing on barriers that might move if teachers, with the principal's support, work at removing them. The touchstones for this part of the exercise are these questions:

     ○ Which barriers might be successfully addressed by establishing a firmer shared vision for school operations?

     ○ Which might give way to professional action by coalitions of teachers?

     ○ Which might be alleviated through joint action with parents and community leaders?

- Taking each barrier in turn, participants generate additional flip chart pages of ideas on how they might be overcome.

- After discussing barriers and creating several pages of ideas on how to address them, participants decide on specific steps that they can take to begin the process of overcoming barriers believed to be significantly inhibiting the development of teacher leadership in their own schools. They also note collective actions to take before their next session. Finally, participants record in their journals a specific action they might take as individuals to help remove a barrier or diminish its effects.

- *Note:* Participants might at this juncture wish to compare the outcomes of CLASS Plan Exercise 7 with the contents of Table 2.2, which we have constructed from synthesis of a number of "Barriers" workshops.

CLASS Exercise 8: The Power of Language

Purpose. Participants inquire into the language of leadership currently in use in their schools. If undertaken as a cross-school cluster activity, this exercise requires sensitivity to the circumstances of individual schools and the styles of their principals and other administrators.

Rationale. How people speak about each other in the course of their work together, even when they use humor or tease, can be indicative of what they value. Shared leadership, in general, depends on factors such as trust, integrity, and goodwill. Parallel leadership, in particular, depends on mutual respect and regard, a sense of shared purpose, and allowance for individual expression. By assessing the leadership language used in a school, participants can develop important insights regarding the extent to which the school culture is amenable to teacher leadership, and whether it is, in fact, a place where teacher leadership and parallel leadership can take hold and thrive.

    Two challenges in this exercise are (a) to avoid intense personal reactions to certain words and expressions, and (b) to resist generalizing about how negative a word or expression may be. For example, the use of "boss" may carry negative connotations in one situation but not in another, for one person but not another. These differences need to be explored, and participants should dig as deeply as they can into their consciousness to identify both positive and negative phrases and terms so that they can have a rich, full discussion of the implications of language for professional relationships and school culture.

Time Considerations and Necessary Materials. The exercise has three parts: (a) an initial discussion, (b) follow-up observations during the course of a week or two, and (c) a synthesizing discussion. Each discussion is likely to take over an hour, and intervening observations an hour or more.

Necessary materials include a data projector or an overhead projector, with transparencies that can be written on, and the Teachers as Leaders Framework enlarged to poster size.

Process

- Participants begin by sharing perspectives on the power of language and how it can be used to achieve certain ends. Participants provide examples of ways they themselves have used language as a tool, considering both what was said and how it was said.
- Referring to the list of phrases associated with four traditional leadership theories (Table 6.2), participants discuss, as a group, their reactions to these phrases.

Table 6.2   Typical Expressions Associated With Four Leadership Theories

Transformational leadership	"We are champions." "Climb every mountain." "Dream the impossible dream."
Strategic leadership	"The buck stops here." "If you can't beat them in the alleys, you can't beat them on the playing field." "Results are all that count."
Educative or advocacy leadership	"Keep the scoundrels honest." "I'm a committed activist." "Against all odds."
Organizationwide leadership	"We're a family." "We're all in this together." "A champion team will beat a team of champions."

- They then brainstorm about possible types of language used among school staff members in the normal course of their school day—for example, hierarchical, encouraging, aggressive, submissive, patronizing, inclusive, alienating, inspirational, confrontational. One member of the group writes the identified headings at the top of a flip chart page. Participants then form groups of three to discuss the words, phrases, and expressions that might fit under the headings suggested.

- The small groups come together and share what they have written, so they can compile a comprehensive, varied collection of words, phrases, and expressions under appropriate headings. Participants ask various contributors to explain the context in which their word or phrase was used, the reactions it elicited, and how it affected relationships among staff members. As many participants as possible should join the discussion, citing similar or dissimilar experiences, and exploring ways that language can be interpreted differently in different situations and why this is.

- Again in groups of three, participants turn to The Language of Leadership in Box 6.5. Each group has a copy, where it records examples of leadership language that contributes to or detracts from the development of parallel leadership and/or teacher leadership in their school. Groups should choose words and phrases bandied about in the halls or staff room that seem to have significant influence—or, on the other hand, very little influence—on major directions the school pursues or major decisions made. In this quest, participants should not overlook language that is not necessarily meant to be negative but that discourages teachers from taking leadership. This can be language that they have heard others use or that they themselves have used. The Teachers as Leaders Framework, mounted on the wall, can stimulate participants to identify words and expressions used regularly in the school that either foster or detract from the fulfillment of the six characteristics of teacher leaders outlined in the framework.

- The task continues over the next two weeks, as participants listen carefully to workplace discussions that reflect professional relationships, as played out in various locales and situations—the staff room, playground, assembly, parent meetings, staff meetings, and collegial conversations. They try to identify phrases, terms, and expressions that demonstrate a broader view of leadership that includes idea generation, identification of key tasks, initiative taking, mutual influence, and shared responsibility. As they encounter these forms of language, they add them to their Language of Leadership list.

- A week or more later, a follow-up session is held. With the completed grid displayed on an overhead projector or wall charts, participants react to the expanded inventory and discuss its implications. The purpose is to shape a rough consensus on the state

Box 6.5   **The Language of Leadership**

Language Perceived as Supportive of Teacher Leadership and Parallel Leadership	Language Perceived as Detracting From Teacher Leadership and Parallel Leadership

of leadership language in the school. Through this analysis, the group begins to understand the magnitude and dimensions of their challenges—or, conversely, the extent of their support base—as teachers begin taking leadership roles in the school and as administrators consider the most effective forms of support to offer. Is the environment a favorable one, that is, is parallel leadership either an emerging reality or, at least, a real possibility? It is important for the group to have an accurate gauge of this crucial aspect of the school's culture before undertaking serious developmental initiatives.

- With the help of the facilitator, participants discuss the meaning and effect of certain phrases and words—and how they feel about that language. It is important to note that terms are not negative unless people in that particular school perceive them to be negative. Participants will benefit from listening to and exploring each other's views and values, and taking special notice of the positive language they want to see used in their school.

CLASS Exercise 9: Creating a Personal Leadership Framework (PLF)

Purpose. This exercise enables participants to synthesize emerging understandings of their personal leadership orientation in an explanatory visual diagram. This exercise is primarily an experience in personal contemplation, interrogation, and imagination but benefits if, at key junctures, a trusted colleague is engaged in the process.

Rationale. Fundamental to becoming a successful teacher leader is insight into the ways that you as an individual relate to authoritative leadership theories. Each of the four areas of leadership theory that is presented in Chapter 2 (Strategic, Transformational, Educative, Organizationwide) derives from a particular value base and also emphasizes particular skills as ways of influencing people in their work and community contexts. In this exercise we use the four areas of theory as the basis for the development of a PLF.

Time Considerations and Necessary Materials. Three resources are required for this exercise:

- The brief descriptions of the four areas of leadership theory that are outlined in Chapter 2
- Table 6.2: Typical Expressions Associated with Four Leadership Theories
- The Leadership Wheel Worksheet, Figure 6.1

Once completed, the results might very productively be shared with a trusted colleague, friend or partner, and comments solicited from that person. Our experience is that prospective teacher leaders (and also principals) very seldom ascertain in one session full understanding of their dominant leadership orientations. Most educators, including ourselves, find the PLF exercise an excellent starting point in determining leadership orientation, but usually require several efforts, over a period of months, before they are able to make the difficult choices between the four leadership orientations that the exercise requires.

Thus, the time required for the exercise is variable—an initial session of an hour, followed by a series of further sessions spread over a period of several months.

Process

- Familiarize yourself with the four leadership theories (Chapter 2) and the Leadership Wheel (Figure 6.1). If you are facilitating a group activity, prepare handouts of the Leadership Wheel for each participant—preferably using large sheets of paper.
- In the outer circle of the Leadership Wheel, identify three to four underlying values that distinguish each theory. Use the descriptions in Chapter 2 in completing this task. Ask yourself: *To what extent does each area of theory appear to capture how I like to think of myself?*
- Now move to the second outer circle. Can you suggest one or more well-known figures who appear to represent each theory? (For example, Martin Luther King Jr. was a charismatic, inspirational *Transformational* leader, as reflected in his "I have a dream" speech in 1963, while President Truman was a very rational, results-oriented *Strategic* leader whose desk contained a plaque with the inscription, "The buck stops here." Mother Teresa, the "saint of the gutters," when she received her Nobel Peace Prize in 1979, spoke to the theme of "Love begins at home" and in so doing emphasized the sanctity of life, particularly childhood, and the need for privileged citizens of the world to share the lives of the disenfranchised and disadvantaged. She reflected the *Educative* leadership tradition, with its emphasis on justice and consciousness-raising. There are no human role models to represent the *Organizationwide* approach to leadership, but sporting teams that take seriously the motto, "A champion team will always beat a team of champions," with its implicit emphasis on participatory decision making, shared responsibility, and interactive learning, seem to us to come close to what Ogawa and Bossert (1995) had in mind when they coined the "organizationwide" terminology.
- Which role models appeal most to you? Whom do you most admire? Your answer will give you an indication of the leadership orientation to which you aspire.
- Proceed to the third circle in the Leadership Wheel. The arts, particularly music, can also provide insights regarding preferred leadership

Figure 6.1   The Leadership Orientations Wheel

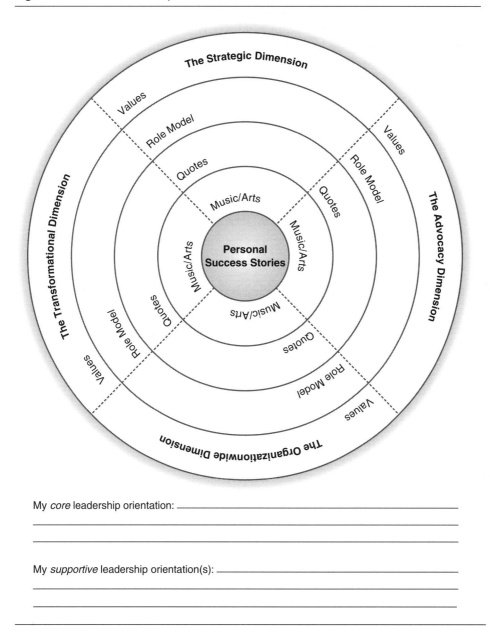

My *core* leadership orientation: _____

_____

_____

My *supportive* leadership orientation(s): _____

_____

_____

orientations. For example, some people are emotionally stirred by inspirational music (*To dream the impossible dream*), others by music that emphasizes individual planning, work, and accomplishment (*I did it my way*), others by human community and perseverance (much *Gospel* music), and yet others by team endeavor (*We are the champions*). Of course, the vast majority of music is devoid of serious value considerations, and some reflects a range of value themes. But having generated a number of musical exemplars of each leadership orientation, ask yourself which exemplar reminds you most of your personal view of the world? In pondering this question you will be gaining further insights regarding your preferred leadership orientation.

- Preferably in conjunction with a number of colleagues, identify significant quotes that appear to reflect the various leadership themes. Examples might include: *Blessed are the poor in spirit for theirs is the kingdom of heaven* (Jesus of Nazareth); *Turn your face towards the sacred mosque* (Mohammed); *I have the heart and stomach of a king* (Queen Elizabeth I); *The only thing we have to fear is fear itself* (Franklin D. Roosevelt); *I have nothing to offer but blood, toil, tears, and sweat* (Winston Churchill); *Freedom of choice is a universal principle to which there should be no exceptions* (Michail Gorbachev); *If you can't stand the heat, stay out of the kitchen* (Harry Truman).

- Ponder the selection of quotes. Which one quote best sums up how you would like to be seen by your colleagues and community members? What does this tell you about your preferred leadership orientation?

- Proceed to the inner circle. Describe a successful experience—professional, community service, voluntary association, family—in which you featured significantly. What was your contribution? What did you do that gave you a sense of achievement and actualization? What does this success story suggest about your actual (as opposed to preferred) leadership orientation?

- You are now hopefully getting to a juncture where you can make choices between the four leadership orientations—all of which are very important, very appealing, and very evident in many school situations. Which single orientation appears to capture your *preferred* leadership orientation? Which appears to capture your *actual* leadership style? (These may be the same, but may not.)

- You have now achieved an important milestone in becoming a teacher leader. But the journey is far from complete. This exercise should be a reference point for you as you proceed to more intensive analysis and thinking over the coming months, and perhaps years.

COMPONENT THREE: DEVELOPING PARALLEL LEADERSHIP RELATIONSHIPS AND STRATEGIES

CLASS Exercise 10: Images of Parallelism in Workplaces

Purpose. This exercise enables participants to explore case study descriptions of parallel leadership and transpose them into meaningful imagery. This exercise is preferably undertaken in a small group arrangement.

Rationale. Successful leadership is closely linked to powerful communications capabilities. A talent for using language, particularly the spoken word, to nurture trust, explain complexity, stimulate inquiry, and inspire passion and loyalty frequently distinguishes influential leaders. In this exercise, participants experiment with their communication talents while developing a metaphor that reflects the particular form of parallel leadership that is depicted in a selected case study. In so doing, they will be gaining expertise in the use of language as a powerful leadership tool as well as enhancing their understanding of the concept of parallel leadership.

Time Considerations and Necessary Materials. This exercise can be completed in one and a half hours. It requires access to the six case studies in Chapters 1–4. A comprehensive thesaurus often proves to be a very valuable asset in exercises such as this.

Process:

- As a small group, agree on a definition of metaphor. Share metaphorical images that you associate with schools in which you have worked (e.g., factory, garden, bridge, ship, circus, Christmas tree, football game).
- In your groups, select one of the case studies from Chapters 1, 2, 3, or 4 and review it.
  - How does the case study reflect our definition of parallel leadership and the underlying values of mutual trust, shared purpose, and allowance for individual expression?
  - What metaphors might be used to describe parallel leadership in this case study? Why? Share your metaphor with colleagues.
  - What do your various metaphors have in common?
  - What do they reveal about the intrinsic qualities of parallel leadership?
- Now consider parallel leadership as it is emerging in your school context. Agree on a metaphor that you would like to see in place in the leadership of your school a year from now. What might your principal, teacher leaders, and other members of your professional community and wider school community do to encourage the maturation of this leadership approach? Which of the four areas of leadership theory (Chapter 2) appear to be most relevant in your metaphor?
- Consider the benefits of transposing your leadership metaphor into a visual image and displaying it in your staffroom, or perhaps presenting it for consideration at a faculty meeting. How might actions of this type be used to enhance understandings of leadership?

CLASS Exercise 11: Leadership and the Arts

Purpose. This exercise enables participants to explore different configurations of parallel leadership through an analysis of dance selections. This exercise is probably best undertaken in a group setting, although whole-school applications have been found to generate deep interest in leadership concepts and processes.

Rationale. The forms of leadership that we exercise, and that we see exercised in our workplaces and communities, are derivatives in large part of our societal processes and cultural values, traditions, and mores. Thus, they show resemblance to other aspects of our way of life, including music, dance, sport, religious devotion and celebration, and core customs. As such, leadership forms can be much more interesting and, indeed, exotic, than textbooks and manuals sometimes suggest they are. They can also provoke significant questions about our societal values and lifestyles that are interesting to ponder.

In this exercise, you analyze a number of dances that appear, through their rhythm, steps, movements, and execution, to relate to parallel leadership as you experience it in your school and as you aspire to experience it. In so doing, you will develop an enhanced appreciation for the subtleties and meanings of parallel leadership. You may also develop new insights into the fascinating world of dance!

Time Considerations and Necessary Materials. This exercise usually takes two hours to complete. A good thesaurus is recommended as a resource—there are about one hundred examples of dance listed in the thesaurus that we use, along with a number of expressions that contain images of dance that have very interesting leadership connotations (*dance on air, dance the night away, dance of death, lead someone on a merry dance*, etc.).

Process

- Introduce the exercise by presenting the group with a number of quotations that center on dance, such as the following:

    All the ills of mankind, all the tragic misfortunes that fill the history books, all the potential blunders, all the failures of the great leaders, have arisen merely from a lack of skill at dancing.

    —Moliere

    Don't dance or ride with General Bangs—a most immoral man.

    —Kipling

If you are going to walk on thin ice you might as well dance.

—Proverb

Dancing is a contact sport.

—Duffy Daugherty

Will you, won't you, will you, won't you, will you join the dance?

—Lewis Carroll

The dancing pair, that simply sought renown, by holding out, to tire the other down.

—Oliver Goldsmith

- What does each quotation imply about the exercise of leadership? (Special note: Each of these quotes—and several others—was used to introduce a chapter in a recent book by Mungo MacCallum [2007] about a political campaign in Australia.) What other quotations come to mind as capturing forms of leadership that participants may have experienced? Ponder the question:

    Why does dance contain such powerful symbols of core cultural processes such as leadership?

- Consider the ways that parallel leadership manifests in each of the following categories of dance.
    o Category One: Line dancing; water ballet; barn dance.
    o Category Two: An indigenous ceremony for inducting young men into adulthood.
    o Category Three: A peacock strutting as a lead-up to mating; an Elvis Presley stage performance.
    o Category Four: An indigenous war dance; a Maori haka performance before an international rugby match.
    o Category Five: Cha-cha; Charleston; Jive.
- Select one example from each category to guide the discussion. Consider:
    o How do the values that underpin parallel leadership (mutual trust, shared purpose, allowance for individual expression) reveal themselves in this dance form?
    o How does each participant in the dance exercise leadership?
    o How would you describe that leadership, using the four areas of leadership theory that are outlined in Chapter 2?
- Now consider three questions that relate to your own workplace and your emerging construction of parallel leadership:
    o What dance form(s) would you suggest describe parallel leadership as you currently practice it in your work setting?

o What dance form would you suggest to describe the form of parallel leadership that you aspire to?

o How might you use the metaphor of dance to enable your professional colleagues to develop enhanced insights into leadership concepts and processes?

CLASS Exercise 12: Parallel Leadership in Diverse Scenarios

Purpose. This exercise increases participants' understanding of the various forms that parallel leadership can take in their school and highlights that different forms of parallelism can each resolve complex educational challenges. The most appropriate grouping for this exercise is probably the school-based project management team, with the principal's participation highly desirable if authenticity is to be achieved.

Rationale. Teacher leadership is a particular form of school leadership different from, yet highly dependent on, metastrategic principal leadership. For it to exist at all, moderate encouragement and support from administrators is required. For it to thrive, substantial encouragement and support are often necessary. This exercise provides the opportunity to develop that understanding. Specifically, it invites participants to depict their organizational dynamics by grappling with a set of hypothetical scenarios for dealing with an educational challenge the school might well face. The assumption underlying the exercise is that participants will, following this professional learning experience, be able to imagine a rich set of possible leadership scenarios to fit the particular needs and conditions of their school.

Time Considerations and Necessary Materials. This exercise requires an hour or more to complete. Participants should have on hand the following:

- the definition of parallel leadership with its three defining characteristics (Chapter 3)
- the challenges for principals in promoting teacher leadership (Table 4.1) mounted on posters or wall charts
- the snapshot from Chapter 3
- an overhead projector and transparencies that can be written on
- a flip chart and markers

Process

- Participants begin by discussing the dynamics between administrator leaders and teacher leaders as described in the snapshot in Chapter 3. In the process, they review together the concept of parallel leadership and its accompanying characteristics, as outlined in Chapter 3, and the new roles of principals as outlined in Chapter 4.

- Participants then read and briefly discuss the hypothetical challenge described below. They also read the four scenarios that follow the presentation of the problem.

The Context and Problem. Chronic environmental problems—persistent automobile and residential fuel shortages, coupled with a series of floods caused by repeated clear-felling near a bordering river—have finally captured the attention of community leaders in a small city. These leaders are now calling for businesses and social institutions, including schools, to do what they can to support more aggressive conservation measures. Schools, in particular, are asked to develop new approaches to the curriculum and to teaching that will increase students' understanding of ecological relationships and make them more knowledgeable about how communities can address proliferating, protracted environmental problems. A strong emphasis on total staff involvement—with planning efforts aimed at engaging students with real-world problems as part of their coursework—is essential.

Four Scenarios

Scenario A. One member of the teaching staff is not only a creative thinker in fields related to the problem but also an instigator of change. She is fully prepared to recommend ways to address the problem. She begins to plan and initiate action. The principal supports, encourages, asks probing questions, talks up her initiative, and celebrates small successes as they occur—after he becomes convinced of the merits of the teacher's approach and sees the positive reactions of her colleagues. He has no perception of his authority being challenged but is a conservative thinker and so needs convincing when new ideas come into play.

Scenario B. A number of teachers, individually and in small groups, initiate and operate specific projects to address the problem in the context of the school's shared vision. They act independently and exhibit a high level of ownership for their initiatives and for the progress of students in the coursework that is developed. The principal, for her part, is perceived as a strong, somewhat larger-than-life leader. She generates enthusiasm for and through the common vision, and she encourages teachers as they look for ways to address the challenges in front of them. Teachers are supported, encouraged, and lauded by both the principal and their colleagues. The high level of energy in the school adds momentum to the teachers' efforts.

Scenario C. A small group of teachers advocates for and designs change. They understand the problem and are prepared to pose solutions. The principal, although working hard on behalf of the students, is fearful that these teachers may somehow threaten the stability of the school and its community. Only when the principal sees that the teachers' initiatives can have a positive impact on the school, and that these successes will enhance his position as principal, does he become supportive and encouraging. There are frequent points of conflict between the teacher leaders and the principal.

Scenario D. The principal has worked hard in the recent past at demonstrating instructional leadership in the school. She has a number of clear preconceptions about how the current challenge confronting the school should be addressed. Teachers, for their part, have mostly receded into the background in the face of initiatives advanced by the principal. Yet implementation of these initiatives has been episodic and uneven. The principal decides it is time to shift the balance of professional relationships, and she openly commits to the possibility that greater leadership by teachers at this juncture might produce more positive schoolwide effects.

- Participants break into four work groups. Each group is assigned one of the four scenarios. In their discussions, each group describes, as specifically as possible, what might occur in the context, given the dynamics of their scenario. The following questions might be posed:
  o What do you envision the teacher or teachers doing?
  o What do you envision the principal doing?
  o What kind of initiatives might each take?
  o What obstacles might the teacher or teachers have to overcome?
  o How would authority be apportioned between teachers and the principal?
  o How might responsibilities be allocated, relationships managed, and tasks carried out?
  o Who would be held responsible for outcomes?
  o What ramifications would all this have on the leadership dynamics in the school?
- The whole group reconvenes to compare their responses to the core problem. They then explore questions such as the following:
  o What impact does the relationship between principal and teachers have on the success of school initiatives?
  o What difference does it make if the principal initiates an action or if a teacher or teachers initiate it?
  o Contrast the dynamics, as you imagine them, between the four scenarios, were they at work in your school.
- And two questions of paramount importance:
  o What impact could the initiation of parallel leadership have on student outcomes in each scenario?
  o What does this imply for your school?

- Finally, the participants, as a whole group, bring their attention back to the three values of parallel leadership and pose this question for individual reflection:
  - What can I do to foster these values in our school?
- After a short reflection time, participants record their intended action in their journals.

COMPONENT FOUR: SUSTAINING TEACHER LEADERSHIP INTO THE FUTURE

CLASS Exercise 13: Linking Metastrategy and Teacher Leadership in Practice

Purpose. This exercise enables participants to explore, in a real-life context, ways of bringing teacher leadership and metastrategic principalship together in your school. This exercise should be completed, if possible, by the principal, other members of the school administration team, and teacher leader cohort. Preferably, members of the administration team will have completed a number of the CLASS Plan exercises and will be familiar with the intents of the program.

Rationale. To this point in the CLASS Plan, exercises have focused mainly on either hypothetical situations or the arms-length examination of school-based situations. But at some point, principals and teacher leaders must come together to share what has been learned and to test their new insights and skills in the context of a significant school development initiative. Participants are now ready for this challenge. They should approach it with enthusiasm, sensitivity, and confidence.

Time Considerations and Necessary Materials. No more than one and a half hours is usually required for this exercise. The resources required are the Teachers as Leaders Framework (Chapter 1), the Functions of Metastrategic Principalship (Chapter 4), the conceptual framework for linking parallel leadership and successful school capacity-building (Figure 3.1), and a healthy dose of goodwill on the part of all participants. The Framework and Functions statements should be incorporated into a large worksheet, as in Box 6.6.

Process

- To get the exercise underway, the teacher leader cohort explains the features of the Teachers as Leaders Framework and addresses any queries that members of the administration team may have. The principal and other administrators then explain the features of the

Box 6.6   **Linking Teacher Leadership Elements and Metastrategic Functions**

Current school development priority:

Teachers as Leaders Elements	Linkages	Metastrategic Functions

Conveying convictions of a better world (Examples)

Facilitating communities of learning (Examples)

Envisioning inspirational futures (Examples)

Aligning key elements (Examples)

Striving for pedagogical excellence (Examples)

Enabling teacher leadership (Examples)

Confronting barriers (Examples)

Building alliances (Examples)

Translating ideas into action (Examples)

Culture-building (Examples)

Nurturing a culture of success (Examples)

metastrategic leadership framework, and answer any queries that may arise.

- The group then reviews the definition of parallel leadership and the ways that it works in practice to enhance school capacity (Figure 3.1). With a firm basis of shared understanding in place, the group addresses two key questions:
  o What is a current developmental priority that we must address as a school?
  o How might the concepts of teacher leadership and metastrategic principalship enable the school to address this priority concern?
- Once a decision has been made regarding Question 1, Box 6.6 can be used to guide analysis of Question 2. Essentially, all parts of the two "Leadership actions" columns should be filled in, with the principal leading discussion relating to the metastrategy column and teacher leaders leading discussion relating to the teacher leadership column. It will be found that the two columns are very much interrelated; adjustments in one column may have to be made periodically to accommodate proposed inclusions in the other.
- After an extensive period of dialogue (e.g., forty minutes) it may be fruitful to take stock of progress with the following questions:
  o What are our major areas of congruence?
  o What areas of incongruence are arising?
  o Why?
- Once a reasonable degree of agreement has been reached, a further critically important question arises:
  o How might we present the outcomes of this meeting to the total staff?
  o What questions might arise at that time and how might they be addressed?

Note: Our experience suggests that principals and teacher leaders who complete this exercise successfully do so with a high degree of professional satisfaction. They should have achieved deep professional trust, shared purpose, and allowance for individual expression—the underlying values of parallel leadership.

CLASS Exercise 14: Staff Meeting

Purpose. The school-based project management team uses a particular everyday educational challenge—organization of a faculty meeting—to apply some of the significant learnings that have derived from the CLASS Plan and to assess their capacity as a parallel leadership team.

Rationale. Staff meeting time is precious because it is represents a rare opportunity for deliberative action. It is, in many schools, the only time that all staff members gather to address issues of common concern. Thus, it provides a challenging venue where participants can test some of the ideas developed in CLASS Plan exercises. Teachers sometimes tend to be frustrated by the way staff meetings unfold, cynical about their usefulness, and unclear about steps that might be taken to improve them. In all too many schools, staff meetings are little more than platforms for information-sharing or for wrestling with current problems of concern to senior administrators.

Time Considerations and Necessary Materials. The exercise should take one to two hours. Participants should have on hand a data projector/overhead projector and transparencies to write on; a flip chart and markers; work products from previous exercises.

Process

- Participants briefly review what they have accomplished in terms of developing their leadership capacity. Within this context, they discuss a new task: designing a structure and agenda for a staff meeting grounded in the group's interpretation of teacher leadership and parallel leadership and its envisioned leadership actions. The proposed structure and agenda should advance the leadership capabilities of the teacher leader cohort and demonstrate some of the outcomes of the CLASS Plan. That this work should be done in partnership with the principal is a given.
- Here is the task: Design a structure and format for your school's next staff meeting. Identify key issues that should be addressed in the meeting, and outline procedures for addressing them. Ground your proposal in concepts of teacher leadership, metastrategic (principal) leadership, and parallel leadership. Consider the following:
  - goals and outcomes sought for each form of leadership (metastrategic goals, teacher leadership goals, parallel leadership goals)
  - necessary agenda items
  - sequence of items
  - need for, and role of, chair or facilitator
  - necessary prior preparation
  - guidelines for discussion, deliberation, and decision making
  - professional development and growth potential that can be built into the meeting
- Work on the task begins in small groups of two to three participants each. Groups discuss possible structures for the meetings in general and also generate specific agenda items.
- The whole group, using discussion skills refined in previous CLASS Plan exercises, formulates a single compelling proposal for staff meetings, including format, agendas for the next several meetings, and shared facilitation responsibilities.

- The final question the group should address is what to do with its proposal. Participants should assume clear responsibility for the next steps—identifying specific actions that are consistent with the principles of parallel leadership as they have developed.

CLASS Exercise 15: Six Months Later and Beyond

Purpose. Exercise 15 draws participants into a process of tracing and documenting ways in which teacher leadership and parallel leadership have impacted their school. This final exercise can be completed wholly by a school-based project management team, or partly by the school-based team and partly by the cross-school cluster.

Rationale. In undertaking this activity six months or more following the completion of the CLASS Plan program, participants look critically at the apparent effects their efforts as teacher leaders are having on the school, including students, staff, and community. Use is made of a process of backward mapping (Padilla et al., 1996). Through this exercise, participants evaluate the authenticity and impact of their professional learning on a continuing basis, and they accrue insights into ways that leadership relates to school outcomes.

Time Considerations and Necessary Materials. This exercise requires a couple of hours each time it is undertaken. Participants need their leadership development journals and the group's key instruments from its leadership development portfolio. In addition, the diagram linking parallel leadership and successful school capacity-building (Figure 3.1) on a poster, a wall chart, or a transparency is the principal focus for the backward mapping that participants do. The questions below should also be listed on a transparency. Finally, a flip chart should be available.

Process

- Given that this exercise causes the group to reassemble after a period of time, it is important to begin by recounting highlights of the developmental journeys that both the group and individuals have taken. Participants reflect openly and share a moment, incident, activity, or discussion that was a significant growth point, either for them individually or for the group as a whole.
- The group then identifies a significant educational event that has occurred in the school and where there is some evidence of improved school outcomes that may relate in part to the "event." The group may need to discuss this for a time to identify and agree on particular events, shifts, or moments that were significant. Examples may relate to a wide range of considerations including

administration structures, classroom support systems, pedagogical delivery, professional learning, community involvement, student voice, collegial supports, a curriculum change, university advisory program, technological innovation, and so on.

- Participants consider the following four questions in relation to the occurrence referred to in the preceding paragraph. Each question is considered individually, with enough time to discuss their ideas about it.
  o What was the nature and extent of educational improvement?
  o What factors were perceived to be responsible for the improvement?
  o What roles did individuals and groups play in bringing about the improvement?
  o What leadership dynamics underpinned the improvement?
- As each question is considered, a member of the group summarizes the responses on a flip chart page.
- Participants then turn their attention to the diagram linking parallel leadership and successful school capacity-building (Figure 3.1) and address this question:
  o Does what we have come up with in our responses to the above questions support, refine, or refute the educational insights represented in the diagram?
- Discussion concludes with participants discussing the following questions:
  o How might enhanced school capacity be defined?
  o How, if at all, have leadership dynamics in the school shifted over the past six, twelve, or eighteen months?
  o How sustainable are the current leadership dynamics?
  o How can we use the understandings we have attained to enhance school capacity further and thus continue to improve student outcomes?
- As a final point of deliberation, the group may wish to consider ways in which it might extend its professional learning in the period ahead. What further use might be made of some, or all, of the fifteen exercises in the CLASS Plan? What additional exercises might be incorporated? What additional members might be included in the group?

Appendix A

Overview of the IDEAS Project

The IDEAS Project resulted from the creation in 1997 of an alliance of the University of Southern Queensland's Leadership Research Institute and the Queensland Department of Education. It was inspired primarily by the findings of University of Wisconsin researchers Newmann and Wehlage and Associates, particularly the power of their concepts of *authentic pedagogy* and *collective professional responsibility* to offset the effects of socioeconomic disadvantage (Newmann & Wehlage, 1995). It was further developed in 2001 to take into account the outcomes of a large scale Australian research project that explored the forms of influence that enable school leaders to impact on student achievement (Cuttance, 2001). Figure 3.1 in Chapter 3 resulted from that research and is fundamental to the IDEAS Project in its current form.

IDEAS incorporates four constructs that extend the Wisconsin research, and international educational theory, into school-based innovation processes.

First is the concept of organizational "alignment." The Research-Based Framework for Enhancing School Outcomes Through Alignment of Key Elements (RBF) that is depicted in Figure A.1 provides teachers and administrators with a way of thinking about their school as an organization that is "in tune" or "in alignment" (or "not in alignment," as the case may be).

Specifically, when the five contributory elements of the RBF are all clearly in evidence in a school's operations, and philosophically "in alignment," resultant school outcomes are postulated to be high. The conceptual research initiatives of Schneider et al. (2003), Leppitt (2006), Voss, Cable, and Voss (2006), Hitt and Ireland (2002), Goold and Campbell (2002), Leana and Pil (2006), and Dunbar and Starbuck (2006), in combination, suggest when organizations such as schools are "aligned" internally and externally they develop enhanced identity, effectiveness, and value-adding capability.

Figure A.1 A Research Based Framework for Enhancing School Outcomes through Alignment of Key Elements (RBF)

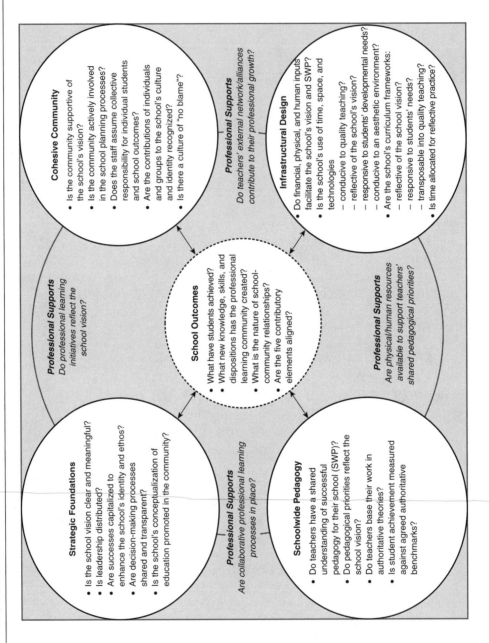

SOURCE: Created by the IDEAS Project team. Printed with the permission of Frank Crowther, representing the IDEAS team.

The conceptual picture of an idealized school that is contained in the RBF provides the basis for survey instruments for teachers and principals as they seek to diagnose their school's strengths, limitations, and overall levels of alignment, and to establish long-term goals and strategies for serious innovation.

Second is the construct of Three Dimensional Pedagogy (Figure 2.2, Chapter 2). This concept recognizes different perspectives on pedagogy that, when taken together, provide what we regard as a plausible image of the twenty-first-century teacher's core work. In putting forward this claim we have written elsewhere that

> 3-DP teachers develop their personal pedagogical self at the same time as they engage with their school's SWP and explore the potential of relevant authoritative theories of teaching and learning to both their personal pedagogy and their SWP. (Andrews & Crowther, 2003, p. 101)

The concept of 3-DP locates the work of teachers, individually and collectively, at the center of a school's operations and emphasizes the importance of sustained pedagogical quality over any other aspect of school practice, including curricula, parent roles, principals' leadership, or systemic efficiencies. In this sense, it represents a radical departure from most approaches to innovation.

Third is the construct of parallel leadership. "Parallelism" in the IDEAS Project draws particularly on the concepts that are outlined in Chapters 1 through 4 of this book, particularly the concept of teacher leadership.

Parallel leadership in the IDEAS Project is asserted to make it more possible for schools to sustain innovative processes than has been possible through traditional leadership paradigms that depend inordinately on individual leaders, particularly principals.

The fourth construct is the IDEAS process of schoolwide organizational development. The IDEAS process is an organizational learning process that is constituted of five distinct phases that are linked in a conceptual sequence, as illustrated in Box A.1. Schools that undertake the IDEAS Project commit to a two to three year period of implementation, encompassing the five stages of the project.

In all five phases of the IDEAS process, the centrality of teacher leaders to processes of successful school reform is asserted. The process requires the identification of one or more school-based facilitators and the establishment of an IDEAS school management team to manage the process with the assistance of an external (university) support team. Facilitators undertake ongoing leadership development, including the fifteen exercises in Chapter 6 of this book, as part of their two to three year engagement in the IDEAS Project.

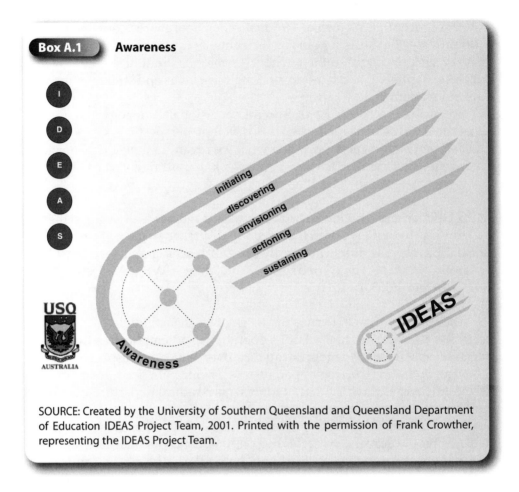

Box A.1   **Awareness**

I

D

E

A

S

USQ
AUSTRALIA

initiating
discovering
envisioning
actioning
sustaining

Awareness

IDEAS

SOURCE: Created by the University of Southern Queensland and Queensland Department of Education IDEAS Project Team, 2001. Printed with the permission of Frank Crowther, representing the IDEAS Project Team.

The IDEAS Project has been implemented in about 350 schools across Australia, with successful trials also conducted successfully in Singapore and Sicily. The Project has been evaluated by authoritative researchers (see Appendix B, Research Phase Four) and the integrity of the underlying concepts, including those of teacher leadership and parallel leadership, as fundamental to successful school reform, has been substantiated.

Appendix B

Overview of the Teachers as Leaders Research Design

BACKGROUND

The research that provided the basis for this book has been conducted in five phases over a period of more than a decade. The first two phases were completed in Queensland, Australia, with the financial support of the Queensland Education Department and the Australian Research Council. The third phase was undertaken as part of an Australia-wide project, with links to Michigan. Phase three was funded by the Australian Commonwealth Department of Education, Training and Youth Affairs (DETYA) and the Australian Research Council. Phase four comprised an Australian national trial and evaluation of a large-scale school revitalization project that is based on principles of parallel leadership (the IDEAS Project). It was funded by the Australian Government. Phase five is a continuing project that involves the implementation of the IDEAS Project internationally (Singapore and Sicily) as well as a number of public and Catholic systems in Australia. It is funded by the systems in question and is currently being evaluated through alliances of the University of Southern Queensland, government agencies, and Nanyang University, Singapore.

PHASE ONE: YEAR ONE (1996)

Research began in disadvantaged communities in the Wide Bay Region of Queensland. The initial purpose was to illuminate the work of extraordinary teachers whose effects on their schools and communities had won the acclaim of their principals and of their colleagues. Some had addressed complex issues involving rural isolation; others had achieved success amid serious prejudice and cultural conflict in Aboriginal communities; and still others had confronted the effects of high-level unemployment in communities where generations of unemployment had been the norm. The following questions guided the Phase One research:

- What characteristics distinguish the work of classroom teachers who have achieved notable success and influence in working in socioeconomically disadvantaged schools?
- What forms of leadership, if any, are inherent in those characteristics?

The following four criteria were created to identify suitable teachers for the research:

- concrete evidence of significant contributions to an aspect of social justice in their school or school community
- high esteem in the community, particularly among socioeconomically disadvantaged individuals and groups
- colleagues' recognition of their influence on school decision making
- a high level of school-based responsibility accorded by colleagues and the school administration

Fifteen school-based educators were identified through these criteria. All agreed to participate in the project on the understanding that their involvement would afford them meaningful professional development.

Two distinct outcomes emerged from this first phase: a preliminary Teachers as Leaders Framework, and a definition of teacher leadership.

The results of Phase One were published in Crowther and Olsen (1996) and Crowther (1996).

PHASE TWO: YEARS TWO TO FOUR (1997 TO 1999)

The two stages of Phase Two were as follows:

- further exploration and validation of the preliminary Teachers as Leaders Framework
- development of leadership materials and processes to implement the refined framework

The following three questions guided this phase of the research:

- What aspects of the preliminary Teachers as Leaders Framework appear valid?

- What changes to the preliminary framework appear necessary?
- What are the key characteristics of a validated framework?

The research was conducted in six schools in disadvantaged communities in Queensland. School administrators, system officials, and teachers in socioeconomically disadvantaged schools were invited to identify highly successful educational responses to a school-initiated reform. Innovative practices that were explored included the following:

- restructuring of a high school program to enhance student retention and vocational placements
- successful establishment of an alternate-campus educational facility for street kids
- development of a highly effective cultural-literacy program in a migrant center
- implementation of a program that involved indigenous parents in student literacy development and community problem solving

The principal research processes used during the Phase Two research were

- on-site analyses of the four case study situations, using observations, interviews, and interactional analysis techniques
- focus groups involving participants from the schools and members of the research team
- post-research analysis and synthesis of the research outcomes by the research team, including validation of these outcomes by the project participants

Data analysis conducted during Phase Two confirmed the essential features of the preliminary Teachers as Leaders Framework but also suggested two necessary adjustments. The first held clearer acknowledgment of the centrality to teacher leaders of teaching, learning, and assessment than the preliminary framework contained. The second was that the full maturation of teacher leadership required the encouragement of principals and system administrators, and this aspect should be explored fully in the next phase of the research. Parallel leadership was identified as important at this stage but not defined or conceptualized. Critical analysis of Phase One and Phase Two outcomes was completed through an international online conference convened by the Australian Council for Educational Administration in September 1999.

PHASE THREE: YEARS FOUR AND FIVE (1999–2000)

Phase Three built on Phase Two. The Innovation and Best Practice Project (IBPP) was instrumental here. A project of the Australian Commonwealth

Department of Education, Training and Youth Affairs, IBPP was directed by Professor Peter Cuttance of the University of Sydney and involved a consortium of four Australian universities: Sydney, Melbourne, Edith Cowan, and Southern Queensland. It was one of the largest educational research projects ever undertaken in Australia, involving 107 schools from all states and territories. Each school researched and reported on innovative practices designed to improve learning outcomes for students, with guidance provided by accredited external specialists—mainly, university researchers.

Nine of the 107 IBPP schools identified as having enhanced student achievement in literacy or mathematics as a result of a school based innovation were selected for specialized analysis of their leadership dynamics by the University of Southern Queensland IBPP team. The nine schools were located in three Australian States (Queensland, New South Wales, Victoria) and encompassed public, Catholic, and independent systems, as well as elementary and secondary levels.

Four questions provided the structure for the Phase Three research:

- What was the nature and extent of the measured improvement in student achievement?
- What factors were perceived by teachers and administrators as accounting for this improvement?
- What roles did individuals and groups play in bringing about the documented improvement in student achievement?
- What leadership dynamics underpinned the improvement?

Researchers, working in pairs, employed a backward mapping strategy (Padilla, Trevino, Gonzalez, & Trevino, 1996) in Phase Three. Student achievement data in a key learning area (literacy or mathematics) were scrutinized for empirical validity. Brief summaries of the findings from two of the case study schools, relative to Research Questions 1, 2, and 3, are contained in Table B.1. Research Question 4 was explored through focus groups involving members of the participating school teams.

As a result of Phase Three research, the concept of parallel leadership was clarified and confirmed. The link between parallel leadership and school capacity building was also explored. Additionally, conceptual links between parallel leadership and enhanced outcomes were established. These are captured in Chapter 3. External validation of Phase Three outcomes was then undertaken through face-to-face discussion with a range of educational groups in Michigan. A summary of the Michigan findings is contained in Appendix C.

Upon completion of the Phase Three research, further analysis was undertaken surrounding the supportive efforts of four of the case study

Table B.1   Research Schools: A Summary of Outcomes and Factors Perceived as Important in Contributing to Successful Innovation in Two IBPP Schools

Elements	West Town High School
Outcomes	• Improved basic math as well as applied-mathematics skills in Grade 8. • Improved parent and student attitudes toward the school. • Enhanced school image in the community.
Strategic Foundations	• Initiated by mathematics department head to improve student achievement and nurture love of math. • Principal supported on basis of consistency with school vision.
Cohesive Community	• Strong alignment between principal, department head, and teacher/coordinator. • Powerful parent and student support. • Labor relations (industrial) issues caused some teacher concern.
Infrastructural Design	• Movable partitions replaced fixed walls. School day extended. • Supportive math curriculum developed for underachieving, disadvantaged students.
Schoolwide Teaching and Learning	• Emphasis on real-life math applications. • Specialist community resource persons brought into the school. • Enhanced student engagement through small group activities. • On-the-spot access to teacher consultations.
Professional Support	• Large budget for professional development. Special program funding accessed. • Principal and senior management supported the initiative.
Synthesis	• This project was distinguished by the initiative of the department head, principal, and teacher in challenging labor relations (industrial) circumstances. • Vision based in department head's and teacher's love of mathematics. Initiative implemented through radical modifications to time, space, and teaching strategies. • Abandoned temporarily with changes in administration and time-tabling limitations.

(Continued)

Table B.1   (Continued)

Elements	Sunbeach High School
Outcomes	• Improved literacy skills, particularly in years 1 and 4 (tested at Grade 1, 4, 7). Improved student attitudes, particularly in Grade 4. • Schoolwide adoption of the literacy program substantiated by Grade 4 success. • Improved public image of education.
Strategic Foundations	• Initiated by learning support teacher inspired by eye-opening professional development experience. • Strong principal and district director facilitation throughout. • School vision modified in response to success of innovation.
Cohesive Community	• Schoolwide workshops implemented by two teachers with principal's encouragement. • Strong parent support and involvement.
Infrastructural Design	• Staged trial used to implement and test effects. Flexible school mechanisms facilitated implementation.
Schoolwide Teaching and Learning	• Focus on metacognitive approach to literacy. Explicit phoneme/grapheme instruction emphasized.
Professional Support	• Teacher-initiated special funding. • School-based funding of professional development. • Links established with other schools for professional development.
Synthesis	• Derived from energy and conviction of a teacher. • Consistency with school vision, and support of principal, important factors. • Program not so consistently successful in other local schools, pointing to importance of particularistic factors at Sunbeach.

principals. Through individual interviews, we inquired into their roles in nurturing teacher leadership initiatives.

The following four aspects of their work were explored:

• the principals' conception of educational leadership
• the distinction between principal leadership and teacher leadership

- the strategies and activities used to encourage, nurture, and develop teacher leadership
- the perceived outcomes of teacher leadership

From this inquiry, the research team formulated seven challenges for the principal in nurturing teacher leadership. These are recounted in Chapter 4. The results of the Phase Three research are published in Crowther, Hann, and McMaster (2001) and in Cuttance (2001).

Limitations

Our Phase Three research had two important limitations. First, it was conducted in schools where successful reform seemed to be widely accepted as achievable. Therefore, leadership concepts and processes that emerged from the research might not have similar application in schools with a history of apathy or failed reform. Second, most of the Phase Three case studies that were integral to the development of the concept of parallel leadership featured reforms that were not initiated as whole-school reform but, rather, were developed from smaller, classroom-based innovations. Therefore all the dynamics of whole-school reform might not have been taken into account in our conceptualization of leadership for successful school reform. In the interpretation of conclusions emanating from the research, these important limitations should be considered. Because of them, we regarded our Phase Three research as incomplete and sought ways to extend it through a Phase Four R&D initiative.

PHASE FOUR: YEARS SIX, SEVEN, AND EIGHT (2002–2004)

In 2002, under the auspices of the Australian Research Council, the implications of parallel leadership for classroom practice were explored by a University of Southern Queensland team. It was found that, when individual teachers construct their pedagogical profiles in the context of an agreed school vision and values, and when they engage in development and implementation of schoolwide pedagogical principles, they begin to see themselves as "three-dimensional professionals." The framework for three-dimensional pedagogy that emerged from this research is presented in Figure 2.2.

Also in 2002, a national trial of the IDEAS Project was undertaken by the Australian Department of Education, Science and Training (DEST) to assess the viability of IDEAS as an approach to school revitalization. The trial and evaluation were managed by Associate Professor Paul Chesterton and Professor Patrick Duignan of Australian Catholic University. The trial was conducted in three Australian states, and involved both state and Catholic schools. The evaluation focused on

- the impact of the implementation of IDEAS on teacher morale and professionalism
- the impact of the implementation of IDEAS on student outcomes
- the impact of the implementation of IDEAS on the development of school-based leadership concepts and processes

The evaluation report that was presented to the Australian Government was entitled *Evaluation of the National Trial of the IDEAS Project*, by Paul Chesterton and Patrick Duignan (Commonwealth Department of Education, Science and Training, 2004). The Introduction to the report noted the key place in the successful school-based implementation of the IDEAS Project of the concepts of teacher leadership and parallel leadership. Of the various conclusions that were reached by Chesterton and Duignan, the following were identified as particularly relevant to the ongoing development of teacher leadership and parallel leadership:

> The successful implementation of IDEAS in schools in the trial schools required a considerable shift in the leadership paradigm of many of these schools. Principals, in particular, had to "let go" of traditional views of power and position in relation to their teachers. . . . Parallel leadership was developing steadily in ten of the twelve schools, and was flourishing in four of the schools. In these latter schools, it was believed there was no going back, even if a new principal with more traditional views of leadership were to be appointed to the school. (p. vi)

> The implementation of IDEAS was found to have positive impacts on teachers in the trialing schools, in terms of promoting pedagogical reflection and discussion, increasing collaboration, increasing involvement in decision making, improvements in teacher morale, and some early beginnings to changes in teacher practices. . . . It (IDEAS) promotes a type of shared leadership that is suited to the professional needs of teachers and school leaders who are expected to produce graduates to serve the emerging knowledge society of the 21st century. (pp. 67–68)

These conclusions from one of the most authoritative, large scale research-based evaluations that is known to have been conducted into the dynamics of shared leadership have been very influential in shaping the recent thinking of the researchers and authors of this book.

PHASE FIVE: YEARS NINE, TEN, AND CONTINUING (2005–ONGOING)

The most recent research and development into teacher leadership that has involved the authors, and that has been used in preparation of the second edition of *Developing Teacher Leaders*, encompassed cross-cultural analyses of parallel leadership and teacher leadership, as well as large scale Australian implementation of the IDEAS Project.

Based on comprehensive trials in Singapore, conducted by Nanyang University researchers under the auspices of the Singapore Ministry for Education, it has been concluded that both concepts (teacher leadership and parallel leadership) have significant appeal to Singaporean educators and have a degree of transferable meaning from American/Australian/British theories of leadership. However, significant cultural mores associated with Singaporean society and nationhood must be allowed for if the concepts are to achieve practical, cross-cultural meaning (Ng & Chew, in press). Similar conclusions are emerging from the trialing of parallel leadership in a Sicilian high school context.

The most recent (2007) research that is drawn upon in this edition of *Developing Teacher Leaders* has involved implementation of the IDEAS Project in new clusters of schools in Australian states and Catholic systems. In one cluster, most of the schools had been designated by system supervisors as "At Risk" (or "Unsatisfactory") at the outset of the three-year period of revitalization (2004–07). In this particular instance, systemically-generated data that were assembled by the schools in question at the end of 2006 provide clear evidence of possible impacts on school outcomes of a process of revitalization that emphasizes parallel leadership.

Figure B.1 contains a synthesised adaptation of the database relating to the sample of schools (one of which is featured in Snapshot Three). It reveals teachers' perceptions of their heightened satisfaction, from 2004–06, with the new approach to leadership (leadership functions 1–5). It also reveals associated improvements (some measured at 0.01 level of significance) in a range of school variables relating to both teachers and students (school outcomes 6–11). Interestingly, no change took place in teachers' perceptions of "work demands" during the period of the school's participation in the revitalization initiative (school outcome 12). While the research associated with this cluster of schools is ongoing, and currently incorporates consideration of 2007 school data and extensive case study analysis, it has been tentatively concluded that successful school revitalization in very challenging contexts is possible, particularly if parallel leadership is used as a foundational strategy.

Figure B.1   Factors Impacting Upon School Improvement, 2004–2006, in a Cluster of "At Risk" Schools

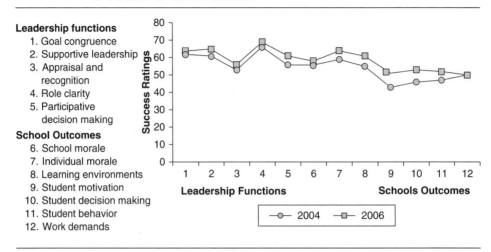

Leadership functions
 1. Goal congruence
 2. Supportive leadership
 3. Appraisal and recognition
 4. Role clarity
 5. Participative decision making
School Outcomes
 6. School morale
 7. Individual morale
 8. Learning environments
 9. Student motivation
10. Student decision making
11. Student behavior
12. Work demands

SOURCE: Created by Frank Crowther from IDEAS Project research data. Printed with Frank Crowther's permission.

Research-based publications prepared by University of Southern Queensland staff and that make use of data collected under the projects outlined above are the following:

Andrews, D., Conway, J., Dawson, M., Lewis, M., McMaster, J., Morgan, A., & Starr, H. (2004). *School revitalization the IDEAS way.* ACEL Monograph, Series No 34, Australian Council for Educational Leaders, Winmalee.

Andrews, D., & Crowther, F. (2002). Parallel leadership: A clue to the contents of the "black box" of school reform. *The International Journal of Educational Management, 16* (4), 152–150.

Andrews, D., & Crowther, F. (2003). 3-Dimensional pedagogy—the image of 21st century teacher professionalism. In F. Crowther (Ed.), *Teachers as leaders in a knowledge society. Australian College of Education Yearbook* Deakin West: Australian College of Educators.

Andrews, D., & Crowther, F. (2006). Teachers as leaders in a knowledge society: Encouraging signs of a new professionalism. *Journal of School Leadership,* Special issue, *16* (5), 534–549.

Andrews, D., & Lewis, M. (2002). The experiences of a professional community: Teachers developing a new image of themselves and their workplace. *Educational Research, 44* (3), 237–254.

Andrews, D., & Lewis, M. (2004). Building sustainable futures. *Improving Schools, 7* (2), 129–150.

Andrews, D., & Lewis, M. (2004). Parallel leadership for 21st century schools. *Access, 18* (4), 5–8.

Andrews, D., & Lewis, M. (2007). Transforming practice from within: The power of professional learning communities. In L. Stoll and K. Seashore Lewis (Eds.), *Professional learning communities: Divergence, details and difficulties.* McGraw-Hill, London.

Crowther, F. (2008). Taking the lead. *Taking the Lead, 15* (1), 3-6.

Lewis, M. (2006). It's a different place now: Teacher leadership and pedagogical change at Newlyn Public School. *Leading and Managing, 12* (1), 107–120.

Lewis, M., & Andrews, D. (2007). The dance of influence: Professional relationships evolve as teachers and administrators engage in wholeschool renewal. *Leading and Managing, 13* (1), 91–107.

Doctoral dissertations that have been completed at the University of Southern Queensland into the dynamics of the IDEAS project are the following:

Atwell, Alison (2007). The impact of a leadership training program on school-based management and school community action in Praya Barat Daya, Lombok, Indonesia.

Conway, Joan (2008). Collective intelligence in schools: An exploration of teacher engagement in the making of new pedagogical meaning.

Fisher, Jennifer (2008). Teacher leadership and organisational capacity: a teacher leader's experience in a p-12 school.

Lewis, Marian (2003). The dynamics, implications, and effects of knowledge generation in professional learning communities: Three case studies.

Morgan, Allan (2008). The principal in a process of school revitalization: A metastrategic role.

Perrin, Cheryl (2005). Nurses as leaders: The nurse-identified attributes of effective clinical nursing leadership.

SOURCE: Compiled by Frank Crowther and printed with Frank Crowther's permission.

Appendix C

A Report on the Michigan Review

With the new millennium just underway, the authors organized a series of focus groups and interviews in Michigan to subject the ideas in the first edition of this book to the scrutiny of teachers, professors of teacher education and educational administration, and other higher education leaders. Four focus groups were held, one with faculty and graduate students at Michigan State University College of Education; a second with teachers and staff from the Michigan Education Association; a third with faculty and administrators from several institutions serving the educational needs of Northern Lower Michigan; and a final one with teachers at Novi, in Southeast Michigan, associated with the Galileo Project (the purpose of which is to create an ongoing forum for teacher leaders to discuss issues of common concern).

These focus groups and interviews pointed to the promise and the problems in the path of teacher leadership. We recount both here. First, the promise is depicted in an interview with the Michigan Teacher of the Year 2000, a person who immediately resonated with the ideas in this book, seeing herself as a teacher leader and perceiving the potential in many of her colleagues. Following the interview report is a rendering of a set of challenging issues that were raised in the several focus groups held in mid 2000.

THE PROMISE: A PERSPECTIVE ON TEACHER LEADERSHIP FROM A TEACHER LEADER

Margaret Holtschlag, Michigan Teacher of the Year 2000, and one of four finalists for the U.S. Teacher of the Year award, is one of those thousands of classroom teachers about whom this book is written: not just an outstanding teacher, an innovative curriculum designer, and a mentor of professional colleagues, but also a true leader in her own right. Here, Margaret discussed with Steve Kaagan (in East Lansing, Michigan, May

2000) the concept of teacher leadership, the Teachers as Leaders Framework in particular, and its relevance to her work.

Kaagan: What do teachers who want to continue their classroom teaching do to lead? How does teacher leadership differ from administrator leadership?

Holtschlag: Teacher leadership starts with a teacher who gets an idea, an idea related to student learning or to making teaching more vibrant. Teacher leadership activities are essentially intrinsic, born of a need to bring all that we can to our children. With an idea in hand, be it about writing or something else, a teacher goes to another teacher or group of teachers and gets them excited about working on the idea. Then a core of people come together to do something significant. School improvement teams (diverse groups mandated by state law to improve the school's performance) can be places where teacher leadership thrives. Yet these teams operate, for the most part, in a top-down way. Their work originates with the principal, who pulls together a group to work on schoolwide problems. In some, but not all, instances, the agenda of these teams is school improvement. But in almost all instances, the agenda matches what administrators had in mind in the first place. The origins were not teachers' views of what needs to be done to improve teaching and learning.

Kaagan: You have seen our tentative Framework for Teacher Leadership, with its six elements (publicly articulates a better view of the world, generates authenticity in teaching, fosters sincerity and trust, confronts structural barriers, builds networks of support, and nurtures a culture of success). Is the framework an accurate rendering of what teacher leadership is all about?

Holtschlag: I was talking with another state teacher of the year recently who was questioning her role and place as a teacher, and I referred to the framework as a means of offering her validation. I was saying, in effect, it's okay to be a teacher leader; go ahead and allow yourself; this is you. She was very grateful. Any one of the elements in the framework is a fine quality. "Publicly articulates a better view of the world" conveys a really positive outlook. I am fortunate in my school, because the attitude among the staff is quite positive. However, one could focus in on a quality like "confronts structural barriers" and say that a teacher who exhibits this capacity is a troublemaker. I don't believe that to be so, but it is one element that some may perceive as two-edged. Another way to respond to your question is to ask, what about a teacher who doesn't show one of the qualities, but shows the other five—for example, the teacher who "fosters sincerity and trust" but does not "generate authenticity in teaching"? Under these circumstances, a teacher would be emitting positive affect but without a foundation in teaching behind it. In the absence of knowing what really works for effective teaching and learning, then all the fostering of sincerity and trust might be empty. On the other hand, if a teacher knows what makes something effective for our children, but does not have communication skills or social rapport, this, too, would be a serious shortfall. So, in the final analysis, I come to the conclusion that all six are essential. When we discussed the framework at the Education Association meeting a few weeks ago, the focus was on the difficulty for many of overcoming structural barriers. From my point of view, the exercise involved with this element is to keep trying until one gets to *yes*. Yet I also believe that if administrators are not open to teacher initiative, teacher leadership will inevitably stay small. I worked in a district once where the principal said, "What you're doing is good, but couldn't you put the desks back into rows?" Another colleague and I were doing some really interesting things with our kids, but under these circumstances, couldn't take it very far. So I finally had to make a decision to move on to another school.

Kaagan: If teacher leadership were an accepted part of a school's functioning, how would the relationship between teachers and administrators shift?

Holtschlag: You have to understand that in many instances, teacher leadership involves a teacher's presenting an idea whose worth has not been proven yet. So, in all likelihood, the administrator does not see the reason for pursuing the idea. The basic shift in the relationship between teachers and administrators, where teacher leadership is present, is that administrators exhibit faith in the professionalism of the teachers to pursue their ideas. They trust that it's going to be okay. Power plays are not part of this shift in relationship. I noted that power was not explicitly mentioned in the framework. Yes, there probably would be a power shift in the relationship between teachers and administrators if teachers were leading. But power shift has too much of a negative connotation. I prefer to say that there would be more of a shared responsibility and mutual honoring for each of the people involved, more like we are all working together, more of a partnership. I recognize that this idea of shared responsibility does not fit the traditional administrative model. A parallel here is what has happened with the old notion that the teachers know all, and the children come to them as empty vessels. That's passed by the wayside. So, too, should the idea that the administrator knows all. Teachers, in fact, come to the table with ideas and decision-making skills of their own.

Kaagan: If teacher leadership were an accepted part of a school's functioning, how would the public respect afforded teachers be affected?

Holtschlag: Oh man, wouldn't that be cool? There would not only be a quite rapid increase in public respect for teachers and for the profession, there would be a lot more community participation in what's going on in the school. Take, for example, a teacher at my school who's doing something very positive with literacy. If she were nurtured in that work and given the space to do that work, there would be a ripple effect, and parents and community would be drawn in to build on the positive effects. After all, don't most people want to become involved with people who are putting into action good ideas? You want to learn from them and contribute to them. I believe that communities everywhere want to be a greater part of what's going on in schools. And this extends beyond the current drives for accountability. Teacher leadership, in effect, could be a powerful way of shaping and making real a shared vision for student learning in the school, between the school staff and the community.

Kaagan: If teacher leadership were an accepted part of a school's functioning, what would be the effect on student outcomes?

Holtschlag: Huge! With the situation of community members who do not have any buy-in to what is going on in the school, there is a lack of respect, and this lack of respect is transmitted to our children. Under these circumstances, the school is functioning in an isolated way. If, on the other hand, there is a push by the school to engage the community in the work of the school; if teachers take, and are encouraged to take, initiatives that do invite the community in, in integral ways the children get the message that their learning is important, and they react accordingly.

Kaagan: Anything I should have asked and didn't?

Holtschlag: Just a couple of final observations. It's not easy to bring lots of people into the process. Teacher leadership takes tons of time—some of it wasted. And one makes a lot of mistakes along the way. I tend to go from one thing to another, to keep on adding things to bring to my teaching. For example, I paired with another teacher once and developed a calendar for kids that had events and activities that matched with key dates in their lives: for example, a set of special activities on one's birthday. I did this originally as a gift. But the idea caught on and was published several years in a row. Then I moved on to technology applications, environmental education, then social and civic education. In each case, I have resisted being typecast. Yet I have second-guessed myself often as to whether the approach I was taking to building myself as a professional was the right one. That day a few weeks ago, at the Education Association, when we discussed teacher leadership, was a day of affirmation. It really is okay, the approach I have taken, to go from one emphasis to another. You didn't know that the ideas presented at the meeting had that effect, did you?

KEY POINTS FROM THE FOCUS GROUPS

At Michigan State University College of Education:

- Teacher leadership is one of a number of roles. Others include teacher as researcher, teacher as instructional expert, teacher as professional learner, and teacher as coordinator of school and community activities. The Teacher as Leaders Framework bears a striking resemblance to models of political efficacy. As such, it could be seen as grounded in principles of liberal democracy, which means relevance in indigenous communities will be a continuing challenge.
- The Framework can also be viewed as a model for excellence in the teaching profession. The concept of structural barriers, that is, those standing in the way of teacher leadership, should be viewed as incorporating technical, hierarchical, resource, and cultural considerations.
- The current global preoccupation with standardization of curriculum and accountability through testing may negatively affect the professional capacity to nurture teacher leadership.
- The concept of teacher leadership implies the presence of leaders and followers in the teaching profession. Formalizing teacher leadership could lead to fragmentation in the profession and in schools.

At the Michigan Education Association:

- The status of the teaching profession is of grave concern in Michigan.
- The absence of a clear concept of teacher leadership fosters adversarial relationships between principals and teacher leaders, with the latter being seen, as a result, as troublemakers.
- Trail blazing is stressful, time consuming, and difficult—teacher leaders can become easily discouraged.
- Principals can easily speak the language of shared leadership but hang onto the status quo.
- People who are accustomed to having decisions made for them may have difficulty accepting the responsibilities that go with teacher leadership—as a consequence, they may too easily relinquish their rights.
- When teacher leaders demand resources, authority figures can feel threatened and so can some teacher colleagues, since resources are a scarce condition that could inhibit the flowering of teacher leadership.
- The growing involvement of parents in schools creates extra demands from parents, which may be constraining for teacher leaders.
- Teachers everywhere lack a forum for exchanging leadership stories.
- Mentoring of young teachers provides a window of opportunity to develop and model teacher leadership concepts. The concept of mentoring needs to be explored in relation to teacher leadership.
- The networking aspect of the Teachers as Leaders Framework can be viewed in terms of workplace sociability—teacher leaders using social activity as a means of developing networks of support, communication channels, articulation of ideas, strategies for political influence, community building, and so forth. This is particularly significant because of the social needs of young professionals.
- Acceptance of the concept of teacher leadership leads naturally to the question of student leadership.
- Teacher leadership is real in Michigan schools, but it is not conceptualized and not formal.
- The concept of parallel leadership needs to be extended and its links to school improvement clarified.

At Northern Michigan College in Traverse City:

- Parallel leadership is an attractive concept because it is not adversarial.
- Most schools contain pockets of greatness, but this does not necessarily enhance the status of the profession. If administrators do not offer recognition, the profession will receive little from the public. Furthermore, pockets of greatness usually imply inadequacies somewhere else, and this could cause divisiveness.

- The training of college professors contradicts principles of teacher leadership. University scholarship encourages questioning and cynicism and, therefore, discourages a culture of success. Universities can douse the flame of leadership when they should be igniting it.
- If teacher leadership is essentially a manifestation of interactivity, what are the implications for isolated teachers and part-time academics?
- The relevance of the newer technologies to the Teachers as Leaders Framework needs clarification.
- Teacher leaders who run into too many barriers either give up or leave the profession. Often these people become known as whiners, cynics, outsiders, or the disaffected. The concept of negative leadership may sometimes be brought about by the denial of authentic leadership opportunities.
- University leadership programs must change drastically. They need to be based on the principle of inclusivity (e.g., teacher leadership), and to encompass the three processes of organizational revitalization: school-wide learning; culture building; and shared approaches to pedagogy.
- In the United States, at the moment, there is a perception in some quarters that the teaching profession is being subsumed in national politics centering on accountability, testing, and litigation.
- Leadership development needs to be approached on many fronts:
  o Revamp university courses and professional training.
  o Develop leadership around a school issue or need and through on-the-job, experiential learning.
  o Cut across processes of organizational renewal, including school-wide learning, culture building, and shared approaches to teaching, learning, and assessment.

At Novi in Southeast Michigan:

- The development of teacher leadership in isolation from the principal's role, and without involvement in processes for holistic school improvement, may not be very purposeful.
- Suggestions for teacher leadership development:
  o Mentoring should encompass demonstrations of pedagogy in real-life situations.
  o Teacher leaders should engage in action that shows that their work is focused on ideals, not on operations.
  o Teacher leadership cannot be separated from communication processes that bring parents into the educative process.
  o There is a need to understand significant negatives, such as complaining teachers, assessment paranoia, and failing schools.
- Teacher leadership may be easier to practice in situations of disadvantage than in situations of abundance, because those with power in well-endowed schools want to maintain things as they are.
- Teacher leaders can use unions and professional associations and networks to promote the professionalism of teachers.

References

Abbott, W. (1966). *The documents of Vatican II.* New York: America Press.

Andersen Consulting Institute for Strategic Change. (1999). *The evolving role of executive leadership.* New York: Author.

Andrews, D., & Crowther, F. (2003). 3-Dimensional Pedagogy: The image of 21st century teacher professionalism. In F. Crowther (Ed.), *Australian College of Education Yearbook, 2003. Teachers as leaders in a knowledge society* (pp. 95–111). Deakin West, Australia: Australian College of Education.

Andrews, D., & Crowther, F. (2006). Teachers as leaders in a knowledge society. *Journal of School Leadership, 16* (5), 534–549.

Apple, M. W. (1992). *Teachers and texts: A political economy of class and gender relations in education.* New York: Routledge.

Argyris, C. (1993). *On organizational learning.* Cambridge, MA: Blackwell Business.

Argyris, C., & Schon, D. (1979). *Organizational learning: A theory of action perspectives.* Cambridge, MA: Addison-Wesley.

Argyris, C., & Schon, D. (1996). *Organizational learning II: Theory, method and practice.* Cambridge, MA: Addison-Wesley.

Armour, S. (2005, November 6). Generation Y. They've arrived at work with a new attitude. *USA Today.*

Avolio, B. J., & Bass, B. (1988). Transformational leadership, charisma and beyond. In J. G. Hunt, B. Baliga, H. Dachler, & C. Schriesheim (Eds.), *Emerging leadership vistas* (29–49). Lanham, MD: Lexington Books.

Barth, R. (2006). Foreward in G. Moller & A. Pankake, *Lead with me. A principal's guide to teacher leadership.* Poughkeepsie, NY: Eye on Education Inc.

Bates, R. (1983). *Educational administration and the management of knowledge.* Waurn Ponds, Victoria, Australia: Deakin Press.

Bates, R. (1992, July). *Leadership and school culture.* Paper presented at the Interuniversity Congress of the Organization of Teaching Faculty of Philosophy and Science, Seville, Spain.

Beare, H. (2001). *Creating the future school: Student outcomes and the reform of education.* London: Routledge/Falmer.

Beatty, B. (2000). The emotions of educational leadership: Breaking the silence. *International Journal of Leadership in Education, 3* (4), 331–358.

Bennis, W. (1999). The leadership advantage. *Leader to Leader, 12,* 18–23.

Blackmore, J. (1996). Doing "emotional labor" in the education market place: Stories from the field of women in management. *Discourse: Studies in the Cultural Politics of Education, 17* (3), 337–349.

Bolman, L., & Deal, T. (1994). Looking for leadership: Another search party's report. *Educational Administration Quarterly, 30* (1), 77–96.

Boomer, G. (1985). A celebration of teaching. *Australian Teachers, 11*, 13–20.

Bryk, A., & Schneider, B. (1996). *Social trust: A moral resource for school improvement.* Chicago: University of Chicago, Center for School Improvement.

Bryk, A., & Schneider, B. (2002). *Trust in schools: A core resource for improvement.* New York: Russell Sage.

Caldwell, B. (1992). The principal as leader of the self-managing school in Australia. *Journal of Educational Administration, 30* (3), 6–19.

Carnegie Forum on Education and the Economy. (1986). *A nation prepared: Teachers find the 21st century: The report on the Task Force on Teaching as a Profession.* New York: Author.

Chesterton, P., & Duignan, P. (2004). *Evaluation of the National Trial of the IDEAS Project.* Canberra: Commonwealth of Australia Department of Education, Science & Training.

Clark, K. E., & Clark, M. B. (1994). *Choosing to lead.* Charlotte, NC: Irongate Press.

Coleman, J. S. (1966). *Equality of educational opportunity.* Washington, DC: Government Printing Office.

Congregation for Catholic Education. (1998). *The Catholic school on the threshold of the third millennium.* Homebush, Australia: St. Paul Publications.

Conley, S., & Muncey, D. (1999). Teachers talk about teaming and leadership in their work. *Theory Into Practice, 38* (1), 46–55.

Cowan, D. (2006). Creating learning communities in low performing sites: A systemic approach to alignment *Journal of School Leadership, 16* (5), 596–610.

Crowther, F. (1996). Teacher leadership: Explorations in theory and practice. *Leading and Managing, 2* (4), 304–321.

Crowther, F. (2003, April). *Smart state, clever country, schools and leadership.* Paper presented to the Inaugural Professional Lecture, University of Southern Queensland, Toowoomba, Australia.

Crowther, F., Andrews, D., Dawson, M., & Lewis, M. (2001). *IDEAS Facilitation Folder.* Brisbane, Australia: Queensland Department of Education.

Crowther, F., Hann, L., & McMaster, J. (2001). Leadership. In P. Cuttance, *School innovation: Pathway to the knowledge society.* Canberra, Australia: Australian Commonwealth Department of Education, Training and Youth Affairs.

Crowther, F., & Olsen, P. (1996). *Teachers as leaders: An exploration of success stories in socio-economically disadvantaged communities.* Brisbane, Australia: Department of Education.

Cuttance, P. (2001). *School innovation: Pathway to the knowledge society.* Canberra, Australia: Australian Commonwealth Department of Education, Training and Youth Affairs.

Darling-Hammond, L. (1997). *The right to learn: A blueprint for creating schools that work.* San Francisco: Jossey-Bass.

Day, C. (2000). Effective leadership and reflective practice *Reflective Practice, 1* (1), 113–127.

Day, C., & Bakioglu, A. (1996). Development and disenchantment in the professional lives of head teachers. In I. Goodson & A. Hargreaves (Eds.), *Teachers' professional lives* (205–227). New York: Falmer.

De Pree, M. (1997). *Leading without power: Finding hope in serving community.* San Francisco: Jossey-Bass.

Dewey, J. (1916). *Democracy in education*. New York: MacMillan.

Dinham, S., & Scott, C. (1997). *The teacher 2000 project: A study of teacher motivation and health*. New South Wales, Australia: University of Western Sydney-Nepean.

Drucker, P. (1946). *Concept of the organization* (Revised ed., 1972). New York: John Day Co.

Drucker, P. (1994). The age of social transformation. *Atlantic Monthly, 274* (5), 53–80.

Dunbar, R., & Starbuck, W. (2006). Learning to design organisations and learning from designing them. *Organisation Science, 17* (2), 171–178.

Duignan, P., & Macpherson, R. J. S. (1992). Creating new knowledge about educative leadership. In P. Duignan & R. J. S. Macpherson (Eds.), *Educative leadership: A practical theory for new administrators and managers* (1–17). Lewes, Australia: Falmer.

Durrant, J. (2004). Teachers leading change: Frameworks and key ingredients for school improvement. *Leading & Managing, 10* (2), 10–29.

Editorial. (2008, January 27). *The Sunday Mail.*

Education Commission of the States Task Force on Education for Economic Growth. (1983). *Action for excellence*. Denver, CO: Author.

Elmore, R. (2000). *Building a new structure for school improvement*. Washington, DC: The Albert Shanker Institute.

Firestone, W., Mangin, M., Martinez, C., & Polowsky, T. (2005). Leading coherent professional development: A comparison of three districts. *Educational Administration Quarterly, 41* (3), 413–448.

Fleming, G. L., & Leo, T. (2000, April). *The role of trust building in its relation to teacher efficacy*. Paper presented at the Symposium at the American Educational Research Association 2000, New Orleans, LA.

Flynn, M. (1979). *Catholic schools and the communication of faith*. Homebush, Australia: St. Paul Publications.

Forster, E. (1997). Teacher leadership: Professional right and responsibility. *Action in Teacher Education, 19* (3), 82–94.

Frost, D. (2006). The concept of "agency" in leadership for learning. *Leading & Managing, 12* (2), 19–28.

Fullan, M. (2005). *Leadership and sustainability: System thinking in action*. Thousand Oaks, CA: Corwin Press.

Glickman, C. (1998). Educational leadership for democratic purpose: What do we mean? *International Journal of Leadership in Education, 1* (1), 47–53.

Goldberg, M. (2000). Leadership for change: An interview with John Goodlad. *Phi Delta Kappan*, September, 82–85.

Goleman, D. (1998). What makes a leader? *Harvard Business Review, 776* (6), 93–103.

Goleman, D., Boyantzis, R., & McKee, A. (2002). *Primal leadership: Realizing the power of emotional intelligence*. Boston: Harvard Business School Press.

Goold, M., & Cambell, A. (2002). Do you have a Well-Designed organisation? *Harvard Business Review*, March, 117–124.

Gronn, P. (1999). *The making of educational leaders*. Management and Leadership in Education Series. London: Cassell.

Gronn, P. (2003). *The new work of educational leaders: Changing leadership practices in an era of school reform*. London: Paul Chapman.

Gutierrez, K., Rymes, B., & Larson, J. (1995). Script, counterscript, and underlife in the classroom: James Brown versus Brown and the Board of Education. *Harvard Educational Review, 65* (3), 445–471.

Hallinger, P. (2003). Leading educational change: Reflections on the practice of instructional and transformational leadership. *Cambridge Journal of Education, 33* (3), 329–351.

Hallinger, P., & Heck, R. (1996). Reassessing the principal's role in school effectiveness: A review of empirical research, 1980–1995. *Education Administration Quarterly, 32* (1), 5–45.

Hambrick, D. C. (1989). Guest editor's introduction: Putting top managers back in the strategy picture. *Journal of Strategic Management,* Special Issue, Summer, 5–15.

Handy, C. (1994). *The empty raincoat: Making sense of the future.* London: Hutchinson Press.

Handy, C. (1996). The new language of organizing and its implications for leaders. In F. Hesselbein, M. Goldsmith, & R. Beckhard (Eds.), *The leader of the future* (3–10). San Francisco: Jossey-Bass.

Hargreaves, A. (1994). Changing work cultures of teaching. In F. Crowther & B. Caldwell (Eds.), *The workplace in education: Australian Perspectives.* Australian Council Educational Administration Yearbook. Sydney: Edward Arnold.

Hargreaves, A. (2003). *Teaching in the knowledge society: Education in the age of insecurity.* New York: Russell Sage.

Hargreaves, A., Earl, L., Moore, S., & Manning, S. (2001). *Learning to change: Teaching beyond subjects and standards.* San Francisco: Jossey Bass/Wiley.

Hargreaves, A., & Fink, D. (2000). Three dimensions of educational reform. *Educational Leadership, 57* (7), 30–34.

Hargreaves, A., & Fink, D. (2006). *Sustainable leadership.* San Francisco: John Wiley & Sons.

Hargreaves, A., & Goodson, I. (1996). Teachers' professional lives: Aspirations and actualities. In I. Goodson & A. Hargreaves (Eds.), *Teachers' professional lives* (1–27). New York: Falmer.

Hargreaves, D. (2001). A capital theory of school effectiveness and improvement. *British Educational Research Journal, 27* (4), 487–503.

Harris, A. (2004). Teacher leadership and distributed leadership. *Leading & Managing, 10* (2), 1–9.

Heenan, D., & Bennis, W. (1999). *Co-leaders: The power of great partnerships.* New York: Wiley.

Heifetz, R., & Laurie, D. (1997). The work of leadership. *Harvard Business Review, 75* (1), 124–134.

Hersey, P., & Blanchard, K. (1969). Life-cycle theory of leadership. *Training and Development Journal, 23,* 26–34.

Hipp, K. (2004). Teacher leadership: Illustrating practices reflective of schools engaged in purposeful efforts to create and sustain learning communities. *Leading and Managing, 10* (2), 54–69.

Hitt, M., & Ireland, R. (2002). The essence of strategic leadership: Managing human and social capital. *The Journal of Leadership and Organisational Studies, 9* (1), 3–14.

Hogan, R., Raza, S., & Driskell, J. (1988). Personality, team performance and organisational context. In P. Whitney & R. B. Oschman (Eds.), *Psychology and Productivity.* New York: Plenum.

Holmes Group. (1986). *Tomorrow's teachers: A Report of the Holmes Group.* East Lansing, MI: Author.

Hooijberg, R., & Di Tomaso, N. (1996). Leadership in and of demographically diverse organisations. *Leadership Quarterly, 7* (1), 1–9.

Hord, S. (1997). *Professional learning communities: Community of continuous inquiry and improvement.* Austin, TX: Southwest Educational Development Laboratory.

Hord, S. (2003). Foreword: Why communities of continuous learners? In J. B. Huffman & K. K. Hipp (Eds.), *Reculturing schools as professional learning communities* (vii-xi). Lanham, MD: Scarecrow Press.

Hord, S. (2004). Introduction. In S. M. Hord (Ed.), *Learning together, leading together: Changing schools through professional learning communities* (pp. 1–4). New York: Teachers College Press.

House, R. (1971). A path-goal theory of leadership. *Administrative Science Quarterly, 16,* 321–328.

Hoy, W. K., & Miskel, C. G. (1991). *Educational administration: Theory, research and practice* (4th ed.). New York: McGraw-Hill.

Hoy, W. K., & Smith, P. (2007). Influence: A key to successful leadership. *International Journal of Educational Management, 21* (2), 158–170.

Hoy, W. K., & Sweetland, S. (2001). Designing better schools: The meaning and measure of enabling school structures. *Educational Administration Quarterly, 37* (3), 296–321.

Ingvarson, L., & Chadbourne, R. (1996). The rise and fall of the advanced skills teacher Australia. *Leading and Managing, 2* (1), 49–69.

Johansson, O. (2004). Introduction. Democracy and leadership—or training for democratic leadership. *Journal of Educational Administration, 42* (6), 620–624.

Kaagan, S. (1999). *Leadership games: Experiential learning for organizational development.* Thousand Oaks, CA: Sage.

Kahn, R. (1956). The prediction of productivity. *Journal of Social Issues, 12,* 41–49.

Kanter, R. (1994). Collaborative advantage: The art of alliances. *Harvard Business Review, 72* (4), 96–108.

Karpinsky, C., & Lugg, C. (2006). Social justice and educational administration: Mutually exclusive? *Journal of Educational Administration, 44* (3), 277–292.

Katyal, K., & Evers, R. (2004). Student learning, engagement with schools, and teacher leadership: Case studies in Hong Kong. *Leading & Managing, 10* (2), 41–53.

Katz, D., & Kahn, R. I. (1966). *The social psychology of organizations.* New York: Wiley.

Katzenmeyer, M., & Moller, G. (1996). *Awakening the sleeping giant: Leadership development for teachers.* Thousand Oaks, CA: Corwin Press.

Katzenmeyer, M., & Moller, G. (2001). *Awakening the sleeping giant: Helping teachers develop as leaders.* Thousand Oaks, CA: Corwin Press.

Kelley, C., & Finnigan, K. (2003). The effects of organisational context on teacher expectancy. *Educational Administration Quarterly, 39* (5), 603–634.

King, B., & Newmann, F. (1999). *School capacity as a goal for professional development: Mapping the terrain in low-income schools.* Paper presented at the Annual Meeting of AlERA, Montreal.

King, B., & Newmann, F. (2000). Will teacher learning advance school goals? *Phi Delta Kappan, 81* (8), 576–580.

Kofman, F., & Senge, P. (1993). Communities of commitment: The heart of learning organizations. *Organizational Dynamics, 22* (2), 4–23.

Kouzes, J., & Posner, B. (2002). *The leadership challenge.* San Fransisco: Jossey-Bass.

Lakomski, G. (1995). Leadership and learning: From transformational leadership to organizational learning. *Leading and Managing, 1* (3), 211–225.

Lambert, L. (2003). *Leadership capacity for lasting school improvement.* Alexandria, VA: Association of Supervision and Curriculum Development.

Leadership Research Institute. (2007). *IDEAS Project Manual.* Toowoomba: University of Southern Queensland.

Leithwood, K. (1994). Leadership for school restructuring. *Educational Administration Quarterly, 30* (4), 498–518.

Leithwood, K., & Jantzi, D. (1998, April). *Distributed leadership and student engagement in schools.* Paper presented at the Annual Meeting of the American Educational Research Association, San Diego, CA.

Leithwood, K., & Jantzi, D. (2000). The effects of transformational leadership on organisational conditions and student engagement. *Journal of Educational Administration, 38* (2), 112–129.

Leithwood, K.. Jantzi, D., Ryan, S., & Steinbach, R. (1997, March). *Distributed leadership in secondary schools.* Paper presented at the Annual Meeting of the American Educational Research Association, Chicago.

Leithwood, K., & Riehl, C. (2005). What do we already know about school leadership? In W. A. Firestone & C. J. Riehl (Eds.), *A new agenda: Directions for research on educational leadership.* New York: Teachers College Press.

Leppitt, N. (2006). Challenging the code of change, Part 1: Praxis does not make perfect. *Journal of Change Management, 6* (2), 121–142.

Licata, J., & Harper, G. (2001). Organisational health and robust school vision. *Educational Administration Quarterly, 37* (1), 5–26.

Lieberman, A., Saxl, E., & Miles, M. (1988). Teachers' leadership: Ideology and practice. In A. Lieberman (Ed.), *Building a professional culture in schools* (148–166). New York: Teachers College Press.

Limerick, D., Cunnington, B., & Crowther, F. (1998). *Managing the new organization: Collaboration and sustainability in the post-corporate world.* Warriewood, Australia: Business & Professional Publishing.

Lindle, J. (2004). William P. Foster's promises for educational leadership: Critical idealism in an applied field. *Educational Administration Quarterly, 40* (2) 165–175.

Little, J. W. (1995). Contested ground: The basis of teacher leadership in two restructuring high school. *Elementary School Journal, 96* (1), 47–63.

Loder, T., & Spillane, J. (2005). Is a principal still a teacher? U. S. administrators' accounts of role conflict and role discontinuity. *School Leadership and Management, 25* (3), 263–279.

Lortie, D. (1975). *Schoolteacher: A sociological study.* Chicago: University of Chicago Press.

Louis, K., Marks, H. M., & Kruse, S. (1996). Teachers' professional community in restructuring schools. *American Educational Research Journal, 33* (4), 757–798.

MacBeath, J. (2006a). Leadership for Learning: A quest for meaning. *Leading & Managing, 12* (2), 1–9.

MacBeath, J. (2006b). *Leadership as a Subversive Activity.* ACEL Monograph Series No 39. Winmalee, NSW: Australian Council for Educational Leaders.

MacCallum, M. (2007). *Poll dancing: The story of the 2007 election.* Melbourne, Australia: Black Ink.

Macquarie Library. (1998). *Macquarie Dictionary* (3rd ed.). Sydney, Australia: Macquarie University.

Marshall, C. (2004). Social justice challenges to educational administration: Introduction to a special issue. *Educational Administration Quarterly, 40* (1), 3–13.

Mayer, J. A. (1943). *Max Weber and German polities.* London: Faber & Faber.

Miller, L. (1992). Unlikely beginnings: The district office as a starting point for developing a professional culture for teaching. In A. Lieberman (Ed.), *Building a professional culture in schools* (167–184). New York: Teachers College Press.

Miller, B., Moon, J., & Elko, S. (2000). *Teacher leadership in math and science: Casebook and facilitator's guide.* Portsmouth, NH: Heinemann.

Mintzberg, H. (1994). The fall and rise of strategic planning. *Harvard Business Review,* January-February,107–114.

Mitchell, G., & Sackney, L. (2006). Building schools, building people: The school principal's role in leading a learning community. *Journal of School Leadership, 16* (5), 627–640.

Moller, G., & Pankake, A. (2006). *Lead with me. A principal's guide to teacher leadership.* Poughkeepsie, NY: Eye on Education.

Morgan, A. (2008). *The principal in a process of school revitalisation: A metastrategic role.* Unpublished PhD Dissertation. Toowoomba: University of Southern Queensland.

Muijs, D., & Harris, A. (2003). *Teacher leadership: A review of research.* Retrieved from www.hesl.org.uk

Mulford, W. (2004). Congruence between the democratic processes of schools and school principal training in Australia. *Journal of Educational Administration, 42* (6), 625–639.

Mulford, W. (2007). *Overview of research on Australian educational leadership 2001–2005.* ACEL Monograph Series, No. 40. Winmalee, NSW: Australian Council for Educational Leaders.

Muncey, D., & McQuillan, P. (1996). *Reform and resistance in schools and classroom: An ethnographic view of the coalition of essential schools.* New Haven, CT: Yale University Press.

Murphy, J. (2005). *Connecting teacher leadership and school improvement.* Thousand Oaks, CA: Corwin Press.

Nash, R. (2005). Cognitive *habitus* and collective intelligence: Concepts for the explanation of inequality of educational opportunity. *Journal of Educational Policy, 20* (1), 3–21.

Newmann, F., & Wehlage, G. (1995). *Successful school restructuring: A report to the public and educators.* Madison, WI: Center on Organization and Restructuring of Schools, University of Wisconsin.

Ng, Foo Seong D., & Chew, J. (in press). *Innovative designs for enhancing achievements in schools (IDEAS) in Singapore: Final Report to Ministry of Education, Singapore.* Singapore: National Institute of Education, Nanyang Technological University.

Nirenberg, J. (1993). *The living organization: Transforming teams into workplace communities.* Homewood, IL: Business One Irwin.

Odell, S. J. (1997). Preparing teachers for teacher leadership. *Action in Teacher Education, 19* (3), 120–124.

Ogawa, R., & Bossett, S. (1995). Leadership as an organisational quality. *Educational Administration Quarterly, 31* (2), 224–43.

Olivier, D., & Hipp, K. (2006). Leadership capacity and collective efficacy: Interacting to sustain student learning in a professional learning community. *Journal of School Leadership, 16* (5), 505–519.

O'Neill, J., (1995). On schools as learning organizations: A conversation with Peter Senge. *Educational Leadership, 52* (7), 20–23.

Owens, R., & Valesky, T. (2007). *Organizational behavior in education.* Boston: Pearson Education.

Padilla, R., Trevino, J., Gonzalez, K., & Trevino, J. (1996, April). *The unfolding matrix: A dialogical technique for qualitative data acquisition and analysis.* Demonstration presented at the Annual Meeting of the American Educational Research Association, New York.

Ponder, G. A., & Holmes, K. M. (2000). Purpose, products and visions: The creation of new schools. *The Educational Forum, 56* (4), 405–415.

Pounder, D. G., Ogawa, R. T., & Adams, E. A. (1995). Leadership as an organization-wide phenomenon: Its impact on school performance. *Educational Administration Quarterly, 31*(4), 564–555.

Rice, E. M., & Schneider, G. T. (1994). A decade of teacher empowerment: An empirical analysis of teacher involvement in decision making, 1950–1991. *Journal of Educational Administration, 32* (1), 43–58.

Rizvi, F. (1992). Educative leadership in a multicultural society. In P. Duignan & R. J. S. McPherson (Eds.), *Educational leadership: A practical theory for new administrators and managers* (134–170). Lewes, Australia: Falmer.

Robinson, V. (2007). *School leadership and student outcomes: Identifying what works and why.* ACEL Monograph Series No. 41. Winalee, NSW: Australian Council for Educational Administration.

Roy, P., & Hord, S. (2006). It's everywhere, but what is it? Professional Learning Communities. *Journal of School Leadership, 16* (5), 490–501.

Rusch, E. (2005). Institutional barriers to organisational learning in school systems: The power of silence. *Educational Administration Quarterly, 41*(1), 83–120.

Sachs, J. (2000). Rethinking the practice of teacher professionalism. In C. Day, A. Fernandez, T. Hauge, & J. Moller (Eds.), *The life and work of teachers: International perspectives in changing times.* London: Routledge/Falmer.

Salt, B. (2006, November 15). Y the younger generation is so different. *The Australian.* Retrieved from newstext@newsltd.com.au

Schein, E. (1992). *Organizational culture and leadership.* San Francisco: Jossey-Bass.

Schneider, B., Godfrey, E., Hayes, S., Huang, M., Lim, B., Nishii, L., Ravewr, J., & Ziegart, J. (2003). The human side of strategy: Employee experiences of strategic alignment in a service organisation. *Organisational Dynamics, 32* (2), 122–141.

Schon, D. (1983). *The reflective practitioner: How professionals think in action.* New York: Basic Books.

Seligman, M. (1998). Positive social science. *APA Monitor, 29* (2), 3–8.

Senge, P. (1992). *The fifth discipline: The art and practice of the learning organization.* New York: Doubleday.

Senge, P. (1997). Communities of leaders and learners. *Harvard Business Review,* September/October, 30–31.

Senge, P. (2000). *Schools that learn*. New York: Doubleday.

Sergiovanni, T. (1994). *Building community in schools*. San Francisco: Jossey-Bass.

Sergiovanni, T. (1998). Leadership as pedagogy, capital development and school effectiveness. *International Journal of Leadership in Education: Theory and Practice, 1* (1), 37–46.

Sergiovanni, T. (2000). *The life world of leadership*. San Francisco: Jossey Bass.

Sharratt, L., & Fullan, M. (2006). Accomplishing districtwide reform. *Journal of School Leadership, 16* (5), 583–595.

Sherrill, J. (1999). Preparing teachers for leadership roles in the 21st century. *Theory Into Practice, 38* (1), 56–61.

Shor, I., & Freire, P. (1987). *A pedagogy for liberation: Dialogues on transforming education*. New York: Bergin & Garvey.

Sinclair, A. (1995). The seduction of the self-managed team and the reinvention of the team-as-a-group. *Leading and Managing, 1* (1), 44–60.

Smith, W., & Ellett, C. (2000, April). *Reconceptualizing school leadership for the 21st century: Music, metaphors and leadership density.* Paper presented at the Annual Meeting of the American Educational Research Association, New Orleans, LA.

Spillane, J. R., Halverson, R., & Diamond, J. B. (2001). Investigating school leadership practice: A distributed perspective. *Educational Researcher, 30* (3), 23–28.

Spillane, J. R., Hallett, T., & Diamond, J. (2003). Forms of capital and the construction of leadership: Instructional leadership in urban elementary schools. *Sociology of Education, 76* (1), 1–17.

Stogdill, R. (1974). *Handbook of leadership: A survey of theory and research*. New York: Free Press.

Tight, M. (2000). Critical perspectives on management learning: A view from adult/continuing/lifelong education. *Management Learning, 31* (1), 103–119.

Troman, G., & Woods, P. (2001). *Primary teachers' stress*. London: Routledge/Falmer.

Voss, Z., Cable, D., & Voss, G. (2006). Organisational identity and firm performance: What happens when leaders disagree about "Who we are"? *Organisation Science, 17* (6), 741–755.

Waller, W. (1932). *The sociology of teaching*. New York: Russell & Russell.

Wrigley, T. (2003). *Schools of hope. A new agenda for school improvement*. London: Trentham Books.

Wrigley, T. (2006). *Another school is possible*. London: Bookmarks Publication. Trentham Books.

Woods, P. (2006). Rationality and the affective roots of democratic leadership. *School Leadership and Management, 26* (4), 321–338.

York-Barr, J., & Duke, K. (2004). What do we know about teacher leadership? Findings from two decades of scholarship. *Review of Educational Research, 74* (3), 255–316.

Youitt, D. (2004). Sailing into uncharted territories: Is teacher leadership the key to school reform? *Leading & Managing, 2* (4), 30–40.

Youitt, D. (2007). Teacher leadership: Another way to add value to schools. *Perspectives on Educational Leadership*. November, Winmalee, NSW: Australian Council for Educational Leaders.

Index

CORWIN PRESS

The Corwin Press logo—a raven striding across an open book—represents the union of courage and learning. Corwin Press is committed to improving education for all learners by publishing books and other professional development resources for those serving the field of PreK–12 education. By providing practical, hands-on materials, Corwin Press continues to carry out the promise of its motto: **"Helping Educators Do Their Work Better."**

The National Association of Secondary School Principals—promoting excellence in school leadership since 1916—provides its members the professional resources to serve as visionary leaders. NASSP further promotes student leadership development through its sponsorship of the National Honor Society®, the National Junior Honor Society®, and the National Association of Student Councils®. For more information, visit www.principals.org.

DATE DUE